Commercial and Economic Law in Nigeria

Commercial and Economic Law in Nigeria

Mike A.A. Ozekhome

This book was originally published as a monograph in the International Encyclopaedia of Laws/Commercial and Economic Law.

General Editors: Roger Blanpain & Frank Hendrickx
Volume Editors: Jules Stuyck & Evelyne Terryn

Wolters Kluwer

Published by:
Kluwer Law International B.V.
PO Box 316
2400 AH Alphen aan den Rijn
The Netherlands
E-mail: international-sales@wolterskluwer.com
Website: lrus.wolterskluwer.com

Sold and distributed by:
Wolters Kluwer Legal & Regulatory U.S.
7201 McKinney Circle
Frederick, MD 21704
United States of America
E-mail: customer.service@wolterskluwer.com

ISBN 978-94-035-4055-9

e-Book: ISBN 978-94-035-4060-3
web-PDF: ISBN 978-94-035-4061-0

The Author

Dr Mike Ozekhome SAN is a scholar-practitioner and the founding partner of a boutique law firm in Nigeria. He is a Senior Advocate of Nigeria and a renowned expert in constitutional law, human rights, and business law. He has acted as the lead defence counsel in many complex disputes involving human rights. He is well sought after for his authoritative knowledge of law and his scholarly abilities in critiquing contemporary social and legal problems in Nigeria. He is frequently consulted to advise on heavyweight matters involving investor-state arbitration disputes: he regularly advises on the grave repercussions of poorly negotiated bilateral investment treaties that functionally deepen the economic crisis of Nigeria and other developing countries. In Nigeria, Dr Ozekhome is fondly called the 'Senior Advocate of the Masses', precisely due to his passion and relentless efforts in pointing out issues of bad governance within the three arms of government through his regular commentaries on national televisions and newspaper articles. He has authored many scholarly works on rule of law and business law, which are the typical areas from which the issues affecting Nigeria and Africa frequently arise. Dr Ozekhome is happily married with children.

The Author

Table of Contents

List of Abbreviations

AfrLR(Comm)	African Commercial Law Report
All NLR	All Nigerian Law Reports
CA	Court of Appeal
CAC	Corporate Affairs Commission
CAMA	Companies and Allied Matters Act
CAP	Chapter
CBN	Central Bank of Nigeria
CSCS	Central Securities and Clearing System
FCCP	Federal Competition and Consumer Protection
FRCN	Financial Reporting Council of Nigeria
FREP	Fundamental Rights Enforcement Procedure
GDP	Gross Domestic Product
HC	High Court
IP	Intellectual Properties
ISA	Investments and Securities Act
KYC	Know Your Customer
LLB	Bachelor of Laws
LUA	Land Use Act
NACCIMA	Nigerian Association of Chambers of Commerce, Industry, Mines and Agriculture
NBA	Nigeria Bar Association
NCNC	National Council of Nigeria and Cameroon
NCX	Nigerian Commodity Exchange
NIMASA	Nigerian Maritime Administration and Safety Agency
NIPC	Nigerian Investment Promotion Commission
NLR	Nigerian Law Reports
NMA	Nigeria Medical Association
NNDP	Nigerian National Democratic Party
NWLR	Nigerian Weekly Law Report
NYM	National Youth Party

List of Abbreviations

SC	Supreme Court
SCN	Supreme Court of Nigeria
SCNJ	Supreme Court of Nigerian Judgment
SEC	Security and Exchange Commission
SMEs	Small and Medium-Scale Enterprises/Entrepreneurs
STMA	Secured Transactions Act in Movable Assets
UN	United Nations
UNCITRAL	United Nations Commission on International Trade Law
WTO	World Trade Organization

Acknowledgements

I want to thank my wife, Josephine Ozekhome, my children and the rest of my family, who supported and encouraged me during the time I was writing this monograph.

Acknowledgements

General Introduction

Chapter 1. General Background of the Country

§1. Geography

1. Nigeria is a Federal Republic with a constitution:[1] it is located in West Africa and it borders with Benin Republic, Chad, Niger and Cameroon.[2] It measures about 933,768 km^2, with its coastline measuring about 853 km. Its landscape consists of lowlands merging into central hills and plateaus as well mountains in the south, and plain land in the northern part. Its territorial sea is 12 nautical miles, with 200 nautical miles forming its exclusive economic zone. Nigeria's climate does not have a common feel; it differs, depending on the part of the country one is. In the south, it is more of equatorial; it is tropical in the centre and arid in the north.

2. Nigeria is endowed with many natural resources, some of which are natural gas, petroleum, tin, iron ore, coal, limestone, niobium, lead, zinc, arable land, etc. The country derives about 90% of its foreign exchange mainly from its crude oil and gas exports. Natural disasters are not so common, but in the past, the recurrent ones include periodic drought and flooding. There are other serious issues of soil degradation due to improper use of farmlands, crude oil and gas mining, rapid deforestation arising mainly from bush burning; urban air and water pollution arising from improper execution of the existing laws on this; oil pollution – water, air, and soil in the Niger Delta area which has suffered serious damage from oil spills from multinational companies whose activities have caused the indigenes a significant loss of arable land.

1. E. Awa, *Federal Government in Nigeria* (University of California Press 1964). Also *see* the Constitution of the Federal Republic of Nigeria, 1999 (now CAP C23 LFN 2004) ('1999 Constitution').
2. For the history of West Africa, *see* J.D. Fage, *A History of West Africa* (Cambridge University Press 1969).

§2. CONSTITUTIONAL HISTORY AND DEVELOPMENT

3. Nigeria is popularly known as Africa's most populous country.[3] It was colonized by Britain in the nineteenth century until 1960 when it regained independence.[4] Before independence, Nigerian founding fathers agitated for independence; a series of constitutions were created. Nigeria's constitutional history is chequered, and can be majorly divided into two periods of time, namely the colonial and post-colonial eras. The colonial period captured five constitutional documents, namely, the 1914, 1922, 1946, 1951, and 1954 constitutions.[5] Then, following independence, Nigeria witnessed the emergence of the following constitutional documents, namely, the 1960, 1963, 1979 and 1999 constitutions. There is indeed a difference, perhaps a radical difference between the making of these two categories of constitutions. While the colonial era constitutions were enacted through an order-in-council of the British monarch, the ones following independence were enacted in two ways: an Act of Parliament and military decree.[6]

4. It is important to note that before the coming of the British colonialists, there was no country called Nigeria.[7] What was in existence were independent groups of people with distinct culture, politics and religions. Nigeria as a country came into existence in 1914 with the Federick Lugard constitution of 1914.[8] That constitution amalgamated, that is, merged the colony and protectorate of Southern Nigeria with the protectorate of Northern Nigeria under the colonial authority of the British government.[9] Following the emergence of Nigeria as a colonial subject, Britain being the colonial master, and administered through an appointed agent called 'the Governor General', Nigeria as one geographic entity was born. The first Governor General of Nigeria was Lord Frederick Lugard. The 1914 Constitution created a legislative council of the colony which made laws only for the colony of Lagos, while the Governor General was with the power to make laws for the rest of the country.[10]

5. Almost a decade after the 1914 Constitution was operative, it was replaced by the 1922 Sir Clifford constitution. This was known for its establishment of a forty-six-member Legislative Council which was empowered to make laws for the

3. *See* generally, A. Burns, *History of Nigeria* (George Allen and Unwin Ltd. 1948); W. Geary, *Nigeria under British Rule* (Methuen 1927).
4. *See* T. Mamman, *The Law and Politics of Constitution Making in Nigeria, 1862-1989: Issues, Interests and Compromises* 49 (Ed-Linform services 1998); Hon. Justice Ayoola, *Rationale, Objectives and the Scope of Law Reform*, in *Law Development and Administration in Nigeria* 21 (Osibanjo and Kalu eds, Intec Printers Limited 1990).
5. *See* generally, The World FactBook, https://www.cia.gov/library/publications/the-world-factbook/geos/ni.html.
6. *Ibid.*
7. A. Oyebade, *The Foundations of Nigeria: Essays in Honour of Toyin Falola, Africa* (World Press Inc. 2003).
8. G. Kirk, *Lugard and the Amalgamation of Nigeria* (Cass 1968).
9. G. Hetherington, *British Paternalism: 1920-1940* (Cass 1970).
10. The World FactBook, https://www.cia.gov/library/publications/the-world-factbook/geos/ni.html.

colony of Lagos and the southern provinces.[11] It also introduced for the first time the elective principle, with Lagos and Calabar being granted the right to elect their representatives to the Legislative Council.

6. The Clifford constitution reigned for about twenty-four years before it was supplanted with the Richard constitution of 1946. This constitution was remarkable as it defined Nigeria for the first time, in terms of regions. Thus, there were three regions, namely, the Northern, Western and Eastern Regions. Richard's constitution came into effect, following the end of World War II.[12] World War II had a significant effect on this constitution and other later constitutions with respect to the governance of the colonial Nigeria, and indeed Africa as a whole, because the returning African war heroes, who were conscripted to fight for Britain were able to understand more deeply the meaning of freedom and sovereignty based on their overall war experience and interactions with other nationals.[13]

7. Additionally, the United Nations Charter adopted after World War II, emphasized on human rights and the right of people to determine and govern themselves. This was a sharp blow on colonialism, and indeed the beginning of liberation movements by the African freedom fighters.[14]

8. The series of events materialized into the creation of the political party known as the National Council for Nigeria and Cameroons, which later became the National Council of Nigerian Citizens (N.C.N.C). This political organization was highly engaged in the active mobilization of the Nigerian people to take advantage of the global movement of self-determination and political independence from colonial rule.[15]

9. Notwithstanding the fact that the 1954 Constitution introduced remarkable and admirable changes in the political landscape of Nigeria, yet, five years later, the 1946 Richards Constitution was thrown to the dustbin in favour of the 1951 Sir John Macpherson Constitution. The charge against the 1946 Constitution was that it was an imposition of the British colonialists without much contribution from the indigenous people of Nigeria.[16] Thus, with the 1951 Macpherson constitution, much consultation with the Nigerian people was recorded. Notably, meetings and consultations that led to its making were held at different levels – district, village, divisional, provincial and regional levels before the National Conference.

---

11. A. Obilade, *The Nigerian Legal System* 24 (Sweet & Maxwell 1979).
12. *See* M. Rahmani, *Constitutional Development in Nigeria 1945–1960* (Doctoral thesis, Liabbes University 2015), Chap 2. Available at http://193.194.79.137/bitstream/123456789/1216/3/D_Ang_RAHMANI%20_Mokhtaria.pdf.
13. For example, *see* T. Obert, *Transport Workers Strikes and the Imperial Response. Africa and Post World War II Conjuncture*, Vol. 31 Afr. Stud. Rev. 26 (1988).
14. L.H. Gann & P. Duignan (eds), *Colonialism in Africa 1870 1900* V 2 (Cambridge University Press 1982).
15. M. Rahmani, *supra* n. 12, 73.
16. F. Toyin, *Colonialism and Violence in Nigeria* (Indiana University Press 2009).

10. The regional conferences that produced a general consensus in favour of a federal system of government were held at Ibadan, Enugu and Kaduna. In the last analysis, the 1951 Constitution which emerged from this wild consultation and indigenous participation marked a major advancement on the constitutional making framework, as the election of majorities in the Central Legislature and in the Regional Houses of Assembly was borne; this gave the legislative houses independent legislative powers in many areas of state activity; also the federal system of government came into being in Nigeria for the first time.

11. At this juncture, it is interesting to note that political awareness had already developed to a self-standing position in Nigeria. Thus, despite the positive changes introduced by the 1951 Constitution compared to its predecessors, within three years of its operation, the expansion of the increased political agitation and awareness which increased regional identities as made possible by the 1951 Constitution made it easy to realize that the Constitution did not offer a sufficient structure to accommodate the quest for national leadership, and the effective management of the arising tensions and conflicts that were brewing at both the national and regional levels as a result of the Macpherson constitution. There were reports of violent attacks that went on in the northern city of Kano which targeted southerners. There was massive loss of lives and property which made the political atmosphere rancorous and ungovernable. Oliver Lyttleton, the then British Secretary of State for the Colonies, intervened by organizing a conference in 1953 whereby the leading political figures drawn from the political parties in Nigeria were encouraged to attend. That conference coupled with the numerous meetings and consultations of the Nigerian people led to the birth of the 1954 Lyttleton Constitution, an improvement on the 1951 version.[17]

12. The 1954 Constitution, as already hinted at, among other novelties that it introduced, granted autonomy to the regional governments, which made them independent of the central government, vis-à-vis legislative competence. This constitution also established a unicameral legislature for the Federal Government and each of the three regional governments. Other notable features of the Constitution were the making of Lagos as the Federal Capital Territory; it was no longer under the control of any regional government. Similarly, there was the establishment of regional public service for the three regions; the judiciary was reorganized, as regional judiciaries were created. Autonomy was also granted to the Southern Cameroons. There was also the novelty introduction of portfolios for ministers. In summary, it could be said that the 1954 Lyttleton Constitution created a sufficient platform, and was indeed a link towards Nigeria's independence in 1960 as federal and democratically elected federal and regional members of the legislature.

13. Nigeria's independence came six years after the 1954 Constitution; Nigeria was granted political independence as a sovereign state. The Constitution that saw this achievement was the 1960 Constitution, which was unique on many fronts. It

17. *See* the Speech of Oliver Lyttleton in the December 1953 Conference – available at http://hansard.millbanksystems.com/commons/1953/may/21/nigeria-constitution.

provided for a parliamentary system of government; it retained the three-region structure of the previous constitutions (i.e., the Northern, Eastern and Western Regions); it provided for a bicameral legislative structure at the federal (Senate and House of Representatives) and regional levels (House of Assembly and House of Chiefs). The legislative powers of government were divided into three lists, namely, the exclusive, concurrent and residual. Notwithstanding the foregoing improvements, the 1960 Constitution bore some features of neocolonialism. For instance, the parliamentary system recognized the British monarch as the Head of State with powers to appoint a resident agent – the Governor General – to exercise executive powers on behalf of the Queen of England, while a Prime Minister elected by the federal parliament acted as the Head of the federal Executive Council.

14. It could be said that considering the heightened level of political awareness already in existence in Nigeria at this time, with many heads of political parties being graduates of notable institutions in the United States and Europe, it was easy to see that, by making the Governor General a representative and agent of the British monarch instead of the Nigerian People, the suspected effect of which was to still render Nigeria a dominion territory, a status which was purely in contradiction with the very struggle and agitation for independence that materialized in 1960, the general impression was that of discontent.

15. This point is further corroborated by the fact that under the 1960 Constitution, the highest judicial body was not the Federal Supreme Court of Nigeria, but the Privy Council – an appellate court under the British jurisdiction, whose decisions stirred the direction of the country in the way the British monarch wanted. These gruesome charges against the 1960 Constitution made it highly unpopular and the agitation to drop its use was high among the Nigerian people, a struggle that led to the birth of the 1963 Constitution. Thus, under the 1963 Constitution, Nigeria for the first time became a republic. Under the first Republic, the parliamentary system of government replaced the Governor General who was appointed by the British monarch, with a President who was elected directly by members of the Nigerian federal legislature. Similarly, in lieu of the Privy Council, the Federal Supreme Court of Nigeria was endowed with the power to act as the court of last instance over any person or matter in Nigeria.

16. The year 1966 was remarkable for Nigeria; its 1963 Constitution was set aside following a military coup d'etat that replaced the first Republic with military dictatorship which lasted for about thirteen years – including the civil war period (1967–1970), under four military Heads of State, ending only in 1979 when the General Olusegun Obasanjo military administration ushered in the second Republic with the promulgation of a new constitution.

17. The 1979 Constitution ushered Nigeria into a presidential system of government with a federal government, nineteen state governments, a federal capital territory, three arms as well as levels of government.[18] Just like the 1963 Constitution, the lifespan of the 1979 Constitution was cut short on 31 December 1983 when the civilian administration of President Shehu Shagari and Vice President Alex Ekwueme was toppled and replaced by the military dictatorship led by Generals Muhammed Buhari and Tunde Idiagbon. Following this new episode, three other extra-constitutional regimes were inspired to replicate the military system of government, namely, the General Ibrahim Babangida military dictatorship (1985–1993), Mr Ernest Shonekan's interim civilian-led regime, General Sani Abacha military dictatorship (1993–1998) and General Abdulsalami Abubakar military administration which successfully brought about the third Republic on 27 May 1999 with the introduction of the 1999 Constitution. The 1999 Constitution was amended in 2011 and remains the most powerful single document in Nigeria.

§3. Cultural Composition

18. Nigerian culture is characterized by a variety of cultures and languages of the various ethnic groups, with over three hundred–four hundred languages.[19] Of all these numerous ethnic groups, three are described as the dominant, while the rest are called the minorities.[20] Given the large number of ethnic groups, only the three described as the majority groups would be skeletally described below.

19. The three major ethnic groups are the Hausa, Igbo, and Yoruba. Apart from these three, there is notably the Edo people who dwell in the region between Yorubaland[21] and Igboland. The Edo people are predominantly Christians due to their early contact with the White Missionaries. Then, there are the Ibibio/Annang/Efik people who dwell in the coastal south southern part of Nigeria; the Ijaw people who dwell in the Niger Delta region of Nigeria, the home of Nigeria's crude oil resources. As a general remark, the people found in the south are predominantly Christians, while the people found in the north are predominantly Muslims, although a small percentage of Yoruba people that dwell in the south are Muslims, and the same is true about some Hausa/Fulani people in the north – a small percentage of them are Christians.

---

18. *See* generally, B. Nwabueze, *Nigeria's Presidential Constitution, 1979-83: The Second Experiment in Constitutional Democracy* (Longman Nigeria Ltd. 1985); Oyediran (ed.), *The Nigerian 1979 Elections* (Macmillan Press Ltd. 1981).
19. *See* PBS NewsHour, *Ethnicity in Nigeria* (5 Apr. 2007), https://www.pbs.org/newshour/arts/africa-jan-june07-ethnic_04-05.
20. *See* Minority Rights Group International, *World Directories of Minorities and Indigenous People* (Jan. 2018), https://minorityrights.org/country/nigeria/.
21. S. Johnson, *The History of the Yoruba* (C.M.S Bookshop 1937).

20. In the north and middle belt parts of Nigeria, the nomadic Fulani people can be found.[22] Due to their nomadic lifestyle, they can be found across the West and Central Africa as well. The Fulani and Hausa people are mainly Muslims, and this was primarily due to their geographical location in the north, the proximity with the middle East, and the trans-Sahara trade with the people of Saudi Arabia.

21. As already hinted at above, two of the Abrahamic monotheist religions are practised in Nigeria – with Christianity being heavily practised in the south, while Islam is predominantly practised in the north. The simple explanation for this is geography. The southern people of Nigeria reside close to the Nigerian coast, which made it possible for the early Christian missionaries who travelled mainly by ships to arrive and settle in the south, while the northerners who dwell in the hinterland, and faraway from the coast, had early contact with the Saudi Arabian merchants who travelled across the Sahara Desert with camels. It should be noted that at this early period, when foreign religions were being introduced to the Nigerian people, there was no entity yet called Nigeria; people only existed independently and had their own cultures and governments.

22. Notwithstanding the heavy presence of Christianity and Islam in Nigeria, about 10% or more of Nigerians practise other religions – notably, the traditional religion that was sought to be wiped out by the Christian missionaries and Arabian merchants. Today, like most minorities in anything, these traditional religious worshippers are discriminated against by the Christians and Muslims who consider their religions as superior over the traditional type. Thus, apart from occasionally burning the traditional worship shrines, Christians and Muslims sometimes assault or even kill most traditional worshippers; and many observers, like the writer of this monograph, consider such aggressive acts as abuse of dominant position.

23. The Nigerian composition is both a complex and interesting experiment; more than three hundred–four hundred ethnicities with varying cultures and languages, trying to live as one people. It has not worked well so far in the writer's opinion. Notwithstanding the numerous languages that are spoken across the country, the English language has been chosen to be the official language, the language of instruction in schools and public and civil service establishments. However, English is not considered the mother tongue in Nigeria. The ability to speak and write it correctly is only acquired from formal education. Thus, considering that a significant percentage of the Nigerian population is not formally educated, most everyday people speak 'pidgin English' which is an adulterated as well as a simplified version of the English language.

24. As a developing country, with not many simplified ways of doing things, a lot of physical activities are required to accomplish daily tasks, ranging from laundry, house cleaning, transportation, manual labour, etc. This reflects the nature of

---

22. *See* The Worldwatch Monitor, *Who Are the Fulani?* Available at https://www.worldwatchmonitor.org/who-are-the-fulani/.

food being widely consumed by the general population, as well. Thus, most Nigerian foods are characterized by high carbohydrates, for example, yam, cassava, maize, etc. Nigerians also have a variety of soups which they eat with pounded yam, wheat, garri, and other pastries.

§4. Political System

I. Introduction

25. The Nigerian political experience is over a century old – and can be subdivided into two broad categories: pre-democracy and post-democracy eras. Whereas Nigeria had its independence in 1960 from the British colonialists, the amalgamation of the southern and northern protectorates in 1914 by Frederick Lugard is considered to be the beginning of the entity called Nigeria.[23] The 1914 amalgamation incident was rather a conclusion of a series of governing processes, which started from the 1884–1885 Berlin Conference that led to the scramble of Africa.[24] Thus, the acquisition and administrative process by the British colonialists started first from trade, then, later the bombardment of Lagos in 1851 as well its annexation sometime in 1861. Pursuant to the blueprint laid down in the Berlin Conference, the northern protectorate was created in 1900, followed by the merger of the Lagos colony with the southern protectorate in 1906. These series of administrative setups were then completed in the 1914 amalgamation of the southern and northern protectorates.

26. Following the 1914 amalgamation, and the naming of the amalgamated entity as 'Nigeria'[25] by Florence Shaw, a British journalist and wife of Frederick Lugard, the political game in Nigeria and the struggle of its people from the former southern and northern protectorates to maintain relevance at the centre stage, became fully on. Self-evidently, the Nigerian entity is an artificial creation which did not take into account the differing cultural sensitivities of the people. This immediately showed in the nature of political parties that were formed after the 1914 amalgamation; they were highly ethnocentric and sought to foster only tribal agendas rather than any national interest and overarching political governance. In this circumstance, achieving any national interest was difficult because the peoples of south and north had Christianity and Islam respectively and hardly saw or see issues from the same perspective.

---

23. B. Nwabueze, *A Constitutional History of Nigeria* (C. Hurst & Co (Publishers) Ltd. 1982); S.G. Ehindero, *The Constitutional Development of Nigeria: 1849-1989* (Ehindero (Nigeria) Ltd. 1991).
24. *See* P. Fordham, *The Geography of African Affairs* (Penguin Books 1965); J. Hargreaves, *West Africa Partitioned* (Macmillan 1974).
25. N. Dumka, *The Ethnic History of Nigeria* Available at https://core.ac.uk/download/pdf/14051828.pdf; O. Omoruyi, *The Origin of Nigeria: God of Justice Not Associated with an Unjust Political Order: Appeal to President Obasanjo Not to Rewrite Nigerian History* (2002) http://www.nigerdeltacongress.com/tarticles/the%20origin_of_nigeria.htm.

27. Cultural differences of the Nigerian people were a big challenge at that time, and more than a century later, not much progress has been made towards dismantling the ethnic barriers that continue to pose as stumbling blocks in the political lives of Nigerians. Truthfully considered, these differences appear irreconcilable because of their special nature, coupled with the architectural design in terms of politics which the British colonialists instituted that seem to favour the people of the northern part of Nigeria.[26] It is widely reported that the British people designed the political architecture in favour of the north because people from that region gave them the least political resistance,[27] unlike the southern people who are more formerly educated and offered a stronger political resistance against British rule and were in the forefront of the agitation for independence.[28] Thus, even after a century had elapsed, people from the north and south in the context of one Nigeria still perceive themselves as political enemies.[29]

§5. A Brief Insight on the Nature of Politics Before the Emergence of Democracy in 1999

28. With these factors in mind, it will be easy to understand why the pre-independence political parties were heavily tribal in their outlook and activities.[30] For instance, and as hinted at in the constitutional history and development section above, following the provision of the elective principle in Clifford's constitution of 1922, Herbert Macaulay, in about a decade after the 1914 amalgamation, formed the Nigerian National Democratic Party (NNDP) in 1923. This was the first political party that contested elections. However, even though the party's name bears a national characteristic, elections were restricted to Lagos and Calabar – electorates were required to be resident in Lagos and Calabar with a minimum income of USD 100. The USD 100 amount was quite high at that period and together with the residential requirement, largely cut off many Nigerians from political participation at that time. The NNDP was widely described as 'Lagos Party' due to its heavy control of the political activities in Lagos.[31]

29. As many new nationalist leaders emerged, the discontent for NNDP grew and intensified. Thus, in 1923 Nnamdi Azikwe, Obafemi Awolowo, Ernest Ikoli and

26. S.J. Hogben & A.H.M. Kirk-Greene, *The Emirates of Northern Nigeria* (Oxford University Press 1966); C.W.J. Orr, *The Making of Northern Nigeria* (Macmillan 1911).
27. *See* Peter K. Tibenderana, *The Irony of Indirect Rule in Sokoto Emirate, Nigeria*, Vol. 31(1) Afr. Stud. Rev. 67–92 (1988).
28. In the southern part, the British people used warrant chiefs to rule indirectly. *See* A.E. Afigbo, *The Warrant Chiefs Indirect Rule in Southern Nigeria 1891-1929* (Longman 1972); S.O. Okafor, *Ideal and Reality in British Administrative Policy in Eastern Nigeria*, Vol. 73(2) Afr. Aff. 293 (1974).
29. *See* C. Robert, *Nigeria in Conflict* (Secker and Warburg 1970).
30. E. Kalu, *Constitutional Development in Nigeria: An Analytical Study of Nigeria's Constitution-Making Developments and the Historical and Political Factors That Affected Constitutional Change* (Cambridge University Press 1960).
31. *See* generally, K.W.J. Post, *The Nigerian Federal Election Politics and Administration in a Developing Political System* (Oxford University Press 1963).

others formed the National Youth Party (NYM) with the ultimate mandate to achieve a national unity which was farfetched at that time and exacerbated by the NNDP's parochial politics.

30. The founders of NYM, predominantly southerners from Igbo and Yoruba origins, fell into the same ditch of ethnocentrism. They were not so different from their NNDP predecessor, and were later overwhelmed by their personality clashes which made them derail from their founding vision of fostering national unity. Following internal scuffles, Nnamdi Azikwe formed the National Council of Nigeria and Cameroon (NCNC) in 1944. While Obafemi Awolowo together with the *Egbe Omo Oduduwa*, a pan-Yoruba group, founded the Action Group (AG) in 1951. The Northern People Congress was founded in 1946 as pro-northern association in counter response to the political activities fronted by the southern political parties.

31. People from the ethnic minority groups soon joined the game of politics in a grandiose scale. Thus, minorities in the Nigerian middle belt founded and promoted the United Middle Belt Congress; the Efik/Ibibio people founded the United National Independence Party which was designed to offer a counter resistance to the Igbo-dominated politics in the then Eastern region, which was and is still home for many minority groups, of which the Igbo people are dominant.

32. The political parties under the pre-democracy era were all guilty of the same charge, the charge of ethnocentrism. Following the emergence of the political parties already described above, many others emerged, all bearing the features of tribalism.[32] For instance, the Alliance for Democracy was dominated by the Yoruba people; the All Peoples Party which was later renamed All Nigerian Peoples Party was dominated by the Hausa/Fulani people and the Igbo people were predominant in the NCNC. With all these events, it could be stated in summary that the Nigerian political landscape in the periods between the amalgamation of the southern and northern protectorates to the declaration of independence in 1960, up until the civil war in 1967, was heavily calibrated with ethnic divisions and rivalries.

33. The unhealthy politicking activities that were clothed in tribal sentiments rather than any national interest culminated into hate and malice among the people from the south and north, eventually leading the three-year civil war (1967–1970), fought mainly between the Igbo and Hausa peoples. The war claimed over two million lives, majority of whom were the Igbos, who were agitating for self-rule under the name 'Biafra'.[33] The Igbo people had complained and still complain that the architectural framework of governance in Nigeria favours the northern people who

32. F. Schwarz, *Nigeria the Tribes the Nation or the Race: the Politics of Independence* (MIT press 1965).
33. R. Sklar, *Nigerian Political Parties: Power in an Emergent African Nation* (Africa World Press 2004).

are comparably less formerly educated than the southern people. The full analysis of the Nigerian civil war, the remote and immediate causes of the war are beyond the scope of this monograph.[34]

§6. A Brief Insight on the Nature of Politics after 1999

34. The Nigerian democracy is slightly more than two decades old; although in comparison with the political landscape in the era before 1999, which featured a lot of bloodsheds and political extra judicial killings, some progress has been recorded. However, there are still major problems with the overall political structure, institutional weakness, and all this constitutes a stumbling block in the realization of the fruits of democracy which includes but not limited to national integration and collective progress of the Nigerian people. The result of the dysfunctional system arising from the improper political set-up has resulted in the poor efficiency of the public and civil services – sectors that still handle and provide some essential services for the Nigerian people. There is a high-level corruption in the employment of public and civil servants with tribe and religion playing essential factors to be considered rather than competent skills and good character. The demotion of merit, which in any event, ought to be an overriding factor in the employment of people in the public service, has culminated into incompetence in services delivery.

35. As a result of this disturbing level of corruption and the lack of requisite competence in the discharge of public duties, basic public goods are in dire lack as well as poorly delivered, thus, plunging most average Nigerians into poverty, which have made them prone to the commission of crimes or being used as political thugs in lieu of meagre handouts by immoral politicians. This high level of poverty and corruption has in the final analysis undermined the security and peace of citizens throughout the country. Given the huge emphasis on tribe and religion as the main factors for promotion in life, rather than merit and judgment of a person based on their characters and skills, ethnic and religious conflicts have worsened and this creates political uncertainties which many financial investors put into consideration when making investment decisions.

36. The foregoing notwithstanding, it should be noted that Nigeria is currently enjoying the longest period of civilian rule since independence. As already hinted at above, the 1966 military coup d'état marked the end of the first civilian rule which started upon the independence in 1960. That bloody 1966 coup has been widely described as being one of the immediate causes of the Nigerian civil war starting in 1967.

37. On a deeper analysis, one realizes why the Nigerian democracy is heavily tainted with a totalitarian outlook and other features that are undemocratic. Between 1966 and 1999, that is, a period of thirty-three years, there were only four short

34. The pre-civil war issues about Nigeria was captured eloquently by: M. Crowder, *The Story of Nigeria* (Faber and Faber 1961).

civilian governments totalling about four years. The rest of the period – that is, about twenty-nine years – was occupied with various military governments. Thus, the adoption of democracy as a system of government in 1999 was done without much experience of democracy in practice, and most of the politicians under the current democratic setting were those who ruled or actively participated during the military era, and therefore could not be true democrats without succumbing to their totalitarian past.[35]

38. Yet, in 1999, following the adoption of democracy as a system of national government, the Nigerian people were overwhelmed with joy and hoped that things would get better in terms of the economy and federal integrating policies which ought to emphasis on merit, justice, and hard work as gateways to every citizen's success. However, today, those genuine expectations have been highly frustrated as the various governments under democracy have failed the people by formulating and championing policies that are infuriatingly ill-conceived. As a result of this multilayered decay in governance, there is high unemployment rate arising from the poor and poorly implemented policies.

39. Corruption is all time high, and has almost been legislated into perpetual existence, as many politicians now seek to legislate matters that will exclusively favour them whether in or when out of office, of course at the expense of the Nigerian people. The deplorable and corrupt state of governance necessitated the former British Prime Minister – David Cameron to describe Nigeria as 'fantastically corrupt'.[36] Whereas this may seem as an exaggeration, it is nonetheless not misleading because the political space in Nigeria has been characterized with intimidation, bribery of the electorate and electoral officials with huge sums of money with the intention to manipulate election results. Thus, there has been a system of operation in the Nigerian politics which tends to unjustly exclude minorities and favour only those with huge wealth and powerful godfathers that can fund financially heavy campaigns.

40. Inherent in politics are also issues about the economic realities of the Nigerian people; the switch from military dictatorship to democracy came with some costs that were largely not visible in 1999 when the democratic era earnestly kicked off. These realities have gradually been unfolding since then, and Nigeria has had to cope with all issues at the same time. For instance, Nigeria has been engaged in reforming its economy from state controlled that it largely was before 1999, especially under the military dictatorship era, to a liberalized, privatized, deregulated downstream sector of the petroleum resources which form about 90% of its foreign exchange. Indeed, in an effort towards a sustainable economy, in 2011, subsidies on petroleum products were removed by the former President Goodluck Jonathan's administration, even though the removal which increased the petrol pump price

35. *See* Omolumen D. Egbefo, *Fifteen Years of Democracy, 1999-2014: Reflections on Nigeria's Quest for National Integration*, Vol. 9(2) Afr. Res. Rev. 59–77 (2015).
36. BBC, *David Cameron Calls Nigeria and Afghanistan 'Fantastically Corrupt'* (BBC News 10 May 2016), https://www.bbc.com/news/uk-politics-36260193.

attracted a nationwide outcry from the masses.[37] There have also been reforms in the civil and public service sectors through an anti-corruption drive starting from 2015 by President Mohamed Buhari. All this has partly been undertaken to restore the eroded confidence of foreign investors.

41. Perhaps, it will be premature to make final conclusions on whether the governments from 1999 till date have failed the Nigerian people by failing to deliver on primary mandates. However, the writer's impression is that the various governments from 1999 till date have not performed their duties in the manner that is sufficient to lift the masses from excruciating poverty. Many issues have exacerbated the ugly condition of things in Nigeria: the reliance on foreign donations which deepens corruption among politicians who misappropriate these funds; non-interest free loans from the World Bank and International Monetary Fund which are not well utilized for the benefit of Nigerians, and therefore having the features of odious debts; the way state-owned assets under the privatization programmes were sold to a few private individuals who were former politicians and have enough money from their loots to buy and control vital services, are all issues of great concern. The result of all this remains the harsh economic conditions many Nigerians currently find themselves in, thus, leading to high insecurity, crime rate, violence and low lifespan. The gist on corruption could be summarized in the fact that notwithstanding that Nigeria is the seventh largest producer and exporter of crude oil, it still imports refined petroleum: due to corruption, it has refused or neglected to revive the existing four petroleum refineries.[38]

42. The level of decay in the Nigerian politics may not be wiped out automatically, no matter the kind of reforms carried out on papers. Much of the reform will have to be culturally rooted, because, political leaders are selected from the pool of citizens; a change in moral values which must emphasize highly on merits, justice, and hard work as gateways to success rather than eulogizing those who obtained wealth by looting public funds and false pretences must be highly emphasized in moral instructions.

43. There are other interesting issues that deserve attention under this heading, but due to the lack of writing space, they will not be considered in detail. For example, as mentioned above, it should be recalled that Nigeria's economy is highly dependent on its crude oil production. It produces about two million barrels a day. The crude oil resource is found and exploited in the southern part of Nigeria, particularly, in the Niger Delta region. Many of the international oil companies own large oil blocks which they exploit and pay some taxes to the Nigerian government. Over the years, there have been serious complaints about the poor methods of

37. *See* Y. Akinbobola, *Bid to End Subsidy Stirs Protest in Nigeria* (Africa Renewal Apr. 2012), https://www.un.org/africarenewal/magazine/april-2012/bid-end-subsidy-stirs-protest-nigeria.
38. *See* C. Eboh, *Nigeria's NNPC Plans to Revamp Refineries to Cut Fuel Imports* (Reuters 22 Mar. 2019), https://www.reuters.com/article/nigeria-refineries/nigerias-nnpc-plans-to-revamp-refineries-to-cut-fuel-imports-idUKL8N2193WQ.

exploitation of crude oil that leaves the environment increasingly inhabitable.[39] The people of the Niger Delta region depend almost exclusively on fishing; as their rivers have been extremely polluted by the exploitation of crude oil, their source of livelihood has become highly threatened. Many of the inhabitants are unable to feed themselves and their families, and the result of this was their frequent resort to violence after the Nigerian government failed to address their concerns any meaningfully.

44. Thus, at various times, many foreign oil workers in Nigeria were kidnapped and ransoms were demanded from their oil company employers. In egregious cases, there were killings of workers, and disruption of exploration activities; there were bombing and vandalizing of oil pipelines and other related infrastructure.[40] While the Niger Delta inhabitants, in their opinion, were doing this to attract the government's attention, and as a way to emphasize their point of being marginalized, the ultimate result was a devastating blow to the Nigerian economy which is highly dependent on crude oil and gas exports; quantity produced fell all time low in 2015, and coupled with a global dip in crude oil price sometime in 2015, the Nigerian economy was brought down to its knees and economic recession kicked in.

45. The disruption of crude oil production by the Niger Delta people is only a superstructure – the main structure that generates the general discontent goes back to how Nigeria is politically wired, wired to favour people from the northern part of the country. For instance, while the crude oil and gas resources are located in the south, about 83% of the citizens who own oil operating licences and oil mining licences are the northerners.[41] Basically, the resources from the southern part are largely used in nourishing, albeit in a bias form, the northern part of the country. Many of the issues that generate strong dissatisfaction among people from the south are immortalized in the extant 1999 Constitution, which have made these contentious issues somehow permanent and difficult to change; they cannot be changed because the northerners occupy more seats in the National Assembly (federal parliament) because they have more states, even though they do not have as much population as the southern people. Thus, no matter how forceful any constitutional amendment is sought by the southerners, the number of votes required to effect the change cannot be exclusively met by them in the National Assembly. In March 2014, former President Goodluck Jonathan inaugurated a National Conference with the aim of finding viable solutions for the multifaceted problems Nigeria faces.

39. M. Eboh, *Oil Firms Spill 3,346 Barrels of Crude Oil in Eight Months Investigation* (Vanguard 29 Sep. 2020), https://www.vanguardngr.com/2020/09/oil-firms-spill-3346-barrels-of-crude-oil-in-eight-months-%E2%80%95-investigation/.
40. B. Adebayo & S. Busari, *Foreign Workers Kidnapped from Nigeria Oil Rig* (CNN 29 Apr. 2019), https://edition.cnn.com/2019/04/29/africa/foreign-oil-workers-nigeria-kidnap-intl/index.html.
41. Premium Times, *83% of Nigeria Oil Blocs Owned by Northerners — Senate Committee Chair Premium Times* (6 Mar. 2013), https://www.premiumtimesng.com/news/123398-83-of-nigeria-oil-blocs-owned-by-northerners-senate-committee-chair.html.

After months of deliberations by various committees, a report of 898 pages was produced to assist lawmakers in reforming the Constitution: no constitutional reform has taken place yet based on the recommendations of National Conference.[42]

46. The issue of population of the south and north is highly contested up till date because it defies migration logic. The southern part which lies along the coast of Nigeria has many rain forests which support life and agriculture unlike the arid north. The north is bigger than the south in landmass while the south has a bigger population and a more fertile land. In migration, people are more likely to move and settle towards the water area instead of moving towards the desert, but the opposite is the case in Nigeria. Furthermore, the creation of local governments which ideally ought to be based on population size was strangely based on land size, such that while Lagos (south) and Kano (north) states have the same population size of about 9.4 million people according to the 2006 population census, Kano has forty-four local governments while Lagos has twenty local governments.[43] These local governments are funded from the federation purse, which means that the financial income of a state unit in Nigeria is based largely on the number of local governments it has. And a state is bound to be rich than its counterparts, if it has a big allocation of funds on the basis of its number of local governments even though in comparison, it has a fewer number of citizens and residents in that state. This and many other issues were chiselled hard in the 1999 Constitution which was written under the supervision of General Sani Abacha, a northerner, who was the military head of state between 1993 and 1998.[44]

47. Even though there is still much to talk about on the political system of Nigeria, there is need to peg the discussion at a point, considering that a full analysis is not really expected here. The 1999 Constitution adopted most of the known fundamental rights. There are freedoms of religion and association, right not to be discriminated against on the basis of gender, birth circumstances, place of origin, and so on. Yet, these rights are frequently violated even by the government. The Nigerian government routinely makes policies that are discriminatory; for instance, the 'quota system' policy requires as a precondition to gaining admission into universities school candidates from the south to score almost ten times higher in national qualifying examinations than their counterparts from the north.[45]

48. Additionally, nearly always, government policies favour the Islamic religion – by providing for Muslim Sharia courts in the Constitution or allowing the compulsory application of sharia law in eleven northern states of Nigeria even though

42. At https://www.premiumtimesng.com/national-conference/download-nigeria-2014-national-conference-report-ngconfab-2/.
43. The Official Census report is available at https://gazettes.africa/archive/ng/2009/ng-government-gazette-dated-2009-02-02-no-2.pdf.
44. *See* K. Awotokun, *Local Government Administration under 1999 Constitution in Nigeria*, Vol. 10(2) J. Soc. Sci. 129–134 (2005).
45. J.C. Omeje, E.I. Egwa & V.O. Adikwu, *Impact of Quota System and Catchment Area Policy on the University Admissions in North Central Nigeria*, Vol. 6(2) SAGE Open (2016), available at doi:10.1177/2158244016654951.

the Constitution guarantees freedom of religion for every citizen and ought to override every other law.[46] It is not therefore surprising that there are many bloody religious and ethnic conflicts in Nigeria, essentially between Christians and Muslims and between southern and northern Nigerians, respectively.

§7. Population, Employment and Production Statistics

49. Nigeria has over 180 million people and a high rate of population growth due to the fact that many of its citizens are not formally educated and do not appreciate birth control measures. Many citizens regard giving birth as an opportunity conferred by their 'creator' and are reluctant towards family planning; many religious sects still consider family planning as sinful and contrary to their religious faith.[47] Thus, even with the current population of 180 million people the sufficient skills for production of goods and services in order to match the necessary demands of the population are seriously lacking.

50. No doubt, since 1999, when Nigeria adopted democracy as a system of governance, and the eventual privatization of the economy, more and more developments have been recorded, such that it could be said loosely that two kinds of Nigeria are emerging – one in which high level and diversified skills are producing goods and services and of course jobs, and one in which workers primarily utilize the traditional methods of production for subsistence. The answer for these two parallel developments is found in the fact that inherent in the 180 million Nigerians are the highly skilled workers, semi-skilled, and those with little or no skill. In the final analysis, it is only a few percentage of Nigerians who are actively producing for the rest of the population who are not in active production but are mainly dependents.

51. The foregoing is reinforced by the fact that even although in principle, there is one country, in reality (as already stated above) there is a geographic divide of the country into south and north – the country has not been able to escape from its historical set-up whereby the peoples of the south and north existed as independent peoples with distinct cultures. In the north where Islam is the dominant religion, there is high-level poverty and human rights abuses because a large percentage of the people are not formally educated and do not have the requisite skills to engage in the production of goods and services using the twenty-first century technology. This is largely the case because in the north, children are sent to Maliki schools where they are taught to recite the Koran rather than being taught science and

46. *See* s. 1(3) of the 1999 Constitution.
47. S.A. Adedini, S. Babalola, C. Ibeawuchi, O. Omotoso, A. Akiode & M. Odeku, *Role of Religious Leaders in Promoting Contraceptive Use in Nigeria: Evidence from the Nigerian Urban Reproductive Health Initiative*, Vol. 6(3) Global Health, Sci. & Prac. 500–514 (2018), https://doi.org/10.9745/GHSP-D-18-00135.

arts.[48] In the south, where the Christian religion is dominant, the story is a lot different. The Christian missionaries in the nineteenth century introduced formal education and building on that, the people of the south are today more educated, possess high-level skills, and even though that the skills required to do many jobs in Nigeria need not be sophisticated, the southern people are in a better position to be more competent participants in the production of goods and services using twenty-first century methods than their counterparts in the north.

52. There should be a qualification to the above assertion that many people from the southern part of Nigeria possess twenty-first century skills. Even though in principle this might sound correct simply by looking at the statistics of university graduates who mainly are in the south, yet, due to the overall large population, the insufficient educational infrastructure has been overwhelmed by the large number of users. This negatively affects the quality of skills transferred to graduates of higher education in Nigeria. Majority of university graduates do not have the requisite competence to solve problems surrounding their degrees.[49] Yet, apart from these poorly acquired skills, many graduates do not have any other skill that can solve problems within the fledgling economy; thus, they remain redundant and unemployed. In the end, those labelled as artisans with semi-skills, for instance, plumbers, electricians, auto mechanics, repairers of fridge, gas cooker, and homes, are better engaged in the largely informal economy of Nigeria.

53. In this circumstance, attaining the middle-class cadre in Nigeria is a Herculean task – and does not come automatically by mere possession of any university degree. Similarly, non-graduates who are either self-employed or engaging in subsistence farming are not performing these jobs with the requisite skills that can lift them out of poverty and unto the middle class as well as create jobs for others.[50] Many people, as a result of the foregoing, do not have any job or income security; do not have health insurance or enough money to cater for themselves in ill health. All this is further complicated by the surging rate of births.

54. To solve the problems surrounding employment and production, attention to key areas must be highly emphasized. And this would entail, among other things, a revamp of the educational sector to stand on its full height; to be able to transfer quality skills that can help school leavers to tackle the challenges surrounding their area of specialization as well as being able to easily create jobs. Admittedly, not everyone can study up to the university level, and it is not even necessary that everyone possesses a university education. What should be emphasized on is a quality delivery of primary and secondary school education which will prepare school leavers to easily appreciate training in vocational schools or the university. If education at the primary and secondary schools is well delivered, Nigeria will have a highly

48. Section 14, Sharia Court of Appeal Law (Northern Nigerian Laws 1963); *see* A.A. Oba, *Islamic Law as Customary Law: The Changing Perspective in Nigeria*, Vol. 51 Int'l & Comp. L.Q. 817 (2002).
49. R.D. Uche, *Quality of University Graduates and Human Resources Development in Nigeria*, Vol. 92(1) Res. in Educ. 49–58 (2014), Doi:10.7227/RIE.0004.
50. Guardian, *Worries Over Declining Training Scheme for Artisans* (The Guardian 21 Dec. 2020), https://guardian.ng/property/worries-over-declining-training-scheme-for-artisans/.

literate population who can easily appreciate the rationale behind birth control, and whose skills can sustain the economy and lift majority out of poverty.

55. But, currently, this is largely not the case. Unlike in well-organized professions like law, medicine and engineering, there is no effort yet to create a system or a certifying board that accredits those with vocational skills; people learn vocational skills these days by enrolling as apprentices with a person who is already practising that vocation, even though the trainer is unlikely to be licensed by any certification body. There is no list of persons who are accredited to accept work orders, and this gap has been negatively exploited by incompetent individuals who declare themselves competent and accept job orders. For instance, there have been cases where self-declared electricians wired houses with grievous electrical faults, which eventually led to the electrocution of some people living in those houses. Given that insurance (to be discussed later) is not well developed, there is hardly a way to recover from errors which led to the destruction of properties due to incompetence of the workers.

56. As already hinted at above, the public service is still slowly recovering from the shackles of military and dictatorial rule that lasted cumulatively for three decades; such that notwithstanding that Nigeria is now under a democratic rule, the attitude towards governance is still largely dictatorial, with much intimidation by politicians to holders of opposing views.[51] Thus, while the government and its politicians are busy with looting activities, the private sector has unfortunately been left with the huge burden of revamping the economy.[52] Even though the private sector is strenuously generating employment, firm growth is simply overwhelmed by the population of unemployed Nigerians. Apart from strengthening education to transfer high-quality skills that can eventually create jobs, the private sector must in any event be supported by the government, through the introduction of favourable and enforceable policies that can, among other things, ensure low level of crime, steady electricity, good roads, pipe borne water, affordable internet and easy access to affordable credit for the ease of doing business. These elements will drive the economy as they are much needed by the private sector to create jobs that will employ citizens in great numbers and consequently alleviate poverty.

57. On another sad note, agriculture in Nigeria is currently in shambles and the neglect of it has caused the country some incalculable fortunes. Before the discovery of crude oil and its boom in the 1980s, Nigeria depended largely on agriculture, having enough for its citizens to consume as well as for exports.[53] It was during this era that much of the quality social and economic infrastructures being used in the country today were built. Agriculture offers two main benefits: it creates jobs and also feeds the population. A well-fed population would likely be more prepared to

51. *See* J.D. Smith, *A Culture of Corruption: Everyday Deception and Popular Discontent in Nigeria* (Princeton University Press 2007).
52. *See* D.U. Enweremadu, *Nigeria's Quest to Recover Looted Assets: The Abacha Affair*, Vol. 48(2) Africa Spectrum 51–70 (2013), Doi:10.1177/000203971304800203.
53. *See* J. Cook, *Tracing the Roots of Nigeria's Agricultural Decline*, Ctr. Strategic & Int'l Stud. (5 May 2016), https://www.csis.org/analysis/tracing-roots-nigerias-agricultural-decline.

think of other pressing issues that threaten their overall development, like civil and political rights, unlike now that no sophisticated thought can be afforded or engaged upon by the Nigerian people because they are largely distracted by the pursuit of everyday needs, hunger and all of its related vices.

58. Agriculture evidently transfers the culture of hard work to citizens – because all of its processes, from tilling the soil to the sowing of seeds to harvesting and selling of produce, involve series of hard work, patience, endurance and accountability. Thus, by engaging in agriculture, the citizens come to understand what hard work means – that harvesting of grains, fruits and vegetables can only come up after efforts have been invested; the benefits of this attitude when it becomes part of a culture cannot be overemphasized. Similarly, a population with such attitude towards work would likely hold their government accountable and demand to know how their hard-earned monies in the form of taxes are utilized. Then in such circumstance, the government is likely to be more accountable and fearful of the people, instead of the other way round. It is from such attitude that strong institutions cmcrgc.

59. But all this is currently not the case; with oil being the largest source of income, the culture of hard work eroded from the minds of many Nigerians. It is the writer's view that Nigerians lost their attitude to hard work with the discovery of oil; an easy way to make money simply by tapping the resources below and selling the same to highest bidders. In that arrangement, whereby not much hard work is required on the part of both government and the people in order to earn a living, laziness of the highest order is bound to set in.

60. As a result, the foregoing 'resource curse' has left Nigeria with very corrupt officials who are scrambling for the oil money to enrich themselves rather than delivering on the electoral mandates.[54] Worse still, majority of the population in their private lives are now lazy and unwilling to engage in activities that do not yield quick and easy money; the incentive for hard work and efforts towards creating a sustainable wealth are vanishing speedily from sight. That same mindset of easy acquisition of wealth without much effort underscored in crude oil export is arguably the reason why obtaining property from another by false pretences have become so prevalent among Nigerians since the 1980s till date. The problem of easy expectation of wealth without investing equivalent amount of efforts in a genuine manner has become cultural, having been the norm for more than three decades, that is a generation.

61. In order to raise a human generation that will appreciate hard work and race to the top in terms of skills acquisition as the sustainable gateways to wealth creation, agriculture must again be welcome to the front seat together with favourable policies that can support the private sector businesses. As a strong necessity, the Nigerian government must invest heavily on data gathering on the various issues

---

54. *See* U. Idemudia, *The Resource Curse and the Decentralization of Oil Revenue: The Case of Nigeria*, Vol. 35 J. Cleaner Production 183–193 (2012).

that plague the country, as that would enable policymakers to plan effectively for the population. Similarly, researchers focusing on Nigeria can only do so effectively having data to work or improve upon, rather than having none at all to work with. It is not an exaggeration to say that a country without sufficient data cannot effectively plan for its population because it would be unable to know exactly what problems exist and their magnitude, and the level of resources they deserve to be properly dealt with.

§8. SOCIAL AND CULTURAL VALUES

I. Languages

62. Nigeria has several languages, currently estimated as numbering over three hundred. Over three hundred languages invariably show that a number of cultures are also in existence. Keeping this in mind, one can see that the over 180 million people in Nigeria see and analyse issues from over three hundred (cultural) perspectives.

63. However, owing to the fact that the country was colonized by Britain, the English language was chosen as the country's official language. English therefore is a unifying language in Nigeria and a conduit pipe through which the various ethnic groups can share their culture and perspectives with their fellow citizens.[55] Even though the English language is tremendously assisting in achieving some progress towards the unity agenda, it should be noted that most Nigerians prefer to communicate in their native languages, especially when they see someone who understands their language; it is even considered rude to speak to an elderly person or someone from your tribe in English because it is often interpreted to mean arrogance and an unnecessary show of brilliance.

64. Thus, it is culturally encouraged to speak in one's native language when communicating with one from the same tribe. The challenge is that this encouragement has sometimes failed to draw the line between official and unofficial communications; people simply speak to those who come from their tribe and are occupying public positions in their common language with the hope to curry some undue favour out of it. This is the case most times regardless of the setting, as it is possible to see a public official speak to a citizen who had come to make enquiries in an official capacity, in their common tribal language. Thus, there is that affinity, that wall that is broken down when a Nigerian is addressed in his/her native language by another tribe person. Many reasons can be responsible for this commonplace behaviour, but in the writer's view, two should be highlighted for lack of

55. *See* generally, O. Benson, L. Anyalebechi & I. Ariole, *Promoting Indigenous Language in Nigeria: Issues and Challenges for the Library and Information Professionals*, Lib. Phil. & Prac. (e-journal) 1472 (2017), http://digitalcommons.unl.edu/libphilprac/1472.

writing space. First, as already pointed out in the beginning part of this work, the Nigerian entity is an artificial creation, and did not emerge as a result of confederation.

65. The peoples that combined to form Nigeria were and still are distinct and have different cultures and religions, and if their opinion were to count, they would have loved to remain on their own if not for the overriding interest of the Berlin Conference of 1884–1885. Thus, it is commonplace, though there are exceptions, for a Nigerian to meet another citizen on a bus and ask him where she/he is from. The answer that follows would likely determine how he would relate with the stranger, whether as a 'brother' or as someone to be treated dispassionately. When the conflicts are not physical among people of these ethnic groups, they are mental, with people of each ethnic group perceiving themselves as being in contest of all kinds with other groups; thus, there is that silent call to assist one's 'brother' to grow and add to the possibility of 'conquering' or resisting intimidations from people of other tribes. In this conundrum, national interest is buried far below the ground and the pursuit of narrow interest is enlarged and made order of the day. Even public office positions which ought to be given based on merit, that is, whoever that possesses the most competent skill, are determined mainly by tribal and/or religious sentiments. Thus, people are more likely to secure an advantage from fellow Nigerian citizens if they speak the same native language, than if they were to speak only English to them.[56]

66. The second reason why English is less preferable for communication is that it is poorly taught in most public primary and secondary schools where many Nigerian citizens receive their basic education. Because it is poorly taught, nearly always, students graduate from primary and high schools with inadequate communications skill in the English language and this makes them unable to sufficiently express their thoughts with the language; they may then resort more frequently to their native language whenever the opportunity presents. Notwithstanding the foregoing, it can still be said that even though English as a first language in Nigeria is only possible among a small minority of the country's urban elite, and is not even spoken at all in most rural places, yet, it remains the language of instruction in schools, official functions and business transactions.

II. Religion

67. Nigeria is a seedbed of many religions – both imported and indigenous religions are practised.[57] Even though the Constitution guarantees religious freedom, nearly always, religion makes its way into the Nigerian politics and seeks to have an overall application. It is dangerous to openly admit that one is a freethinker – in Islam, it cannot go without a death punishment for a family member to disclose to

56. *See* generally, M. Ogunmodimu, *Language Policy in Nigeria: Problems, Prospects and Perspectives*, Vol. 5(9) Int'l J. Human. & Soc. Sci. 154–160 (2015).
57. *See* C. Meek, *The Religions of Nigeria*, Vol. 14(3) Afr.: J. Int'l Afr. Inst. 106–117 (1943).

the rest of the family about his unbelief in the faith; apostasy attracts a death sentence under sharia law: this applies in many states in the northern part of the country. Christianity is predominantly practised in the southern part. Even though southern Christians are not as violent as their northern Muslim counterparts when it comes to enforcing breaches of the injunctions ordained in their holy books, they nevertheless are guilty of the charge of intolerance. The intolerance of varying viewpoints is intrinsically problematic; the various denominations of Christianity in the south are at loggerheads regarding whose spiritual methods are biblically sanctioned and should therefore prevail.

68. Similarly, there is a double standard practice among Christians and Muslims vis-à-vis their attitude towards traditional religion. While they openly reject traditional religion as diabolical and inefficient, nearly all the time, one realizes that many Christians and Muslims indeed consider it as more powerful, and that traditional worshippers possess enough spiritual powers that can tremendously harm them. Sometimes too, Christians and Muslims merge their beliefs with the traditional religion and even consult the chief priests of traditional religion for answers to what they consider a spiritual challenge. The deference to traditional religion by Christians is often depicted in Nigerian Nollywood films. On a deeper probe, one realizes that the reason for this oscillation by Christians and Muslims between the Abrahamic religions and the traditional one lies in the fact that whereas the former is less than two centuries old in Nigeria, the latter has always been with the Nigerian people and indeed commands more loyalty even when many would not acknowledge it.

III. Family

69. In Nigeria, loyalty to one's family is greater than the one held for the country. This is due to many reasons too numerous to highlight here. But suffice it to mention that given the lack of vital provisions of life at the national level, the responsibilities of shelter, food, education, health, security are almost exclusively provided by one's family. If one's family does not provide these basic amenities of life, chances are high that such individual will be socially disadvantaged and would unlikely succeed in life. The extended family system is the norm because one needs as many family members as possible for assistance through life because one's success in life is difficult to achieve without some basic assistance.[58]

70. Given that the government is not satisfactorily responsive to these issues, the extended family system, in large part, acts as a viable alternative to the government. Thus, grandparents, cousins, aunts, uncles, sisters, brothers, parents, to in-laws, are all important allies in one's journey through life. As there is no viable system that supports access to credit for the ease of doing business, or scholarship funds or loans

58. *See* generally, E. Fapohunda & M. Todaro, *Family Structure, Implicit Contracts, and the Demand for Children in Southern Nigeria*, Vol. 14(4) Population & Dev. Rev. 571–594 (1988).

for educational pursuits, individuals always turn to their family members for financial assistance; there is that general responsibility on everyone to look out for one another. In the extended family system, age is a big player and determines hierarchy and seniority; opinions are not weighted based on actual knowledge of the subject of discourse but on the general experience about life, which is, of course, measured by age. The general behaviour of members of a family is largely influenced by the family's social status; thus, a family known to be honest in their dealings always spend more time to encourage their members not to involve in activities that will tarnish the family's image.

71. Today, the role of the extended family is gradually paling into insignificance because many Nigerians now travel to different parts of the country or even outside the country to pursue their dreams, and it is increasingly becoming difficult to reunite with family members at any one time. The inability to accomplish one's dreams in his locality and the eventual need to travel out has been a big factor in the disintegration of the extended family system, and the promotion of the nuclear family type.

IV. Communication Style

72. It should be noted that the common way to greet strangers in Nigeria is a handshake with a warm welcoming smile; people even offer welcoming drinks or snacks to strangers even before they disclose their intention for visiting. Male persons, in greeting someone elderly, may bow their heads while female persons may genuflect, all as signs of respect. It is extremely valued by a visitor if his host can show that he is happy about the visit. The visitor would have to monitor whether enough signs have been shown by the host; this will determine how long the visitor will stay. Similarly, it is considered rude to rush over greetings; when greeting, people use the opportunity to enquire about the other's health, the health of their family members, and how their lives have been generally. However, the mode of greeting is different for Christians and Muslims. While the foregoing description depicts what the case is in the south, in the north which is predominantly Muslims, it is likely that observant Muslims will not shake hands with members of the opposite gender.[59]

73. It is common knowledge that Nigerians like to be addressed by their titles: academic, professional or honorific titles and their surname; surnames in many cases carry prestige, especially if one's family members are very important or political individuals. The case is different in informal settings, as friends or relatives may address their members by the first name or even by their nicknames.

59. *See* N. Princewill, *Of Our Indigenous Greeting Culture* (The Guardian 16 Jun. 2017), https://guardian.ng/opinion/of-our-indigenous-greeting-culture/; Also *see*, 'A guide to Nigeria – etiquette, customs, clothing and more' *Kwintessential,* https://www.kwintessential.co.uk/resources/guide-to-nigeria-etiquette-customs-culture-business.

74. Furthermore, if one is invited for a dinner or for any event by a family, he or she is expected to bring some fruits, or anything of value for the host. In fact, the visitor would be more welcome if they bring some gifts for the children and are able to call them by their names; that way, the host feels that the visitor is one of them. In presenting the gifts to the family, the right hand or both hands should be used. Using the left hand to shake or present gifts to any person is considered extremely rude and unacceptable, and could change perceptions about the person who extended the left hand. To digress, there is no reasonable explanation for the discrimination of the left hand except that most people in Nigeria are pattern-seeking in nature and would easily object to anything that is not prevalent or commonplace; for example, it is common knowledge that albinos, gays, transgender people, and most other minority groups are discriminated even when the Constitution guarantees their freedom and rights.

75. During Ramadan (a period of intense fasting and prayers in Islam), it is customary for people of the Islamic faith to share gifts among themselves. And due to the heightened attention given to sex by most religions, especially among Muslims, gifts from a man to a woman has to be characterized as proceeding from the man's wife or mother, sister or any other female relative, but not from the man himself. Without saying that the gift comes from any of these persons, a high-level suspicion of adultery can be mentally established against the recipient, that is, the woman. Unlike in other cultures, in Nigeria, gifts are not always opened in front of the giver; opening it is reserved until the giver has left.

76. There is no single Nigerian way to communicate; styles differ considering that over three hundred–four hundred cultures exist. In the south where the Igbo, Yoruba and other tribes reside, people often employ proverbs in the course of communication. This means that most times, it is not encouraged to be direct with one's communication; proverbs in Nigerian languages, like the English figures of speech, exist to provide indirectness, to pass on uncomfortable meanings in a rather euphemistic manner. Although the use of proverbs and other unique communication styles is more intensively used while speaking in any of the native languages, these styles and use of proverbs have been extended to when speaking English as well. Thus, it is possible that in speaking English, many people who think in their native languages literally translate words and expressions into English.

77. The Igbos and Yoruba[60] employ humour as well when speaking, as they believe that is a way to retain the listener's attention and also as a way to chisel most information into the memory, especially in the olden days when there was no lasting (written) form of recording or keeping information for a long time. Thus the use of humour and proverbs was meant to assist the human memory, to link the humours and proverbs to a particular discussion. In addition to the foregoing, facial expressions are important and can be used to determine the level of sympathy or indifference one has over an issue; sometimes, facial expression is the only evidence to prove guilt or innocence over certain issues.

---

60. Olatunde O. Olatunji, *The Yoruba History, Culture and Language* (Ibadan University Press 1970).

§9. Economic System – The Role of Markets and Government in Economic Life

78. Nigeria, Africa's most populous country with a mixed economy, currently has severe economic policy challenges necessitated by corruption, lack of transparency in governance, and the overreliance on crude oil export as the main source of earning foreign exchange. Before the discovery of crude oil in commercial quantity sometime in the 1980s, the country's foreign exchange came mainly from the export of agricultural products. However, the discovery of oil changed the country's economic focus and methods. Agriculture was immediately relegated to the background, while corruption and all the features of 'resource curse' were present in the oil boom era, and even today.

79. After being ruled by several military and dictatorial regimes for a cumulative period of twenty-nine years since the independence in 1960, during which time the economic system was more of state controlled, in 1999, democracy was adopted as a system of governance, and the economy was eventually liberalized and privatized. Many of the state-owned assets were sold; though most of the sales were not transparent, and there were issues of collusion and sale of government property and businesses to cronies who did not have the resources and skills to revitalize and effectively deliver the services surrounding the businesses that were purchased from the government. Even though the government still manages some sectors, like water board, prison, and schools, some of the services it used to exclusively provide in the past have now been privatized.[61]

80. Privatization notwithstanding, old habits die hard: even though the government has liberalized and privatized the economy, and democracy being the system of government, oftentimes, the government falls back to its old habits of heavy-handedness and over intrusion into private businesses. In fact, there are vital services, e.g., health, power, security, and education, etc., that determine a good enabling environment for business that are still being rendered clumsily by the government. The bad news is that government officials do not deliver these services properly and timely and the outcome affects the growth of businesses in Nigeria.[62] For instance, the registration of business organizations at the Corporate Affairs Commission (CAC), which is managed by the government, requires a lot of protocols, with officials often demanding bribes as a precondition to facilitate one's official requests. Indeed, it is more correct to say that the government still retains the exclusive right to produce more than half of the needed services in Nigeria, especially those contained in the exclusive list of the extant 1999 Constitution, even when it does not do so efficiently and effectively.

---

61. *See*, generally, K. Mohammed, Dutsin-Ma, A. Bello, *The State of Nigerian Economy in the 21st Century; Privatization and Commercialization Programmes under Obasanjo/Atiku Regime*, Vol. 9(1) Eur. Sc. J. 88–98 (2013), https://core.ac.uk/download/pdf/328023776.pdf.
62. T.C. Obiwuru, O.B. Oluwalaiye & A.T. Okwu, *External and Internal Environments of Businesses in Nigeria: An Appraisal*, Vol. 12 Int'l Bull. Bus. Administration 15–23 (2011).

81. Ideally, the government is supposed to focus mainly on the provision of an enabling environment that will encourage the growth of businesses, but that is largely not the case. Thus, electricity, security, roads, etc., which the government ought to ensure are sufficiently in existence as economic drivers, are in dire lack, and this affects businesses and even discourages potential investors from investing in Nigeria. The government has also failed to effectively play the role of a competent regulator of businesses. Businesses are not well regulated;[63] it is possible to sell items of extremely poor quality, fake, or even dangerous items in the Nigerian market, yet, such a heinous act would hardly be detected, challenged or punished by the government.[64] There seems to be little incentive for honesty and good faith behaviour since those who negatively and illegally exploit the market usually go undetected or unpunished. Indeed, consumer protection is hardly in place, such that from telephone companies to those selling fake baby foods and drugs in the market, the government keeps a blind eye to all this because its officials can easily be bribed and they are also ill-equipped to deal with the level of market abuses that deeply threaten the lives of Nigerians on a daily basis.[65]

82. Property rights are not well protected as well even though section 33(2)(a) of the 1999 Constitution provides that a person can take lawful steps to protect their property. Contrary to section 44 of the Constitution regarding adequate compensation for compulsory acquisition of property, there have been instances where the government refused to pay compensations to citizens after it had compulsorily acquired their lands and buildings on the excuse of overriding public interests. Section 44 of the extant 1999 Constitution provides for government's adequate compensation in the event of expropriation but as research shows that is hardly the case.[66] This same attitude has spilt into the behaviour of many Nigerians who obtain other citizens' properties by forceful or non-legal means without any reasonable justification. They do this, knowing well that little or no consequences would inure, especially when the police can easily be bribed. Thus, survival tilts heavily in favour of the fittest and day by day there is a growing spirit of intimidation across the country.

§10. The Legal System

83. Given that Nigeria was colonized by Britain, its legal system shares a lot in common with the English common law legal tradition. Thus, after the colonial rule

63. I. Anyaogu, *How Poor Regulation Is Hurting Nigeria's Small Businesses* (Business Day 29 Jul. 2020), https://businessday.ng/features/article/how-poor-regulation-is-hurting-nigerias-small-businesses/.
64. NAFDAC, *Curbing Substandard, Falsified (SFS) And Counterfeit Medicines* (NAFDAC 11 Nov. 2019), https://www.nafdac.gov.ng/curbing-substandard-falsified-sfs-and-counterfeit-medicines/.
65. IBRD, *Doing Business in Nigeria*, Comparing Bus. Reg. Domestic Firms in 36 States and FCT Abuja with 189 Other Economies 33–56 (2018), https://www.doingbusiness.org/content/dam/doingBusiness/media/Subnational-Reports/DB_in_Nigeria_2018_w-bookmarks.pdf.
66. Victor O. Ige & Rasidat A. Oladapo, *Variation in Compensation for Compulsory Property Acquisition: Ondo State, Nigeria Experience*, Vol. 24(2) Pac. Rim Pro. Res. J. 139–148 (2018).

which impressed the English legal tradition on Nigeria, the country realized that it is not possible to invent a new legal system overnight. Therefore, much of English law was borrowed to form part of Nigerian law, and that is still the case.[67]

84. The sources of Nigerian law today are, namely:[68]

a. the Constitution,
b. statutes,
c. received English law,
d. customary law,
e. sharia law,[69] and
f. judicial precedents, otherwise known as case law.

85. Each of these sources will be briefly explained below.

I. The Constitution

86. The Constitution governs the relationship between one arm of government and another on the one hand and between the government and citizens on the other hand. The 1999 Constitution was enacted by the Abubakar Addusalami military administration in 1999 after the death of Sani Abacha who was the military head of state between 1993 and 1998. The 1999 Constitution replaced the 1979 Constitution that was enacted by the Olusegun Obasanjo military administration in 1979. The Constitution is the most powerful source of law in Nigeria, and when there is a conflict between its provisions and any other law, that other law becomes void to the extent of its inconsistency with the Constitution.[70] The Constitution contains fundamental rights that are universally recognized and enforceable in Nigerian courts. In 2009, the Chief Justice of Nigeria, pursuant to section 46(3) of the Constitution, developed the Fundamental Rights (Enforcement Procedure) Rules, which confer *locus standi* on any person to enforce the breach of another person's fundamental rights.[71] This is a major improvement in the country that was ravaged by military rule during which issues were mainly resolved outside the purview of rule of law.[72]

67. *See* s. 14 of the Supreme Court Ordinance, 1914 which provide that 'subject to the terms of this or any other Ordinance, the common law, the doctrines of equity and statutes of general application which were in force in England on the 1st of January 1900, shall be in force within the jurisdiction of this court'. Also *see* s. 45 of the Interpretation Act Cap 123 LFN 2004, which provides for the same thing.
68. *See* generally, C. Okonkwo, Introduction to Nigerian Law (Sweet & Maxwell 1980).
69. The Islamic religion is predominantly practised in the northern part of Nigeria, and by s. 14 of Sharia Court of Appeal Law (Northern Nigerian Laws 1963), sharia law is the applicable law.
70. *See* s. 1(3) of the 1999 Constitution.
71. *See* the Fundamental Rights (Enforcement Procedure) Rules, 2009.
72. *See* E. Nwauche, *The Nigerian Fundamental Rights (Enforcement) Procedure Rules 2009: A Fitting Response to Problems in the Enforcement of Human Rights in Nigeria?*, Vol. 10 Afr. Hum. Rts. L. J. 502, 503 (2010).

87. After the adoption of democracy in 1999, ten years down the line, it was realized that many people still haunted by their military past abused the fundamental rights of citizens, rather than resorting to the rule of law. A source of confusion to Nigerian courts prior to 2009, related to the interpretation of Order 1 Rule 2 of the Fundamental Rights Enforcement Procedure (FREP) Rules 1979, which provided that 'any person who alleges that any of the fundamental rights provided for in the Constitution and to which he is entitled, has been, is being, or is likely to be infringed may apply to the court in the state where the infringement occurs or is likely to occur, for redress.' Courts interpreted this to mean that only a person whose fundamental rights were breached, and no other, had the *locus standi* to sue: it was not possible to sue on behalf of another person whose fundamental rights were breached. Any such legal action was nullified for want of *locus standi*.[73] This prevented many victims who were financially unable to pursue the enforcement of their rights to go without a remedy. Apart from instances of judicial activism, e.g., the case of *Captain SA Asemota v. Col SL Yesufu and Another*[74] where the court amended the petitioner's application *suo moto* in order to achieve the aim and objectives of the 1979 FREP rules, the issue of lack of *locus standi* to sue on behalf of another raged until the statutory amendment in the FREPs Rules, 2009.[75]

II. Statutes

88. Laws enacted by the National Assembly (Nigeria's highest lawmaking body) are called 'Acts'. An Act of the National Assembly is a federal law that generally applies across the country, while laws made by any of the legislatures of the thirty-six state units are called 'laws'. When there is conflict between a law made by a state legislature and that made by the National Assembly, the latter prevails. Before 1999, the laws that were made by the various military regimes were called 'decrees'; they were passed without any legislative procedure.[76] Thus, in 1999, these decrees were revised and those that were compatible with democratic principles were recognized and retained by the Constitution; the 1999 Constitution under section 315 designates those surviving decrees as 'existing laws', and the President reserves the right to modify an existing law to align with the provision of the Constitution.[77] They are valid and continue to apply to individuals and governments. The decrees that were incompatible with the principles of rule of law and democracy were repealed in 1999.

---

73. Some of the cases include: *Olusola Oyegbemi v. Attorney-General of the Federation* (1982) 3 NCLR 895; *Alhaji Shugaba Abruraham Darman v. Minister of Internal Affairs* (1981) 2 NCLR 459.
74. (1981) 1 NSCR 420.
75. *See* generally, A. Sanni, *Fundamental Rights Enforcement Procedure Rules, 2009 as a Tool for the Enforcement of the African Charter on Human and Peoples' Rights in Nigeria: The Need for Far-Reaching Reform*, Vol. 11 Afr. Hum. Rts. L. J. 511–531 (2011).
76. *See* generally, A. Obilade, *The Nigerian Legal System* (Sweet & Maxwell 1979).
77. *See AG Abia v. AG Federation* (2003) 19 WRN 1. In this case, the Supreme Court upheld the Adaption order that was published in the Statutory Instrument No. 9 of 2002 to bring the revenue allocation (federation accounts) in alignment with the 1999 Constitution.

89. Another way statutes are made in Nigeria can be found in section 12 of the 1999 Constitution. Thus, treaties and conventions that have been signed and ratified by Nigeria have to pass through section 12 in order to be domesticated. The effect of domestication is that such treaty ranks equal with locally made statutes. There have been questions as to what may happen in the event a treaty that was domesticated is in conflict with a locally made statute.[78] Courts are divided on this: while a school of thought believes that whenever in conflict a treaty turned statute should prevail because it embodies Nigeria's commitment with the rest of the world; another view is that both are equal and prevalence should be based on which was later in time, that is, the doctrine of implied repeal.[79]

III. Received English Law

90. As earlier stated, Nigeria fashioned its legal system in line with the English common law tradition. Thus, all statutes in force in England on or before 1 January 1900, common law, the doctrines of equity are deemed to be part of Nigerian law. Even though it is now the case that whenever there is a local statute that provides for what is contained in a statute of general application, the local statute should prevail, yet, this still poses a lot of difficulty because the statutes of general application that were in force in England on 1 January 1900 are too many and do not govern everyday transactions in Nigeria, but are tactically used as 'ambush laws' to surprise opponents in court. Another challenge is that statutes of general application (i.e., statutes older than the year 1900) are old and do not always reflect modern-day realities in Nigeria; some of them have been repealed in England or amended to reflect modern-day realities. However, given the dearth of laws in Nigeria, the statutes of general application still unfortunately find relevance in the legal system.

IV. Customary Law

91. In the southern part of Nigeria, customary law (largely unwritten) refers to the customs and practices of the people.[80] Given that Nigeria has fashioned its legal system with much of borrowing from the English common law, it realized to its chagrin that common law cannot truly supplant the people's cultural perspectives on law and justice overnight. Thus, even though the English type of law forms the major part of the legal system, some recognition is accorded to customs, especially in respect of property rights and celebration of marriages.[81] Customary courts are in the lowest cadre of courts, and deal with matters that are entirely hinged on customs; the presiding judge need not be a lawyer, even though lawyers do sit with non-law judges so as to guide them on the broader law perspectives.

---

78. *See* generally, A.A. Oba, *The African Charter on Human and Peoples' Rights and Ouster Clauses under the Military Regimes in Nigeria: Before and after September 11*, Vol. 2 Afr. Hum. Rts. L. J. 275 at 280 (2004).
79. *See* the Supreme Court case of *Abacha v. Fawehinmi* (2000) FWLR (Pt.4) 553 at 586.
80. *See* A. Obilade, *The Nigerian Legal System* 83 (Sweet & Maxwell 1979).
81. T. Olawale Elias, *The Nature of African Customary Law* 55 (Manchester University Press 1956).

92. In the superior courts of records, like the High Court, National Industrial Court, Court of Appeal and Supreme Court, customary law is treated as facts and must satisfy the test of reasonability and good conscience.[82] This is because more than three hundred customs exist and sometimes retain practices that contrast with the broader principles of law contained in statutes or common law. Judges are deemed to know the common law and statutes, but not customary law, which embodies the various customs and practices of the over three hundred ethnic groups. As already hinted at, these customs have to be proven to exist before a court of records can accept them as applicable to a circumstance. The way to prove a custom's existence is to call on custodians of the said custom, e.g., the village chiefs or traditional rulers who are deemed to be versatile about the people's customs and traditions, to explain whether an alleged custom is indeed part of their tradition and how it applies in the circumstance.

93. In Nigeria, the customary law of individuals, in the absence of any will of a deceased person, governs the devolution of their personal property, especially if the deceased person's lifestyle suggested a deference to their customs. Today the value of customary law is increasingly diminishing because, nearly always, customary practices come in conflict with the provisions of the Constitution, especially those sections on fundamental rights of the citizens. For example, in Igboland, there is the discriminatory practice of 'osu'[83] *Osu* refers to the derogatory designation given to people whose ancestors centuries ago were banished from their communities into exile. Today, they are generally discriminated against on the basis of this circumstance that surrounds their birth. Similarly, there is a widespread discrimination of the female gender especially in the Igboland, whereby male offspring are considered superior to the female counterparts; this gender-based discrimination finds expression in many aspects of social life among the Igbos and other ethnic groups in Nigeria, especially in the devolution of family property.[84]

V. Islamic Law

94. Whereas customary law is typically unwritten, same cannot be said of Islamic law, which is written down, with clearly defined and articulated principles, many of which apply across the globe. Sharia law is derived from the Koran and Hadith and is largely observed by Muslims in the northern part of Nigeria as personal law due to their history and trade relations with the Arabian merchants in the

---

82. *See* s. 18, Evidence Act 2011.
83. *See* Franklin Ugobude, *"Culture: The Osu Caste System in Igboland"* *The Guardian* (The Guardian 18 Nov. 2018), https://guardian.ng/life/culture-the-osu-caste-system-in-igboland/.
84. Interestingly, the Court of Appeal held in *Mojekwu v. Mojekwu* [1997] 7 NWLR 283 that gender-based discrimination in devolution of property is contrary to s. 42 of the 1999 Constitution which prohibits discrimination, including on the ground of sex (gender). However, on appeal to the Supreme Court (2004) 11 NWLR (Pt. 883) 96, the court held that the *oli-ekpe* custom which denied women the right to inheritance is a valid custom. For an expert critique of this Supreme Court decision, *see* E. Worugji & R.O. Ugbe, *Judicial Protection of Women's Rights in Nigeria: The Regrettable Decision in Mojekwu v. Iwuchukwu*, Vol. 16 Univ. Botswana L.J. 59 (2013).

nineteenth century.[85] In eleven states in Nigeria, sharia law is applicable and governs the Muslims in those states; the implication of having the sharia legal system within the broader democratic system is that it introduced religious-oriented punishment to offences as instructed in the Koran or Hadith.

95. In the writer's view, sharia law is largely antithetic to the Constitution which ought to override any law in Nigeria in the event of conflict; virtually all the provisions on fundamental right guaranteed in the Constitution are contradicted by sharia law. Similarly, there ought not be a basis to assert that sharia law should trump over statutes made by the National Assembly, which apply generally across the country. The adoption of the sharia legal system by the eleven northern states in Nigeria surprisingly started after the adoption of democracy as the country's system of government.

96. There is no Supreme Court decision yet that pronounces on the constitutionality of certain offences and punishments under sharia law, whether, for instance, the discrimination of women, the stoning to death on the charge of adultery, the amputation of hand for the guilt of theft, death penalties for blasphemy and apostasy, and fair hearing issues should be expunged or kept for the sake of religious tolerance. In the writer's view, these aspects of sharia law in Nigeria cannot meet the validity test of the Constitution and should be addressed by the lawmakers to provide full clarity.

VI. Judicial Precedents

97. Inherent in the common law system is the use of judicial precedents, also known as case law.[86] The use of judicial precedents implies that the previous decisions of the Supreme Court would bind it when determining current matters. By section 230 of the 1999 Constitution, the Supreme Court is the apex court and its decisions bind the Court of Appeal and the High Courts. The Court of Appeal established in 1979 has ten judicial divisions which are located across the country, but are considered to be one court. Its decisions bind it and also the high courts. Below the Court of Appeal are five courts of coordinate jurisdiction, namely, the State High Courts, Federal High Courts, National Industrial Court, Customary Court of Appeal and the Sharia Court of Appeal. These courts are bound by the decisions of all the courts above them, while decisions from their peers are only of persuasive and not binding value.

98. In determining what part, or how a decision in a previously decided case binds a current case, the facts of the previous case must be materially similar to the current case, and the *ratio decidendi* must have been predicated on the facts of the

85. Y. Sodiq, *A History of the Application of Islamic Law in Nigeria* (Palgrave Macmillan 2017), Chap 6. Available at https://link.springer.com/content/pdf/bfm%3A978-3-319-50600-5%2F1.pdf.
86. *See* J.H. Farrar & A.M. Dugdale, *Introduction to Legal Method* 84 (Sweet &Maxwell 2nd ed. 1984).

previous case which are materially similar in the current one.[87] In determining what could be binding, the obiter dictum or *dicta* of the judge are not considered to have a binding value; it is only persuasive to the court that made it or to a lower court judge.[88]

VII. Arms of Government

99. This section would be incomplete without commenting on the arms of government. Unlike the English Parliamentary system which was in vogue in Nigeria between 1960 and 1966, currently, the presidential system of government which is akin to the United States system is being practised. Thus, the first arm of government is the legislature whose primary function is lawmaking. The legislature at the national level[89] is bicameral, and made up of the Senate and the House of Representatives. The Senate is made up of 109 elected members, comprising of 3 senators from each of 36 states, and 1 senator from the Federal Capital Territory. Members of the House of Representatives are 360 in number, with 10 representatives from each state. Each state has its own lawmaking body, known as the House of Assembly. Also, all legislators whether in the National or State Assembly[90] are elected for a constitutional period of four years' term, though the electorates have the constitutional right to recall their legislator.

100. The second arm is the Executive arm of government, which is vested in the President, who is the commander in chief of the armed forces. The legislature's primary function is to enforce the law. The President's powers are also exercisable through his vice president and all the ministers, whom he delegates powers to perform certain duties. At the state level, the executive power is vested in the Governor of the state, who is designated as the chief security officer of his state. The Governor's power is also exercisable through the deputy governor and commissioners whom the Governor assigns or delegates powers to perform certain duties.

101. The third arm is the judiciary. The judiciary interprets the law by stating what they think was the intention of the lawmakers with respect to a particular legal provision. Given that the Nigerian legal system is hinged on common law, the decisions of courts operate to enrich and fill gaps in the black letter law. The Constitution established the High Court, National Industrial Court, the Customary Court

---

87. A. Obilade, *The Nigerian Legal System* 113 (Sweet & Maxwell 1979).
88. *See* Black's Law Dictionary 1100 (West Group 7th ed. 1999).
89. The federal legislature legislates exclusively on matters on the exclusive list, and shares legislative competence with state houses of assembly with respect on the concurrent list. See the second schedule, part I of the 1999 Constitution.
90. Each state house of assembly has the constitution power to legislate on the concurrent list found in the second schedule to the 1999 Constitution. The Supreme Court has held that the concurrently shared legislative powers between the state legislatures and the federal legislature do not entitle the latter to make laws that make laws that empower its agencies to carry out acts that will interfere with the planning powers of the state. *See* the case of *AG Lagos v. AG Federation* (2003) 35 W.R.N 1.

of Appeal, the Sharia Court of Appeal of the Federal Capital Territory, the Sharia Court of Appeal of each state, the Court of Appeal, and the Supreme Court. These courts are known as superior courts of record. The Constitution also empowers the National Assembly and the Houses of Assembly to establish courts that are inferior to the High Court, and any court established pursuant to the Constitution is deemed not to be a court of record. Examples of these courts are the Magistrate court, the District Court, Area/Sharia Court, and the Customary Court.

102. By far, high courts are the busiest and important courts because they deal with issues of both facts and law. Their findings of facts and the application of law to them, known as judgments, are reconsidered upon appeal by the Court of Appeal. The Court of Appeal does not deal with issues of facts; they consider issues of law except it can be shown that the trial court, that is, the High Court, refused to carry out its duty of fact-finding. In that case, the Court of Appeal can under section 16 of the Court of Appeal Act step into the original jurisdiction of the High Court and entertain facts at the appeal level in order to know whether the applied law was appropriate in the circumstance.

Part I. Commercial Law

Chapter 1. Concepts and Sources of Commercial Law

103. Commercial law refers to the body of laws that govern business transactions between two companies or a company and an individual on the one hand and between two individuals on the other hand. In Nigeria, the body of law called commercial law is a series of distinct aspects of laws governing commerce. These include but are not limited to contract law, agency, sale of goods, hire purchase, banking, employment and trade union laws. There is no independent body of law that governs the activities of merchants, the equivalent of *lex mercatoria* in other jurisdictions. If any of such exists in Nigeria, they exist not in a code-like form, but scattered across the aspects of laws forming commercial law. These laws will be analysed generally, just to give the reader a fair view of Nigeria's commercial law.

§1. Contract Law

104. Under Nigerian law, a contract is an agreement which the court can enforce.[91] Whereas not all agreements are contracts, every contract is an agreement. The Nigerian contract law is a mirror image of the English law of contract. Thus, for a contract to be valid and enforceable, the elements of offer, acceptance, consideration and intention of parties to enter into a legal relation must be present.

105. A contract could be oral or written, and should generally be supported by a consideration.[92] However, a contract under seal need not be supported by a consideration to be enforceable. Section 4 of the Statute of Frauds 1677, which is a statute of general application in Nigeria, provides for contracts that must be in writing. In determining the existence of a contract, the court could see whether the facts establishing its existence are express or implied. In the event, the 'Composite Document Rule' in essence states that in determining the existence or otherwise of a contract, the court could look at a series of documents that refer to one another as if they were one.

91. The most authoritative text on Nigerian contract law is unarguably by: I. Sagay, *Nigerian Law of Contract* (Spectrum Law Publishing 2nd ed. 2001). The first edition was in 1985 by Sweet & Maxwell, London.
92. *Ibid.*, at p. 59.

106. A contract can be unilateral or bilateral. In a unilateral contract, such as the famous *Carlill v. Carbolic Smoke Ball Company*,[93] the offer is made by the offeror who binds himself by offering to fulfil a particular promise if anyone fulfils the offer. In such circumstance, only the offeror binds himself, and upon the fulfilment of the condition by any person, that person becomes entitled to claim the reward. In a bilateral contract, two parties are involved from the beginning, bargain and agree on terms which are supported by a consideration that flows from the offeree.

107. The starting point in the making of a contract is the existence of an offer.[94] An offer refers to an offeror's willingness to enter into a contract with the intention of being bound in the event the contract is accepted by the offeree. An offer must be accepted in its totality; where the offeree modifies it, it cannot be said to be a valid acceptance of the offer. If the offeree qualifies or modifies his acceptance, the modification of the original offer would be deemed to be a counter-offer; a counter-offer is a fresh offer that must be accepted or rejected.[95]

108. Offers are often times confused with invitations to treat, but it should be noted that no matter the similarities they may share in common, they are legally different nonetheless. An invitation to treat may refer to the series of preliminary negotiations that precede an offer. The main feature which the court looks out for when trying to fathom whether what was termed an invitation to treat was indeed an offer is to see if there was any element of an intention to be bound. If it can be shown that the parties did not intend to be bound by their preliminary negotiations, the court would hardly term it an offer that is capable of being accepted.

109. Furthermore, offers do not exist in perpetuity; once the time stated has elapsed, it will cease to be a valid offer and can no longer be accepted. Where no time within which it would elapse is stated in the offer, then the lapse of reasonable time would suffice. An offer can also cease to exist if the offeror revokes it before it is accepted.

§2. CONSIDERATION

110. Consideration is vitally important in common law contracts, and consists of something of value which proceeds from the promisee.[96] Except contracts under seal, courts would require that as a condition to validate a contractual agreement, some consideration must have proceeded from the promisee. Consideration has been defined in several court decisions, and the embattled meaning now seems to be well settled in the contract law jurisprudence. Consideration does not need to be

93. [1893]1 QB 256.
94. *See Orient Bank v. Bilante Intl* [1997] 8 NWLR (Pt. 515) 37 at 76.
95. *See Major General George Innih (rtd) & ors v. Ferado Agro and Consortium Ltd* [1990] 5NWLR (Pt. 152) 604.
96. *See* B. *Stobiliri & Co Ltd v. Obasi* [1997] 9 NWLR (Pt. 520) 293 at 305.

sufficient; it must be adequate. It can even be a promise. Courts do not make contracts for parties and would be reluctant to annul a contract (except in the context of vitiating elements) simply because the consideration that was offered was far less than the foregoing market rate. As a rule, courts do not make contracts for parties.

111. Apart from two notable exceptions,[97] it has been well settled in the contract law jurisprudence that consideration must not be past;[98] it must be made in contemplation of the offer. Courts allow executory consideration as being sufficient to enforce a contract. It is important to point out instances that will not be deemed to have conferred a valid consideration. These would include an instance whereby a promise is made to perform a subsisting obligation; where a duty is imposed by law, the performance of such duty would not sufficiently constitute a consideration; performance of a duty imposed by contract with a third party; waiver of right in property being subsequently sought to form a valid consideration.[99]

§3. Intention to Enter into a Legal Relation

112. Courts would be wary to enforce a contract where the parties did not show enough intention to enter into a legal relationship. This means that even if other vital elements of a valid contract were present, the lack of an intention to be bound is material and goes to the enforceability of the contract. Two types of contract in this regard have been considered to be generally unenforceable due to the lack of intention to be bound. They are: social and domestic contracts.

113. It is reasonably believed that agreements of purely domestic nature are not to be binding. For example, agreements entered into by two family members, say between a husband and wife, parent and child, between two siblings are usually not binding in law; courts are reluctant to enforce domestic contracts due to the presence of informality, and the impropriety of delving deeply into family matters, matters that may ruin family relations if not carefully handled in the context of litigation. However, where that familial element is in fact lacking, for instance, where a husband and his wife are living apart and have a strained relationship, or where there is a strained relationship between a parent and child, the court may proceed to enforce the contract.

114. Similarly, promises or agreements made in the context of social arrangements can hardly qualify for enforcement because the law generally regards them as mere puffs. For instance, where a promise is made by a person to his other friends during a drinking binge, or where someone promises to make a donation at a social

97. Where a debt is barred by a statute, the debtor's written acknowledgement to resuscitate the debt may suffice. *See* s. 37 of the Limitation Act. The second is that provided by s. 27 of the Bill of Exchange Act which endorses the use of antecedent debt or liability as being valuable consideration for a bill.
98. *See Akenzua II, Oba of Benin v. Benin Divisional Council* [1959] WRN LR 1.
99. *See* Sagay, *Nigerian Law of Contract*, *supra* n. 91 at pp. 72–88.

event. These are regarded as mere bluffs and are not reasonably expected to bind the promise maker due to an expected understanding of lacking intention to be bound.

115. An important point should be made at this juncture; whereas in domestic and social contracts, lack of intention is typically presumed, that presumption is not extended to commercial contracts because it is reasonably expected that parties dealing on that level expect to be bound by their promises. However, there is a recognized instance whereby a contract would be deemed to be devoid of any intention to create a binding obligation regardless of its commercial outlook. Thus, where parties insert honour clauses or any functional equivalent in a contract, it would be understood that the parties do not wish such contract to have a binding legal effect.

116. At common law, collective agreements between trade union representatives and corporations were deemed to lack the intention to be bound.[100] The rationale behind this was not to discourage corporations from entering into negotiations with trade unions about the welfare of workers. Thus, such negotiations and agreements were left to bind only in honour. However, this common law position has been reformed by the Wages Board and Industrial Council Act which gives a binding effect on the recommendations made by the Wages Board. Similarly, the Minister of Labour is empowered under section 2(3) of the Trade Dispute Act to make a collective agreement legally binding.

§4. Contents of Contract

117. Every contract in the context of litigation is self-evidently disputed. In determining the general and specific obligations of the parties, the court would have to consider the contents or terms of the contract. In considering the terms so as to ascertain the scope of obligations, it may be realized that not every term of the contract is express or written; some might be oral or implied,[101] and the court has the duty to consider all of these types of terms in order to give the contract an interpretation that has the most real connection with the parties' common intention. This can further be achieved by considering a series of documents that have relevance to the formation and execution of the contract, except the contract has an entire agreement clause that bars the court from considering any extraneous documents.

118. In interpreting terms of a contract, the court assigns different weights to them; some are of heavyweight (conditions) and therefore regarded as fundamental, while some others might be of lightweight (warranties) and therefore regarded as minor terms. The difference between these two goes to the nature of remedies that

100. J.R. Carby-Hall, *The Collective Agreement-Legal Enforceability?*, Vol. 35(1/2) Managerial L. 1–24, pp. 3–4 (1993).

101. The implied terms under Nigerian contract law are terms implied by custom: *see Oyenuga v. International Computers (Nigeria) Ltd* (1991) 1 NWLR 415.
By statutes: *see* for instance, ss 12–15 of the Sale of Goods Act 1893; By courts: *see Shirlaw v. Southern Foundaries Ltd* (1939) 2 K.B 206 at 227.

the innocent party to the contract is entitled to enjoy upon breach.[102] Where a breach is fundamental, say the breach of a condition, the innocent party is entitled to both damages and rescission of the contract. Where the breach is minor, say, the breach of a warranty term, the remedy may be restricted to damages only.

§5. VITIATING ELEMENTS OF A CONTRACT

119. There are elements that can vitiate the binding effect of a contract. Being that ascertaining the existence of a contract is a question of fact, courts are minded about the circumstances surrounding the formation of a contract. Over the years, some elements have been recognized as capable of vitiating the effect of a contract. When properly established, they go to either the validity or enforceability of the contract. Under Nigerian law, mistake, misrepresentation, illegality, undue influence, duress and legal incapacity have been established to be the elements that vitiate contracts. In the paragraphs below, a skeletal description of each of them will be attempted.

§6. MISTAKE

120. Mistake refers to the ignorance of material facts at the time a particular contract was formed, such that if the complaining party were to be aware of the existence of such facts, they would not have signed or entered into the contract.[103] Different categories of mistake exist, namely, common mistake, mutual mistake, and unilateral mistake. A common mistake refers to a situation whereby both parties are mistaken about the same set of facts that necessitated their entry into contract. An example may be where both parties at the time of entering into a contract for sale of goods did not know that the subject matter of sale is no longer in existence.

121. There is a minor similarity between a mutual and common mistake – that similarity is that in both situations, the two contracting parties are mistaken. While in a common mistake, both parties do not know the existence of a material fact affecting their contract, in a mutual mistake, both parties are mistaken but not with respect to the same fact. For instance, using the same contract of sale of goods, if a buyer and seller agree on a price over a car, mutual mistake in that instance would refer to their mistake over the brand. The seller might have offered his Toyota Camry 2013 for USD 20,000, whereas the buyer thought that the USD 20, 000 price referred to the seller's 2016 model.

122. The third kind of mistake is the unilateral mistake. When a mistake is unilateral, only one party is mistaken; that is, the other party knows the true set of facts.

---

102. *See* generally, Sagay, *Nigerian Law of Contract*, *supra* n. 91 at pp. 125–127.
103. *Ibid.*, at 237–295.

This type of mistake is more in sale of goods, whereby the seller may hide some of the facts which if they were known to the buyer, the latter would not have offered the same price or buy it at all.

123. Given that inherent in the formation of contract is the presumption of *consensus ad idem*, that is, a belief that both parties had a meeting of the mind, courts are highly reluctant to enforce a contract when mistake is sufficiently pleaded. Thus, since the existence of any mistake capable of affecting the enforceability of a contract must be a question of fact instead of law, the burden of proof is on the party alleging or relying on the mistake. The standard of proof in non-criminal matters is the balance of probabilities. And in doing so, the court could put itself in the position of a reasonable person and decipher from that point of view whether a case of mistake has been established.

124. Courts in Nigeria treat issues of common mistake as having the capacity to render a contract null; because even though the parties were clearly in agreement, the subject matter underscoring the contract is not in existence, therefore, making the contract impossible to perform. When a mistake is mutual, courts look at the circumstances objectively to know whether any of the mistaken party had acted reasonably in the circumstance. If it is established that one of the parties, especially the party alleging the mistake, acted unreasonably, the court would likely validate the contract and order for its performance or damages in lieu of performance.

125. However, it should be noted that superior courts in Nigeria combine common law and equitable jurisdictions; the latter would enable the court to exercise its moral conscience to mitigate the full effects of a mutual mistake. Thus, depending on the circumstances, when a case of mutual mistake is not accepted, the court may refuse to specifically order the party being asked to perform, especially when in total consideration of the circumstances, it would be cumbersome and burdensome for that party to perform the contract. The effect of a unilateral mistake goes to the nullity of the contract because it has some element of deceit; one party intentionally obtained the interest of the other party to enter into the contract. It should be kept in mind, though, that where a unilateral mistake is pleaded, that is, the party relying on it pleads that had he known the true identity of the other party or object of the contract, he would not have entered into the contract. Courts easily nullify such contracts because there was no meeting of the minds; consent was fraudulently obtained and therefore cannot sustain a contract between the parties.

126. In conclusion, mistake is a very serious vitiating element and frequently rears up as defence against the enforcement of a particular contract. When a contractual document was mistakenly signed, the innocent party would likely be relieved from performance if he can successful plead the defence of *non est factum* – a Latin maxim that literally translates to 'not my deed'. Although, initially, this defence was exclusively reserved for visually challenged persons as well as illiterates, it has today been extended to any person who can show that he was tricked into signing a contract. This defence would hardly be successful if the signed document being challenged was prepared or emanated from the party wishing to set it aside on the ground of *non est factum*; in which case, the doctrine of *contra proferentem* would apply to prevent the party who prepared the document from stating that one or all of its contents exist outside his consent or knowledge.

§7. MISREPRESENTATION

127. Before entering into a contract, it is likely the case that both parties had claimed the existence of certain facts, the consideration of which induced one or both parties to enter into the contract.[104] Where it turns out that the statements which induced a party towards entering into a contract were untrue, such is regarded as misrepresentation. Misrepresentation frequently arises in the context of sale of goods and services, whereby the seller employs the use of hyperboles, and exaggerates certain facts. For example, where a second-hand car dealer advertises his cars on a website using digitally doctored photographs that give the impression that the cars are almost brand new, and on the basis of which a buyer accepts to pay a price he would not have agreed to pay had the real look of the cars been presented. If later he realizes that the car being delivered is very old and incongruous with the one that was advertised, or where the car dealer in this case states that a particular car had covered, say, 30,000 km, whereas the car had indeed covered about 60,000 km, both situations would easily be regarded as misrepresentation.

128. It should be boldly underlined that in the context of contracts, misrepresentation refers only to facts which were falsely alleged; it does not refer to law or a statement of intention. The reason for this is because, in all legal systems known to the writer, ignorance of the law is hardly excusable; and no one especially in the absence of a moral duty can be held liable for expressing their opinions because the right to freedom of thought and expression is guaranteed in the highest rights documents, the Constitution. With respect to misrepresentation of law, an exception should be noted. Nigerian courts treat foreign law and customary laws of the various parts of Nigeria as facts which must be proved. In that case, a misrepresentation of foreign law or customary law would likely constitute a sufficient actionable ground.

129. Similarly, while silence does not usually constitute a misrepresentation, in instances where a party has the duty to disclose facts which are within his personal knowledge, the non-disclosure of such facts could make the contract voidable. It should be noted as well that in instances where duty is not imposed on a party to disclose, silence would not usually constitute a misrepresentation. But if that party discloses, the disclosure must be accurate and not misleading. Where a party to a contract makes certain statements which in his belief are true, but unknown to him that the statements are false at that time, equity imposes on him the duty to disclose the true nature of the circumstances as soon as he learns about them. In the context of insurance (to be discussed later in the insurance section), whereby one party does have full knowledge of the material facts, the law requires that party to disclose all

104. *Ibid.*, at 295–340.

such material facts which shall form the basis of fixing the premiums by the insurer. Where such material facts are not disclosed in the beginning, such failure can cause the contract to be rescinded.

130. Given that misrepresentation is ideally seen as a set of untrue facts that affected the plaintiff's judgment, the plaintiff must prove how the misrepresented facts influenced his entering into the contract. This would mean that regardless of the nature of misrepresentation, if the plaintiff was never aware that it was made or cannot show how his belief of the facts influenced him, the plea of misrepresentation would not be sustained.

131. Over centuries, courts in the common law systems have developed two kinds of misrepresentation, namely, innocent and fraudulent misrepresentations. A misrepresentation is innocent where the party making the misrepresentation believes his statements to be true and does not have any intention to deceive the defendant towards entering the contract. The effect of an innocent misrepresentation depends largely on whether it is first of all a term of the contract. Where it is determined to be a term, a further enquiry would be whether it is minor term (warranty) or a condition which is a fundamental term. Where it is a warranty, only damages would inure, while damages or rescission of the contract would be available for the innocent party to choose from in the event the misrepresentation was with respect to a fundamental term.

132. Where a misrepresentation is fraudulent, the party making it must not have honestly believed it to be true. Thus, to establish a fraudulent misrepresentation, it has to be shown that the party who made it did not believe it to be true and that the statement was false. In establishing this, only these two elements have to be proved; it is not important for the plaintiff to show the motive for the defendant's fraudulent misrepresentation. When the misrepresentation is fraudulent, courts are highly reluctant to listen to any defence that suggests that the plaintiff would have avoided or discovered the falsity of the representation if he had been duly diligent. The effect of a fraudulent misrepresentation is that the contract would be voidable at the instance of the plaintiff, who could also ask for damages depending on the nature of the term that was fraudulently misrepresented.

§8. ILLEGALITY

133. Another vitiating element of a contract is illegality.[105] Illegality of contract refers to the infringement of a provision of a statute, common law, or public policy; for instance, contracts in restraint of trade would generally be adjudged to be against public policy because of its possibility to stifle competition or the progress of individuals to do business and create jobs. A contract can be illegal by statute and this can possibly occur in two stages of a contract. In instances where a contract

105. *Ibid.*, at 359–457.

infringed a provision of law from the beginning or at any state before the final performance of the contract, the result is that that contract would be void and unenforceable. Similarly, it could happen that a contract was validly entered into by the parties, but the manner or method of performing the contract may bring it within the confines of illegality.

134. Given the heightened sensitivity of the legal system in relation to crimes, every aspect of a contract can be dissected and examined thoroughly to ensure that there is no illegality. For instance, in holding whether or not a contract was illegal, the courts even probe the legality of the consideration being offered. Where the consideration given to the promissor is characterized with fraud, the contract itself may not escape illegality. The subject matter of the contract may also be an illegal one and the court in determining this can look objectively or reasonably at the intention of the parties. Thus, where a person hires a truck which on its own does not constitute an illegality, however uses the truck being hired to traffic underaged girls across a national border, it can then be said that the hiring was characterized with fraud.

135. The usual consequence of illegality is the unenforceability of the contract. The rule of *impari delicto* would apply which seeks to keep the costs wherever it has fallen and prevents a party from seeking to recover the money it had spent; this is because allowing such party to recover would be tantamount to the court enforcing the illegal contract, by providing a remedy. There are peculiar and justifiable circumstances whereby the court in total consideration of the facts, and in determining that a party was not involved in the illegality, permits such innocent party to recover, for instance, where the innocent party can sufficiently show that he repudiated the contract before it was performed and that the repudiation was voluntary and was not triggered by an intervening third party, say, the law enforcement agents.

136. Also, where the entire contract is not entirely illegal, the court may apply the doctrine of severance, that is, severe the illegal part and enforce the remainder part. In any event, it is not possible under Nigerian law to enforce an illegal contract as that itself will jeopardize public morality and the overall welfare and development of the Nigerian society. In fact, given the peculiarity of this type of vitiating element (illegality), it is immaterial that one of the parties did not plead it, as the court under its inherent jurisdiction to do justice is empowered to raise the illegality issue by itself and address it accordingly.

§9. Duress

137. Inherent in the formation of a valid contract is the existence of a mutual consent of the parties; the lack of consent vitiates the contract and courts do not enforce obligations against a party whose intention to assume such obligation was never truly obtained.[106] Thus, if duress is established, the contract becomes voidable at the instance of the innocent party. Case law forming around duress has been those instances whereby actual violence or threat was used to procure consent of a party to a contract. The oppressed party must have believed that his life was in imminent danger and refusal would lead to a bodily harm, if not death. A case in point would be where the oppressed party was asked to sign a contract document under a gunpoint or the threat of harming or torturing his spouse or family.

138. It should be pointed out immediately that not all threats would materialize into duress; where the threat if carried out would not amount to illegality, for instance, a threat to carry out an act which in itself would not be illegal even though such act might boil down to be detrimental to the party alleging the duress. In the process of solidifying the jurisprudence on duress, courts have wobbled a bit in their perspectives; from restricting duress to only those instances of actual physical violence, such that a threat to seize one's property unless he paid his debts or conferred certain benefits to the party issuing the threats was considered insufficient to vitiate a contract. However, that narrow construction or perspective of what constitutes duress is no longer in vogue as courts have extended duress of goods to be sufficient to vitiate a contract.

§10. Undue Influence

139. Unlike duress that considers the use of actual threat or violence, undue influence has an equitable feature as well as a wider application in the context of contract. It would cover those instances that necessitate a party from independently arriving at the decision to enter into a contract. For instance, in fiduciary relationships, where one of the parties owe the other the duty not to exploit and take advantage of the vulnerability or naivety of the other party, the court would stringently require the party having the fiduciary duty to prove that the contract was entered into by the vulnerable party after being told the true set of facts or after that other party had received an independent counselling.

140. Given that undue influence has a wider coverage than duress, its establishment in a contract is a strong question of fact, and a series of facts could be analysed to show that one of the parties has a stronger influence, influence which could be remote or actual, and as a result of which, the will of the vulnerable party was completely emasculated. It is immaterial that the stronger party who benefitted from the contract by applying some undue pressure did not make any statements of persuasion.

141. Certain relationships, say doctor-patient, parent-child, husband-wife, lawyer-client, etc., presumptively suggest that one party is weaker and therefore could have unduly been influenced due to certain emotional considerations, the absence of which would have necessitated a different outcome in relation to the

106. *Ibid.*, at 340–359.

decision to enter into the contract. Even though in the early development of contract law, the literature in relation to undue influence was much more about the abuse of fiduciary duties, today, it has been extended to instances of unconscionable bargains predicated on the abuse of a stronger or dominant position.

§11. INCAPACITY

142. Entry into contract has been generally limited to adults because of the issue of consent and capacity to make a binding decision against oneself.[107] Decisions matter and the law is wary of the consequences that can arise from decisions made without much experience and knowledge of the necessary facts to be considered: improperly thought-out decisions can negatively shape the future of a person. For instance, an improperly thought-out decision to enter into a contract may result in a huge amount of debt, which may lead to personal bankruptcy of a minor and make it difficult for him to rise in life. In Nigeria, where there is still a bankruptcy stigma that negatively affects a bankrupt's reputation,[108] declaring oneself bankrupt due to the overwhelming amount of debts being owed would most likely jeopardize one's future. In view of all this, the decision to enter into a contract has been generally limited to adults who presumably are equipped to analyse issues in their complexities before making decisions that would bind them.

143. Thus, since the reasonable ability to give consent is material to a valid contract, minors under 21, illiterates and corporations enjoy special status in relation to the formation of contracts. In the case of registered corporations which are regarded also as persons, the capacity to enter into certain contract is determined partly by its memorandum and articles of association and partly by the Companies and Allied Matters Act (CAMA) 2020. In the case of human persons under 21, who are generally regarded as infants for the purpose of contract, the Infant Relief Act 1874 which is a statute of general application in Nigeria, and common law, applies. Based on the Infant Relief Act, infants under 21 are not allowed to enter into a trading contract except contracts for necessaries,[109] and beneficial service, like apprenticeships.

144. Another category of persons are illiterates in the language of the contract; to them, the Illiterate Protection Act governs their contractual activities. Nigerian law also protects people of unsound mind from being bound by their contractual duties, especially if it can be reasonably shown that at the time of entering the contract, the plaintiff ought to have reasonably ascertained that the defendant was of

---

107. *Ibid.*, at 457–488.
108. See the Bankruptcy Act 1990 and its negative attitude towards an undischarged bankrupt.
109. What is a 'necessary' depends on the social status of the infant; it differs from one person to another. It is therefore a question of mixed law and fact. *See* s. 2 of the Sale of Goods Act which defines the goods that would be considered necessaries. But the factual aspect of denoting what is a necessary refers to the child's social status. Thus, the child of a rural farmer, even though has the same constitutional rights as the child of a politician, what the latter may consider as a necessary may be super luxurious for the rural farmer's child.

unsound mind. Different considerations may however apply if at the time of entering the contract, it can be shown that the defendant was of sound mind and reasonably understood the consequences of his actions. For instance, there are persons who have the challenge of periodic insanity which comes up during a particular period of the year due to a certain unfavourable weather condition; they would not ordinarily be bound for decisions made during the period of lunacy.

§12. Privity of Contract

145. So far, what has been established in the discussion of contract law in Nigeria is that, a contract is entered into between two consenting and capable parties. Even though there are instances whereby it appears on a first look that more than two parties are involved, on a deeper look it would show that the third party's interest draws from one of the two parties. Thus, in enforcing a contract, the court would generally require that the person asking for enforcement offers some consideration. So, where parties to a contract agree to confer benefits or impose certain obligations on a third party, the general rule is that that third party would not be compelled to perform such obligation, neither would he be sufficiently entitled to enforce and enjoy the conferred benefits.

146. The doctrine of privity[110] evolved out of the high degree of sanctity accorded to the common decision of two consenting and capable parties to do as they please within the confines of contract law and general law. Initially, during the early development of contract law jurisprudence in England, courts typically discouraged all manners of intrusion into the valid contract of parties; courts even declared at any given opportunity that their duty was not to make contracts for parties, but to enforce them. But as it later showed, the doctrine of privity which is largely predicated on the assumption that contractual parties will exist perpetually and in good sound minds started to occasion injustices, especially in situations where the original parties are no longer in the picture, either as a result of death or other kinds of incapacitation that make it impossible for them to enforce the contract by themselves. In view of this inconvenience posed essentially by a strict regard to the privity rule, courts began to gradually mellow down, and thus, created exceptions to accommodate certain peculiar circumstances.

147. The first notable exception is restrictive covenants. Restrictive covenants which run with the land would continue to be validly enforceable against any person holding interest in the land, even though the original party had sold his interest in the land to the third party whom the restrictive covenant is being enforced against.[111] Thus where a party knowingly acquires a parcel of land with certain covenants which restrict him from doing certain things, those covenants can be enforced against him even though he did not originally contract them. He cannot successfully plead that he did not contract to be restricted by those covenants

110. *See* generally, Sagay, *Nigerian Law of Contract*, *supra* n. 91 at 489–517.
111. *Ibid.*, at 495.

because, given that he was aware or ought to be aware of their existence before purchasing the land, the courts would presume that he understood the implications of their existence and was comfortable to deal with them, hence, his decision to acquire interest in the land.

148. Second exception can be found in insurance contracts; a case in point being section 6(3) of the Motor Vehicles (Third Party) Insurance Act, which provides that an insurer will indemnify a third party who has suffered injuries caused by a party to the insurance contract, within the stated coverage. Thus, the injured party can claim directly against the insurance company for the injury caused by a party to a third-party insurance contract, even though the third party had no contract with the insurance company.

149. The third exception is trust, express trust in particular. Trust exists to solve various problems, including to set up financial sources for children under the age of 21 (infants) who cannot be bestowed with the management of certain properties or businesses. A person with children under the age of 21 may guarantee their future to a good extent by creating a trust, and bestowing the trustee with the legal title to manage the property for the benefits of the infant children until they attain majority.

150. The fourth exception is a banker's commercial credit.[112] In commerce, the use of credit letters serves to douse the mutual fears of the seller and buyer, especially when both stay in different countries and have no easy way of ensuring mutual performance. Thus, to bypass the fear and the ensuing consequences, the seller may require the buyer to obtain a letter of credit for the former's benefits, so that if the buyer's bank can assure that the buyer has deposited some money for the benefit of the seller, the seller may ship the goods and present the bill of lading and any other stated document to the buyer's bank and get paid without any obligation on the paying bank to verify whether the shipped goods by the seller are in conformity with the contract terms. In the unlikely event that the buyer's bank did not in fact hold any money for the benefit of the seller, such misrepresentation would entitle the seller to sue the buyer's bank for reimbursement; and this is regardless of the fact that the buyer's bank was not part of the original contract between the buyer and the seller.

151. The fifth and the last to be considered here due to the lack of writing space is agency. There is a time honoured rule that whoever acts through another person is deemed to have acted by himself. Thus, the act of an agent when dealing with a third party can bind his principal whether the principal was disclosed or not to that third party at the time the agent was entering into the contract, and the third party can sue either the agent or the principal, just like the principal can sue the third party even though he was not part of the contract between his agent and the third party. Similarly, it makes commercial sense to sue the principal of an agent who may have a deeper pocket compared to his employee or agent acting on his instructions.

---

112. *Ibid.*, at 515.

152. In conclusion, a common theme that runs through these exceptions is the recognition that commercial transactions would hardly be possible on the strict application of the privity rule. While contract retains its original conferment of sanctity, these exceptions, which continue to be expanded by courts, continue to oil the wheels of commerce.

§13. Discharge of Contract

153. Once a contract is validly entered into, some obligations arise and continue to subsist until performance has been completed. Thus, there are different circumstances that can warrant a discharge; discharge as used here means that the underlying obligations of both parties are no longer operative, and they are therefore relieved from performing them. Discharge can come in various ways, namely, by complete performance of the contractual obligation; when there is an agreement of parties to terminate a previous contract they entered into; when a party to a contract has breached a fundamental term; and when the contract itself has been frustrated.[113] Three out of the four ways listed above are straightforward and need no further elucidation. However, the last one, that is discharge by frustration would be briefly explained. Frustration refers to a situation in the life of a contract whereby the subject matter of contract ceases to be in existence before performance. An example may be where a seller offers his house for sale and the buyer agrees to purchase it but before performance, it happens that the property has been gutted by fire.

154. In that case, both parties become discharged in their respective obligations. The situation would be the same if the parties based their contract on what was expected to occur, but for reasons beyond their control, the event did not occur. There are many shades of frustration that should not necessarily be discussed here due to space; however, the vital point to note with respect to frustration is where the life of a contract has been predicated on a thing that exists or is expected to be in existence at a particular time, and it happens that such material thing or event is not in existence by the deadline of performance, and its non-existence cannot be reasonably traced to a party's fault, then under Nigerian law, it can be said that the contract has been discharged by frustration.

§14. Remedies

155. The essence of any contract or the general expectation when parties enter into a contract is that it would be performed. Given that a contract is the exchange of promises, courts consider it to be in accordance with public policy and good morals that parties honour their promises as much as it is reasonably practicable. No question of contractual remedy would arise if a contract is fully performed. However, there are instances that necessitate the breach of a contract; a breach could be

113. *Ibid.*, at 518–565.

wilful or not. Courts routinely award remedies whenever it can be established that a contract was not fulfilled as agreed; that is, it was breached.

156. At common law, during the early period of contract law, only damages (monetary loss) existed as a contractual remedy. Soon it was realized that damages were insufficient as a remedy for breach due to those special factors that form the basis of a contract, the satisfaction of which cannot adequately be achieved by the award of damages. The performance of certain contracts was highly sacrosanct for many people, and it was unfair that a party to a contract could easily discharge his obligations, simply by paying damages. Similarly, English/Nigerian law does not generally exempt a counterparty from performance solely on account of hardship: this position is equally meant to discourage the economic analysis of performance which could occur if the cost of performance outweighs the foreseen amount of damages. The court of equity regarded this as unfair and created other equitable remedies like specific performance and injunction to ensure the regular performance of contracts.

157. Courts in Nigeria in considering the award of damages ascertain whether it is remote as to deserve compensation; the guiding rule on this was enunciated in the case of *Hadley v. Baxendale*.[114] Having ascertained that damages in a contract are not remote, the next issue that must be determined relates to the measure of damages. In contracts where liquidated damages, that is, a stated amount of money the breaching party would pay, are inserted, there would be no need in considering the measure of damages provided the liquidated damages sum is a reasonable estimate of loss and not designed to be a penalty or windfall; if reasonable, the court would simply order the breaching party to pay that amount, plus, the costs of litigation incurred by the innocent party, if the latter pleads it in his statement of claim.

158. Since July 2000, the decision in *AG v. Blake*[115] provides for the disgorgement of profit made from a wilful breach of contract. Although very likely, there has not been any opportunity yet in Nigeria, especially at the Supreme Court level, to test the acceptability of the *Blake* type of damages. In the United Kingdom, *Wrotham Park*[116] damages are used in assessing the cost of breach of covenants; although both Blake and Wrotham Park damages can apply in Nigeria persuasively, there are currently no local equivalents. In Nigeria, damages in contract, unlike in tort, must be specifically proved; the loss of bargain is what the court is interested in compensating. The court, not being a Father Christmas, will hardly turn damages into a windfall. The onus is therefore on the plaintiff to prove exactly his loss, the amount of money he exactly lost due to the defendant's breach. This, therefore, is a question of fact geared at putting the innocent party in the position he would have been had the contract been performed. As far back as 1965, the Supreme Court

114. [1854] EWHC J70. Sagay, *Nigerian Law of Contract, supra* n. 91 at 618–669.
115. [2001] 1 AC 268.
116. *See Wrotham Park Estate Co Ltd v. Parkside Homes Ltd* [1974] 1 WLR 798.

already provided guidance in *Chanrai v. Khawam*[117] regarding the absence of 'general damages' in contract under Nigerian law; in other words, general and punitive damages exist only in tort circumstances. Courts are quite wary when awarding damages in tort, because while in contract a party's actions only affect the other party to the contract; in tort, a party's action could affect the entire society: this is one of the reasons courts award punitive and general damages to serve as deterrence, even if the injured party cannot prove specifically the damages being claimed.

§15. Specific Performance

159. As earlier stated, initially at common law, damages were the only remedy. However, it later proved itself inadequate in all circumstances, if not totally counterproductive in some cases. Being that the essence of contract is also about profit maximization, contractual parties started to breach contracts if the cost of performance was higher than the benefits to be obtained from the contract. This defeated one of the reasons for entering into a contract: the certainty about the performance of certain obligations in the future even if it becomes difficult to do so. Hardship is not considered a sufficient reason not to perform a contract under English/Nigerian law because commerce needs a high level of predictability in order to thrive.

160. Equity intervened by way of specific performance: it is an order of court that a party to a contract should perform a certain obligation. A refusal to obey an order of specific performance would be adjudged as contempt of court and could lead to imprisonment of the party refusing to obey it. The view of English courts in *Ryan v. Mutual Tontine Association*[118] has been treated as part of Nigerian law. Thus, Nigerian courts will only order for a specific performance where damages would not be an adequate compensation. The court on its own would not be able to arrive at the conclusion of awarding a specific performance order unless a party pleads for it and takes steps to furnish convincing reasons on why damages will not be a sufficient compensation in the circumstances. Where damages would be sufficient, the court will be reluctant to order the breaching party to specifically perform because the measure of damages in contract is special damages which compensate for what was monetarily lost; or recently restitutionary damages that seek to disgorge the breaching party the profits of breach, as a way to discourage wilful breach generally.[119]

---

117. *Chanrai v. Khawam* [1965] 1 All NLR, 182.
118. [1893] 1 Ch. 166 at 126.
119. *See AG v. Blake* [2001] 1 AC 268.

§16. INJUNCTION

161. Injunction is also an equitable remedy which compels a person from performing or not performing certain acts in accordance with the contract.[120] An injunction could be temporary (interim) or permanent (perpetual). When an injunction is sought in the course of enforcing a contract, it will operate to preserve the subject matter of contract until the court is able to determine the substantive issues in the contract. The main function of an injunction in the context of litigation is to ensure that the court's final judgment would not be in vain, which would be the case if the subject matter is destroyed before a court judgment is made.

§17. THE LAW OF AGENCY

162. The Nigerian law of agency is heavily sprinkled with English law vocabulary because, since the reception of common law into the Nigerian system, not much has changed with respect to commercial law in general and the law of agency in particular.[121] It should be noted that agency law is a slight variation of the privity rule (discussed earlier). The privity rule generally prevents non-parties to a contract to enforce its provisions. However, there are exceptions and it could be said that agency is one of them.

163. Commercial life would be generally impracticable or difficult without the law of agency: this is because there are instances whereby a person (a principal) cannot undertake certain tasks by himself for many cogent reasons, reasons ranging from the principal's lack of expertise to negotiate and conclude a contract to his general lack of time to do so. In that case, the engagement of an agent becomes necessary. Similarly, corporate bodies, regarded as legal persons, cannot negotiate and conclude contracts by themselves without acting through their human agents, their directors and secretaries.[122]

164. The governing rule as established by the Supreme Court ensures that a person does not hide under the shadows of another whom he could easily control to commit a wrongful act: a person who procures another to do a thing is considered to have done it by himself.[123] This rule makes sense because the essence of hiring an agent is to do a thing the principal would have ordinarily done if he was disposed to do so. This means that the principal should ensure that the agent has the requisite expertise and good character. The agent must act within the scope of authority given to him by the principal; this authority can be actual, apparent or ostensible.

---

120. Sagay, *Nigerian Law of Contract*, *supra* n. 91 at 670–675.
121. *See* generally, K. Igweike, *Nigeria Commercial Law: Agency* (FAB Educational Books 1993).
122. On the presumption of regularity regarding the activities of a company, *see* ss 93 and 94, Companies and Allied Matters Act (CAMA) 2020.
123. *See James v. Midmotors (Nig) Ltd* (1978) 11–12 SC. 21.

165. There could be many reasons to appoint an agent, to act generally for the principal or to act in a specific task in which case his authority would come to an end after he has completed performance of the specific task. The scope of the agent's powers is usually contained in the instrument that appointed him. Thus, being a kind of contract, the general elements of contract would have to be present; essentially, there has to be an offer and acceptance as well as the mutual intention to be legally bound.

166. There are instances whereby a person holds himself out and acts in a way that makes people believe that a certain state of facts exist, and a third party may have made his decisions on the basis of the agent's representations. In such case, the agent will not be allowed to renege on his representations without some liability: this is known as agency by estoppel.[124] In any event, the notion of agency supposes that the agent acts on behalf of the principal before a third party with the purpose of creating a legal relationship between himself and the third party on the one hand and between the third party and the principal on the other hand.

§18. Agency Distinguished from Other Sister Relations

167. Generally, agency has a resemblance of trust[125] because a trustee acts on behalf of the beneficiary and makes binding decisions that are directly enforceable against the beneficiary. Similarly, both an agent and a trustee owe fiduciary duties to their principal and beneficiary respectively because of the sensitive information in their possession which generally enables them discharge their tasks effectively. However, while a trustee is bestowed with a legal title of the trust property he is charged to manage for the beneficiary, an agent does not have any legal title to his principal's property which he deals with, and cannot validly dispose of them as his own. Similarly, the act of a trustee in relation to a trust property is distinct and in his own name because he has the legal title, while the act of an agent is that of the principal. Furthermore, courts in Nigeria have the power to remove a trustee in line with the CAMA,[126] while in relation to agency, only the principal can remove an agent because their relationship is not statutory but contractual.

168. Another legal relationship that might be confused with agency is the relationship between an employee and his employer. In Nigeria, an employee that is acting in the course of his employment can validly bind the employer if the former injures a third party in the process. However, labour statutes govern employee and employer relationships and do not extend to cover agency relations; agencies generally presuppose that the agent will act based on his thoughts and discretion while it is expected that an employee takes instructions from as well as remain under the

124. *See Bamgboye v. University of Ilorin & Ors* (1991) 8 NWLR 129.

125. *See* generally, J.O. Fabunmi, *Equity and Trusts in Nigeria* (Obafemi Awolowo University Press 2006).

126. For example, *see* s. 201 CAMA 2020.

control of his employer. Thus, while a principal can at any time terminate his continued willingness to be represented by an agent (e.g., due to a negative discovery about the agent's character), an employee cannot be fired without being issued with a termination notice or salary in lieu of notice in accordance with section 11 of the Labour Act 1990.

§19. Types of Agent

169. Different types of agent have evolved from case law over centuries of the common law existence.[127] The description of agents as having apparent, real, or ostensible authority is a broad categorization of their identities and function, and may not be a helpful tool in knowing concretely what the various agents are and the legal implications surrounding their nature.

170. The first is 'attorney' which simply means an agent or a representative of another person. Nearly always, the appointment of an attorney is made in writing and such instrument is usually known as a 'power of attorney'. In the context of legal practice, if a lawyer (donee of power) is appointed by his client (the donor of power) to represent him in court or legal matters, the former will be referred to as an 'attorney at law', and has the authority to make legal representations of his client within the confines of his authority. Just like in other jurisdictions, lawyers are regulated in Nigeria by the ethics and codes of the legal profession, and are required to act at all times in accordance with the Rules of Professional Conducts. If a lawyer breaches the code of conduct, he can be liable to disciplinary actions from the Legal Practitioners' Disciplinary Committee. Similarly, while acting for his client and using his professional discretion which binds the client, a lawyer may be liable in negligence if he acts carelessly to the detriment of his client.

171. The second type is auctioneers under the Auctioneer Laws of the various states in Nigeria.[128] They are appointed specifically for the purpose of conducting public or private sale of properties. Where an auctioneer is appointed, he becomes primarily the seller's agent and would have to comply with instructions regarding the sale of the property. For instance, where it is required that the property cannot be sold below a stated price, the auctioneer has no power to sell below that price; if he does, the sale will not be binding because he had gone beyond the scope of his authority. Similarly, where he is instructed to specifically sell by a public auction, he cannot neglect the instruction and afford to sell by a private arrangement. Further, as in all public auctions, the idea is to sell to the highest bidder without considering sentiments and the personality of the buyer; sale becomes completed and binding on both the seller and buyer when the hammer of the seller (auctioneer) falls.

127. *See Freeman and Lockyer v. Burkhurst Park Properties Ltd* (1964)1 ALL E.R. 630.
128. For example, *see* CAP A12, Laws of Lagos State, https://laws.lawnigeria.com/2018/02/27/sales-by-auction-law/.

172. The third type is brokerage contracts, whereby a broker acts as a middleman and brings together a buyer and seller for negotiation and possibly entering into a contract. He is rewarded by commission. The nature of his function does not typically confer him with the possession of any property or subject matter of the contract. Thus, he cannot sue or be sued in his own name except through the person he represents. Brokerage contracts are common in insurance, stocks and real estate.

173. The fourth type of agent under consideration is 'the factor'. The statute governing this in Nigeria is the Factors Act of 1889, a statute of general application. A factor is a commercial agent who thrives on commission by selling the principal's goods. Each good he sells entitles him to an agreed commission. A factor does not have a discretion to sell below a stated price even though unforeseen market realities may require such immediate decision. He must first discuss and obtain the principal's consent to sell below that instructed price. Where he fails to do so and proceeds to sell below the stated price, the principal reserves the right to approve the undervalue sale or demand for the original price. Similarly, a factor can sell above the price he was instructed to sell without any duty to render accounts to the principal. Also given that a factor is not an employee of the principal but an independent contractor, he is liable for the costs incurred in the course of marketing/selling the principal's goods; it is understood that his commission would take care of his expenses; he also can act as a factor to one or several principals.

§20. Creation of Agency Relations

174. Given that agency is a specialized contract, the general principles of contract law apply. Thus, the parties to an agency relationship must be legally capable of entering into such contract, and given that agency presupposes the notion that a person acts through another, it is legally impossible to appoint another person to do what the principal is legally incapable of doing. Cases in point would be those situations whereby an infant who is legally incapable appoints an adult to perform a task. Such engagement would be legally void. This is also true in a situation whereby an incorporated company that is not authorized to perform an act based on its constitutional documents authorizes an agent to do that which it is not empowered to undertake; such act would be deemed ultra vires, and thus null and void.[129]

175. Earlier on, the different types of agent were highlighted. It is important to quickly offer a brief overview regarding the various ways by which an agency agreement can occur. The first is hinged on the actual, implied and usual authority of the agent. This occurs when he is expressly appointed to do a specific thing. This type of contract, regardless of its express component, can be in writing or oral since there is no statute, including section 4 of the Statutes of Frauds 1677, which mandates an agency contract to be in a written form.

129. *See* s. 343 CAMA 2020.

176. However, the burden of proving that an express agency contract exists is on the party alleging its existence, and it is left for him to figure ways by which he could prove his claim in line with the laws of evidence. It should be noted that inherent in any express authority to do a specific thing is the implied authority to do things that are naturally incidental to the acts expressly authorized. There is no closed list of acts that can be impliedly derived from an express authority to perform an act. However, it is a question of fact than law and in determining whether an act was incidental to an express authority, Nigerian courts would apply the reasonable person's test to decipher whether the agent's implied act was necessarily an offshoot of his express authority.[130]

177. There is also the usual authority which is a mixture of express and implied authority. For example, in partnership arrangement, each partner is an agent of the partnership as well as to the other partners, such that his usual authority to act in the ordinary course of business would bind the firm and his partner colleagues.[131] Similarly, Nigerian law still retains the old English practice of a wife or mistress of a man, being his agent and capable of, or having the authority to pledge his credit in the obtainment of necessaries.[132]

178. The second is that which is hinged on estoppel. Estoppel is the brainchild of equity, and seeks to disable a person from approbating and reprobating, especially where he has made representations which a third relied and acted upon; the principal would also be held liable if he knew or ought to know about the representation and refused to take any step to stop it. In determining this, the court considers the overall circumstances to know whether, in fact, the doctrine of estoppel should apply to prevent the agent and/or his principal from denying liability in the hands of the third party.

179. The third is by ratification. Where an act is done by an agent without any authority from the principal, it will become binding on the latter if after due consideration, he accepts it as valid and capable of binding him. In that case, an agency by ratification comes into existence, and this can be done either expressly or impliedly. In Nigeria, under section 96 of the CAMA 2020, the existence of any incorporated company is first of all heralded by the incorporation activities of its promoters. The contracts entered into by the promoters (agents of the company) can only be valid and binding on the company if it ratifies it upon coming into existence. Where the company refuses to ratify, the agent who entered into the contract would be personally liable for their obligations.

180. Lastly, it should be noted that the possibility to ratify an agent's contract rests squarely on the rules on validity of a contract. For instance, where the principal is incapable of entering into a contract, he cannot ratify it if, legally speaking,

---

130. *See Electronics Ltd v. Akhter Computer Ltd* (2001) 1/BCLC/433.
131. *See* s. 5 of the Partnership Act 1890.
132. *See Webster v. Webster* (1916) 1 K. B. 714; *see* G.H. Treitel, *The Deserted Wife's Right to Pledge Her Husband's Credit for Necessaries*, Vol. 16(2) Mod. L. Rev. 221–225 (1953).

it is beyond his power to do so. Similarly, contracts that are void cannot be ratified by the principal and a valid ratification must hinge on the knowledge of the full facts surrounding the contract.

§21. Rights of the Agent

181. An agent, having performed his duty as contained in the agency contract, has the right to be paid his agreed fees and even be indemnified of any expenses incurred in accordance with the agency contract. Nigeria ranks poorly (about 146 out of 180) in the Corruption Index of Transparency International, 2020. For an agent, this could pose a challenge in practice owing to the difficulty in obtaining services from the public sector offices without occasionally being requested to pay bribes. Thus, an agent who has offered a bribe (an illegal act) in the course of accomplishing his agency tasks may not be reimbursed by the principal as of right: no cause of action can validly inure from the latter's refusal to reimburse. The rule is that an agent can only be reimbursed for expenses reasonably incurred in the course of his duty and such expenses must not have been expended on illegal acts, unless the agent can sufficiently show lack of *mens rea*, i.e., that he was unaware of the fact that that particular act was illegal.

182. Apart from enforcing the right to be repaid through litigation, an agent (where applicable) can also enforce this right via self-help;[133] for instance, by lien and/or by set-off. In Nigeria, lien can arise by contract or by operation of law, e.g., judgment of court, tax lien, maritime lien under section 70(2) of the Maritime Shipping Act 1990. Thus, an agent can exercise his mechanic lien right over the principal's property or title documents until his money has been fully repaid. He can also set off the debt by retaining the principal's money in his possession or by assigning the debt to a third party who is being owed by the principal.

183. It should be pointed out that an agency contract could be terminated in two main ways, ways similar to how contracts are generally terminated. That has been discussed above in detail. Here, however, it is sufficient to mention that an agency contract could be terminated by the parties to it, and by the operation of law. One party or both parties can terminate the agency contract in line with the provisions of contract. It is likely that an agency contract would stipulate that either of the parties wanting to terminate the contract should give at least a month notice; where this or any other requirement is not observed, the breaching party would be liable in damages.[134] When an agency ends by operation of law, it refers to those supervening circumstances that are beyond the control of the parties – issues ranging from a change in law that makes that nature of agency contract illegal, force majeure, to a sudden incapacity of one of the parties, say, insanity or death.

---

133. *See* s. 40 of the Secured Transactions in Movable Assets Act 2017 now authorizes self-help repossession of collateral.

134. *See Esso West Africa Inc v. Alli* (1968) 3 ALR Comm 317; *Akinfosile v. Mobil Oil (Nig) Ltd* (1969) 3 ALR Comm 141.

184. Lastly, termination of an agency contract does not affect the existing liabilities of the parties; it only prevents further liabilities from being incurred. This means that upon termination the principal will not be liable for the agent's further dealings with a third party; the agent has the duty to inform a third party about the termination so that agency by estoppel will not be invoked by the latter to bind the agent.

Chapter 2. Economic Operators

§1. Personal Status of Merchants

I. Legal Capacity of Minor

185. A minor is not allowed to enter into contract in Nigeria except for necessaries and beneficial services, which he can ratify upon attaining adulthood of 21 years. A minor cannot be sued in his name unless through his guardian. To that end, a person intending to do business in Nigeria with any natural person must first ascertain whether he is an adult or minor and based on that information ascertain whether they have capacity to enter into the contract for which they have shown interest. The Infant Relief Act 1874 is the principal law that governs infants and their commercial activities.

186. There are other supplemental laws that pertain to infants, depending on what is the circumstance at a given moment. The Constitution of Nigeria stipulates that 18 years is the age for adulthood for the purpose of performing civic duties. Section 30 of the Criminal Code Act stipulates that a person of 17 years and above who is convicted of a capital offence is eligible to serve such punishment. While the Child Rights Act 2003[135] stipulates that a child is a person less than 18 years, and sexual intercourse with a person less than 18 is considered a rape, regardless of whether the child consented to it. However, while different ages exist when the definition of a minor or child is considered, in relation to contract or commercial activities, 21 is the age that is applicable.

II. Foreigners

187. A foreign person for the purpose of doing business in Nigeria could be either a natural person or a legal entity. A natural person intending to do business in Nigeria would require a business permit issued by the Ministry of Interior. The requirements for obtaining a business permit are numerous but could change from time to time, thus, necessitating the need to contact the Ministry's website in order to ascertain what the latest requirements are.[136] The law that governs the obtainment of business permits by foreigners is primarily the Nigerian Investment Promotion Commission (NIPC) Act. Sections 22–24 of the NIPC Act stipulate the various fiscal incentives available to foreign direct investors in Nigeria, while section 25

135. The Child Rights Act 2003 is a special legislation and does not apply uniformly across Nigeria, especially in the northern part due to the minimum of 18 years being the age of adulthood. Under sharia law which applies in the Northern Nigeria, women can be married before they attain the age of 18 years.

136. The Ministry of Interior's website is accessible at https://interior.gov.ng/.

thereof guarantees against expropriation and section 26 provides for International Centre for Settlement of Investment Disputes Arbitration for dispute settlements involving foreign investors.[137]

188. A foreign company that desires to physically do business in Nigeria must do so by incorporating a local company according to section 78 of CAMA 2020. By registering a local company, they would be liable to pay taxes and also improve business opportunities in Nigeria, and can sue and be sued.

III. Married Women

189. In principle, the Nigerian Constitution recognizes the equal rights of men and women. However, in practice, this is not truly the case due to the pluralistic legal system which allows the operation of customary law alongside the received English common law. Under certain customary laws, women do not enjoy the same level of rights as their men counterparts and over time they have come to accept this as the norm. Thus, certain issues like land ownership and inheritance are still hotly contested in some customs in Nigeria as to whether a woman can partake in them in equal measures as their male counterparts.[138]

190. In the Nigerian Constitution, one example is obvious in section 25 on the acquisition of citizenship by an alien. While a foreigner's marriage to a Nigerian man can confer citizenship to the foreigner, the converse is not the case in respect of women, and to that extent, it is gender discriminatory. All this notwithstanding, women can do business in Nigeria without legal restrictions even though at the family level, her husband or family members might disallow her from doing certain kinds of business which they think is 'unsafe' for her.

191. In fact, certain types of business might require her husband to give consent, especially if execution of such business will require her to be absent from her husband and family. There is the discomfort that some Nigerian men have when their wives are progressing more economically than they do; they begin to worry that she might stop being 'loyal' to them, and might plan with her male colleagues to get rid of him. These feelings are usually false and ill-conceived, yet unfortunately, a woman's economic success still unsettles some men who could engage in negative acts towards curtailing her progress. Men typically have unrestrained right to do any business they like, and can travel to any place, spend some time away from family if the nature of his business entails that; it is even encouraged that he possesses such unlimited freedom provided that through such efforts, he is able to provide the basic needs for his family.

---

137. The NIPC Act is freely downloadable at https://investmentpolicy.unctad.org/investment-laws/laws/234/nigeria-nigerian-investment-promotion-commission-act.

138. *See Mojeku v. Mojeku* (2004) 11 NWLR (Pt. 883) 96 where the Supreme Court decided favourably for a custom that bars women from inheriting land.

§2. PARTNERSHIPS AND CORPORATIONS

192. In Nigeria, personhood is divided into two, namely, a natural person and a legal person. A natural person for the purpose of doing business constitutes all adult persons that are twenty-one years and above in age, and can sue or be sued in their name. A natural person above the age of 21 can do business, although CAMA 2020 requires a minimum of 18 years[139] to be able to register a business name at the CAC Nigeria, which is the Commission that is charged with administering the provisions of the CAMA 2020. Business names are governed by Part B of CAMA, and a registered business name is not separate from its owner; it does not have a separate legal personality that can sue or be sued.

193. The second type of personhood is the legal personality of incorporated companies. A company could be limited by shares (private or public), or by guarantee. If a company, public or private, is limited by shares, the shareholders' liability to the company and its creditors are limited to the number of shares they hold in the company. A minimum of one[140] shareholder and a maximum of fifty[141] can form a private company, while a minimum of fifty shareholders can form a public company. A company could also be limited by guarantee, and in that case, the members are limited to the minimum amount (NGN 100,000) to the company's creditors.[142] While the shareholders of a private and public liability companies can be entitled to vote and share in dividends from the profit made by the company in which they hold shares, members of a company limited by guarantee cannot share profit made by the company as such profits must be used to advance or promote the objects of the company. Private and public liability companies as well as companies limited by guarantee are governed by Part A of CAMA.

194. Part C of CAMA governs incorporated trustees. The legal personality is vested in the trustees of the company who can sue and be sued in their names on behalf of the organizations. Companies registered under Part C of CAMA are non-profit in nature, and just like companies limited by guarantee, their members do not share profits, and instead, any profit made by the organization is used in the promotion of its aims and objectives.

195. Partnerships in Nigeria are generally governed by common law except if a state in Nigeria, like Lagos state, has a partnership law. There is no law that governs partnership at the federal level except the old English Partnership Act 1890, statute of general application. Partners are governed primarily by their partnership agreement, and liability is usually severally and jointly. If each partner dies, the *jus accrecendi* unless otherwise agreed would apply to transfer the deceased partner's rights and responsibilities to the living partners; the rights in the partnership do not go to the deceased partner's estate.

---

139. Section 106(2) CAMA 2020.
140. Section 105(3) CAMA 2020.
141. Section 22(3) CAMA 2020.
142. Section 26(12) CAMA 2020.

196. Most professional service providers render their services through partnerships because partnership is a more trusted business vehicle by clients who know that liability for any service that is negligent and causes the client to sustain damages would be recovered directly from the partners through a court action, and their liability will not be limited to their shares unlike a limited liability company. Given that the partners are aware of their unlimited liability, they are careful enough to ensure that their professional services are of high quality and devoid of negligence.

Chapter 3. The Economic Institutions

§1. Professional Organizations

197. There are over two hundred registered professional organizations or bodies in Nigeria that regulate the standard and practice of certain professions. The majority of the professional organizations are established by an Act of the National or State House of Assembly and they cover all professional disciplines in Arts and Sciences. These bodies ensure that their member-practitioners adhere strictly to the relevant codes of conduct and are disciplined in the event of breach. The main essence of these bodies is to ensure that the members of public who rely on the services and judgments of these practitioners are not hurt by poor and irrational judgments of professionals.

198. These organizations sustain through membership dues and are strong pressure groups to the government for narrow interests that affect members both of their groups and those of the general public. Professional bodies in Nigeria serve as avenues through which their members advance and improve knowledge relevant to their careers as they are able to interact and learn from among themselves in the various conferences and seminars that are organized: a comprehensive list of these professional organizations is available.[143]

§2. Chambers of Commerce

199. In Nigeria, Chambers of Commerce are organized as non-profit organizations that promote commerce and trade relations. They are incorporated under Part A of CAMA 2020, as companies limited by the guarantee of its members. Section 26 of CAMA gives detailed descriptions of how companies limited by guarantee should be organized. The relevant highlights of section 26 are that a company limited by guarantee cannot be registered with a share capital; members do not share profit; profits are ploughed back and utilized in promoting the company's objectives; if the company ever carries on business with the objective of making profit and distributing to members, but incurs debts and liabilities, the officers and members who knew about the transactions would be jointly and severally liable.

200. The memorandum of a company limited by guarantee cannot be registered without the authority of the Attorney General of the Federation. In the event of winding up, members cannot contribute less than NGN 100,000, and after winding up, any remaining property of the company after all debts and liabilities have been discharged cannot be distributed to the members, but must be transferred to another company limited by guarantee with similar objects.

143. *See* https://educeleb.com/professional-bodies-in-nigeria-websites/.

201. Chambers of Commerce in Nigeria, whether city/state/bilateral, can register with the Nigerian Association of Chambers of Commerce, Industry, Mines and Agriculture (NACCIMA), as members. *See* www.naccima.com. NACCIMA is the umbrella association that plays a representative role of the various Chambers of Commerce in the country; it represents and advocates for their collective interests before the government.

202. Finally, and very importantly, the Financial Reporting Council of Nigeria (FRCN) had issued the National Code of Corporate Governance 2016 (the 'Code'). The Code drew life from the powers of the FRCN under sections 50 and 51 of the FRCN Act 2011, which commenced in October 2016. The Code was issued in three parts: the Code of Corporate Governance for the Private Sector; the Code of Governance for Not-for-Profit entities; and the Code of Governance for the Public Sector. The code for the Not-for-Profit entities operates on a 'comply or justify non-compliance' basis as stipulated under section 7.3 thereof. Therefore, Chambers of Commerce are governed by the Code of Governance for Not-for-Profit and, of course, also by CAMA 2020.

§3. Advisory Bodies and Committees

203. The need for a body that is charged with providing researched opinion is vital for the success of any government agency or any organization for that matter. Most agencies set up by law have legal provisions for advisory body or committee charged primarily with the duty to provide researched opinions, analysis of data and expert opinion that can guide the executive body charged with the day-to-day execution of the law and thus too busy to think of fresher ways of performing the duties.

204. The opinions of advisory bodies are not binding and can be fully accepted, modified or rejected by the executive to which the opinions are given. For instance, under the Nigerian Oil and Gas Industry Content Development Act, section 104 establishes the Nigerian Content Development Fund for the empowerment of Nigerians in the oil and gas exploration. To ensure effectiveness, the Act provides for the establishment of an advisory committee that would be charged to provide the management board with fresh and efficient ideas to manage the fund. The crucial role of research and development in any organization cannot be overemphasized and government establishments are set up alongside advisory bodies.

205. Similarly, in relation to committees, the various arms of government in Nigeria have their committees that are charged with executing specific functions. The federal legislative committees are more than fifty, each charged specifically with the task to examine issues that affect a particular sector or people in the country and where there are problems, it could under the power conferred to them by the Constitution – sections 88 and 89 – summon individuals to testify before it. There are also the federal executive committee and national judicial council charged with the duty to look into matters affecting the relevant arm of government in the discharge of their functions.

§4. Commercial Courts and Commercial Arbitration

206. In Nigeria, there are high courts and the national industrial court which is a specialized court; the latter is charged with the duty to resolve labour and commercial trade disputes in Nigeria. An appeal from the National Industrial Court goes to the Court of Appeal.

207. The High Court and Federal High Court also have jurisdictions for all commercial disputes. The High Court has unlimited jurisdiction and entertains issues relating to bankers and their customers, tort, criminal matters, etc. The Federal High Court has limited jurisdiction and the matters which fall under its purview are listed in section 251 of the Constitution – thus, if a matter whether in a commercial transaction or tort falls under the items listed in section 251, the Federal High Court would have jurisdiction; otherwise, the High Court of the state would entertain the matter. By section 252 of the Constitution, it has all the powers of a High Court even though it has unlimited jurisdiction.

208. The Nigerian Judicial System is generally slow in dispensing justice. For example, a commercial dispute typically lasts for five years at the Court of First Instance (High Court, Federal High Court or National Industrial Court) and about four years at the Court of Appeal, and six years at the Supreme Court. The Nigerian Supreme Court is the apex court and its decision in respect of any matter is final.

§5. Commercial Arbitration

209. In Nigeria, arbitration arises per contract, and is based essentially on party autonomy. Compared to litigation, it is a faster method of resolving dispute in commercial relations. Parties to a contract have the liberty to choose arbitration as a method of resolving their commercial disputes. Nigeria is a signatory to the 1958 New York Convention pertaining to arbitration and has a national law – namely the Arbitration and Conciliation Act 1990, which mirrors the principles of the New York Convention and the United Nations Commission on International Trade Law (UNCITRAL) Model Law on Arbitration.

210. Sections 3, 4 and 5 of the Arbitration and Conciliation Act are imperative given that they reinforce the principle of party autonomy, and also, parties who have elected to resolve their commercial dispute by arbitration must first exhaust that channel before going to court to review or enforce the award. Thus, in many instances, Nigerian courts have, in deference to the party autonomy doctrine of arbitration, reinforced the view that it is not possible to abandon an agreement to arbitrate in preference to litigation because an arbitral clause is itself an enforceable contract.

211. The principle of separability is recognized in Nigerian arbitration jurisprudence. If a contract which contains an arbitration clause is found invalid or generally unenforceable, the arbitration clause would not be impacted; the parties' right to arbitrate would still be enforceable regardless of the invalidity of the general agreement.

212. Parties to an arbitration are at liberty to choose the forum of arbitration as well as their arbitrator(s), whether it is in the ad hoc or institutional context. The chosen venue could be within or outside Nigeria; given the factors inhibiting effective and speedy arbitration in Nigeria, nearly always, wealthy individuals choose arbitration forums outside Nigeria; the London Court of International Arbitration has been the most patronized. Nigeria has many institutional arbitration forums – for instance, the Lagos Court of Arbitration is effective, and many commercial arbitration disputes in Nigeria are brought before it. Its rules are patterned according to the Model Law on arbitration by the UNCITRAL. Parties can choose a sole arbitrator to decide on their dispute or three arbitrators whereby the two arbitrators chosen by the parties choose the third (chief) arbitrator.

213. Once an arbitral award is rendered by the arbitral panel, it becomes binding on the parties according to section 51 of the Arbitration and Conciliation Act, and if a party fails to comply with the award, it can be enforced after an application has been made to a High Court to enforce same as its judgment. The application which is made by a motion on notice has to be accompanied with the arbitration agreement, the award, the name and place of business of the person against whom it is intended to be enforced and a statement that the award has not been complied with.[144]

144. *See Imani & Sons Ltd v. BIL Construction Co Ltd* (1999) NWLR 12 (Pt. 630) 253 at 263, CA.

Chapter 4. General Obligations of Economic Operators

§1. Commercial Registers

214. Commercial registers exist as a way to prevent fraud arising from ostensible ownership, whereby a person in possession of property that is subject of encumbrances or superior ownership deceives a third party into acquiring it on the basis of his purported clean title. In Nigeria, there are different commercial registers that reveal encumbrances on properties, or the activities of companies.

215. First, in relation to companies, the CAC registry exists to accommodate records in relation to corporate borrowings and charges registered against the company's assets, changes in the activities of a company, for instance, any change in the directors, secretary, and all other officers of a company, are reflected in the CAC registry. It is also in this registry that the annual filings of companies are registered for public perusal. Any member of the public can pay a search fee to peruse through and if possible obtain a certified true copy of all the filed information in the CAC registry regarding the companies whose information is registered there in compliance with all statutory filings as stipulated by the CAMA, 2020.

216. Second, the Federal Inland Revenue Service is the public agency in charge of collecting tax revenues from personal and corporate tax incomes.[145] They have a public registry that enables a member of the public to peruse through a company's tax history and ascertain whether such company has been paying taxes.

217. Third, there are land registries in each state of the federation. Land is governed by the law of the state where it is situated. Thus, each land registry of a state harbours information regarding the ownerships of registered pieces of land and all transactions alienating interests in land or in which a particular land or building was used as collateral to secure transactions.

218. Fourth, in respect of movable asset, there is a centralized, internet-based collateral registry domiciled with the Central Bank of Nigeria (CBN), whereby through an internet search, all encumbrances in respect of a borrower's collateral, which were registered by secured creditors, are discovered. Given that the Secured Transactions in Movable Assets Act (STMA), which gave birth to the CBN collateral registry, was enacted in 2017 by the National Assembly, the National Collateral Registry, although functional, is still at a nascent stage.[146]

219. Fifth, there is a registry for personal intangible property – the Intellectual Properties (IPs). There is the trademark registry where trade names or marks are registered such that if there is a passing off claim, evidence of first to register could easily be obtained from the trademark registry.

---

145. The Finance Act 2020 is the law applicable to income taxes and other types of tax in Nigeria.
146. The National Collateral Registry is accessible at https://www.ncr.gov.ng/.

§2. Opening a Bank Account

220. In 2005, the Nigerian banking sector was reformed and each bank was compulsorily required to have a minimum capital of NGN 25 billion, deposited with the CBN, as a reassuring collateral for depositors in the event of a bank's insolvency. Owing to this huge sum, many of the banks folded up, while some merged with other viable banks to be able to comply with the reform standards. Since 2005, the banks have become sufficiently strengthened and reputable and most of them can compete with their counterparts in other parts of the world.

221. Opening a bank account is continuously made easier nowadays. It is now possible to open certain kinds of bank account online by providing the necessary identification documents without physically appearing in the bank's physical office; this is mainly convenient for those that are residing outside Nigeria. There is also the requirement by the Nigerian Central Bank to all banks to engage in certain verification and due diligent activities known as 'know your customer'. This entails verifying all the submitted documents, including visiting the physical address of the potential bank customer to ascertain whether they live there. With this and many other measures, banking fraud has reduced. The legal tender in Nigeria is the 'Naira' and it is illegal to refuse to accept it as a means of payment. However, parties to a contract can agree to transact in any currency of their choice, provided that none of the parties is forced to accept any other currency other than the Naira.

222. Ideally, a bank account could be opened in one business day and basically requires that the potential customer supplies a copy of his valid identity card, a passport photo, filled bank account opening, and the customer's other biometric details. There are more than thirty commercial banks in Nigeria and all of them provide mobile internet banking services, which provide customers the possibility of downloading a bank's mobile application on their mobile devices and being able to make payments as well other related transactions without visiting their banks' physical locations.

223. There is always a confidentiality clause in the account opening forms, between a bank and its customer, but this is usually overridden if the bank is required via a court order or by the Central Bank which is the apex regulator, to produce certain information relating to a customer. Similarly, a bank could be required by a court order to freeze a customer's account or towards satisfying a debt owed by a customer to a third party; a bank could be mandated by a garnishee order to divulge whether or not it maintains an account for the judgment debtor-customer.

224. Where there is a dispute arising from an agreement between a bank and its customer, the appropriate court to entertain the dispute is the High Court of the state where the facts of dispute, that is, the cause of action, arose. In any case, where a customer is unsatisfied with the conduct of a bank and does not wish to litigate the same, such customer can petition the bank to the Central Bank which is the regulator of banks and other financial institutions in Nigeria.

Chapter 5. Business Assets, Goodwill and Commercial Property Rights

§1. Business Assets

225. In Nigeria, business assets can be categorized into personal (movable) and real (immovable) properties. At common law, a personal property is any property that is not real or immovable. Personal property can further be divided into two categories, namely, personal tangibles and personal intangibles; the latter would be discussed later below. Personal tangible property includes all assets that are movable in nature, for instance, cars, computers, clothing, gold, etc. While personal intangible properties are properties that cannot be physically felt and are thus considered as choses-in-action, for example, debts, accounts-receivable, intellectual property, etc.

226. Similarly, land or building is considered a real property (immovable) because they can be physically felt and are immovable in nature. In Nigeria, land or building can be used to secure a payment obligation, and such transaction must be registered in the land registry of the state where the transaction occurred. If an owner of land alienates interest in the land, either via sale for statutorily allocated lands or via assignment for land that has government's certificates of occupancy, such transaction must be in writing according to section 4 of the Statute of Frauds, 1677. For sale or assignment of interests in land transactions, the Stamp Duties Act[147] requires the payment of stamp duty ad valorem in respect of such transactions, as a prerequisite of perfection of interest in land property.

227. In respect of personal property, the STMA Act 2017 is the law that is applicable when personal property, whether tangible or intangible, is used to secure a repayment obligation. Thus, a person could use his equipment, inventory (goods of sale) to secure debt obligations, and the secured creditor is required to register his security interest in the collateral registry, which is managed electronically by the CBN. Where the debtor is a company, the secured creditor is additionally required to register a copy of the charge against the company in the CAC registry, as a prerequisite of perfecting his security interest in the collateral.

§2. Intellectual Property

228. Copyrights, trademarks and patents are fully recognized in Nigeria as IP, and each of these IP rights are afforded full protection under their respective legal regimes. The three IP rights would be addressed below.

147. *See* Ch. 10 below for more details.

I. Copyright and Neighbouring Rights

229. Copyright is a legal and moral right that accrues to the creator of an original work, which enables the owner the exclusive right to distribute the work for economic benefits. In Nigeria, the Copyrights Act is the applicable law, together with the Berne Convention 1886, which Nigeria is a signatory to. Both acts generally provide that a copyright owner has a moral right to his work; this means that while it is possible to assign the economic rights emanating from a copyright, it is impossible for a person to assign the moral right; moral rights are factual and basically, no contemporary legal system has yet afforded to endorse the notion that a person who performed an act can afford to deny such fact.

230. The Nigerian Copyrights Commission is charged with the responsibility of administering or enforcing the copyrights law within their administrative competence. Thus, even though the creator of a work of copyright is not required to register as a precondition for effectively asserting his right of ownership, it is advisable to register it with the Copyrights Commission so that in the event of dispute regarding ownership of a particular work, a certified true copy can always be obtained from the Copyrights Commission to prove who was first in time in creating the disputed work. However, in this era of internet, it has become easier to prove copyright ownership in works, especially if they were published online, and the date of publication may be used to ascertain which author or creator was first in time.

231. Copyrights law in Nigeria allows fair use; a person may, without a prior permission first sought and obtained from the owner of a copyrighted work, make use of it fairly either for personal use or for educational or non-commercial purpose. A breach of copyright entitles the owner some damages and may require the wrongdoer to account for profits or a damages sum that is sufficient to disgorge the wrongdoer may be awarded by court to compensate the owner and also serve as deterrence to potential wrongdoers. The court that has the original jurisdiction to entertain any dispute emanating from copyright in Nigeria is the Federal High Court pursuant to section 251 of the Nigerian Constitution.

232. A copyright lasts for a lifetime, and continues for seventy years after the death of the creator, when it enters the public domain. It is a universal right and does not need to be registered in the countries of non-origin in order to be effective there. Works in the public domain can be copied or used as pleased without violating the economic right of the creator; however, the moral right of the author is never extinguished and requires that the creator be acknowledged whenever the work is utilized for innovation. Thus, even though a person may not be in breach of the economic aspect of a creator's copyright, use without acknowledgement of the author can expose the user to the liability of misconduct which affects integrity; for instance, plagiarism is highly punished in academic institutions and could be a ground for disqualification for certain political positions.

233. Section 26 of the Copyrights Act provides for Neighbouring Rights. Basically, every song harbours two copyrights. The first is the composition right which accrues to the songwriter. The second is the performance right (neighbouring right) which accrues to the artist that recorded the song, and the right extends to public performance of the song. Section 26(1) states that a performer shall have the exclusive right to control in relation to his performance the following acts: recording, broadcasting live, reproducing in any material form, and adaptation of the performance.

II. Trademark

234. Trademarks and service marks are recognized as intellectual property rights in Nigeria under the Trademarks Act 1990.[148] Essentially, it is a symbol, word or words that are registered with the aim of exclusively identifying a company or product. For a trademark to be effective and capable of conferring a legal right, it has to be registered with the commercial law department of the Ministry of Trade and Investment in Nigeria. Thus unlike copyright which naturally accrues to the creator of an original work, a trademark that is unregistered cannot validly confer ownership right on the alleged owner.

235. By Sections 14 and 23 of the Trademarks Act, a trademark can be registered for an initial period of seven years and can be renewed subsequently for a period of fourteen years at any one time. If it is not renewed and the grace period of one year elapses following reminders from the registrar of trademarks, such marks can be acquired and registered by another person. Registration of trademark confers a legal right that entitles a person to maintain a legal action against a person who infringes on the trademark right – that is, uses a mark or name that is similar to the registered one to the extent that members of the public who are accustomed to the registered trademark may be misled. Non-registration of trademark entitles the holder to an equitable right which is sufficient to sue (for passing off) an unauthorized user who has also not registered the used mark.

236. A registered trademark in Nigeria is protected outside Nigeria because Nigeria is a signatory to the Paris Convention of 1883, and a person desirous of protecting his trademark around the globe or in any country must take steps to register the same in the desired country. The protection of trademark registered only in Nigeria is territorial and a Nigerian court cannot exercise power over a claim of ownership of trademark (property) registered elsewhere unless it is also registered in Nigeria. Needless to add that a trademark can be commercialized through exclusive or partial licensing. If the licensing is partial, it means that the licensed user uses it alongside other users, by incorporating it on their products. If it is exclusive, the licensed user uses it solely and can sue any person that uses it on their product during the duration of licence.[149]

---

148. The Act is accessible at https://nigeria.tradeportal.org/media/Trade%20Mark%20Act.pdf.
149. *See* s. 26 of the Trademarks Act.

237. Lastly, a trademark registered solely in a particular colour does not extend to protect the same mark in another colour. However, if the registration of the trademark is in grey colour (black and white), the protection would extend to any such mark or words in any other colour.[150] Per section 251 of the Constitution, the court that entertains dispute or matters arising from trademarks in Nigeria is the Federal Court in the division of where the cause of action arose.

III. Patent

238. Patent is an exclusive right which a country grants to an inventor for a design, model or inventive steps, which provide a new method of doing something or provide a new technical solution to a recognized problem. In other words, it seeks to protect the intellectual right that emanates from uncommon scientific invention or discovery out of nature. In Nigeria, patent is governed by the Patents and Design Act (PDA) 1970[151] and is administered by the registrar of patents and industrial designs under the Federal Ministry of Commerce, Abuja. Nigeria is also a signatory to the Paris Convention for the protection of industrial property, 1883, and also the Agreement on Trade-Related Aspects of Intellectual Property Rights 1995.

239. By section 17 of the PDA, protection of a registered patent is limited to a period of twenty years in Nigeria, and if the patent is registered in other jurisdictions, it equally receives protection afforded by both local law and the Patent Convention if the country is also signatory to the Convention. The Patent Convention affords one-year protection as grace period for a patent to be registered in another country that is signatory to the Patent Convention.

240. A patent can be commercialized through licensing which can be exclusive or partial in exchange for something of value which can be money or other kinds of property. The law accords protection on the statutory inventor; that is, the person who registers the patent first as opposed to the inventor who failed to register. Thus, the regime recognizes the first to file as an evidence of ownership because the backbone of patent is dependent on information contained in the patent registry in relation to state of the art.

241. A patent that is not renewed after the initial period of registration has elapsed and after a grace period of six months can lose protection under the Nigerian law. Towards encouraging innovation, the government, relying on the PDA and TRIPS Agreement provisions, can cause a patent owner to compulsorily grant another person a licence if that third party requires it for innovative works. A matter ensuing from patent is entertained in the Federal High Court pursuant to section 251 of the Nigerian Constitution.

---

150. *Ibid.*, at s. 16.
151. The Act is accessible at https://lawsofnigeria.placng.org/laws/P2.pdf.

§3. TRADE SECRETS

242. Nigeria does not have a local legislation that provides for the protection of trade secrets; protection typically comes from contract, tort and other principles of law. However, Article 39 of the TRIPS Agreement provides for the protection of trade secrets, and as Nigeria is a member of the World Trade Organization (WTO), the agreement is binding on Nigeria, although it is subject to the ratification of the National Assembly under section 12 of the Nigerian Constitution. However, TRIPS sets out what the minimum standards should be in respect of inventions that qualify as trade secrets; namely, such confidential information must be a secret that is not generally known to the public; it must have commercial value; and the holder must exert some reasonable efforts to keep it secret.

243. It should be noted that under the Nigerian law, not all inventions are patentable due to failure to meet the rigorous requirement of novelty and public morals; other times, it is due to the nature of information involved, for instance, customer lists, pattern, formula, technique or process that affords a person or business entity some competitive edge. Even at that, not all inventors are desirous of patenting their inventions because it provides the public an opportunity to study the invention and perhaps come up with innovations through compulsory licensing. Due to the risk involved in public registration, many business people keep their inventions or certain sensitive information as trade secrets. While this protects the owner of the trade secret from public sight, the risk is that the trade secret could be stolen by an insider and sold to a competitor who would quickly register it, thus acquiring legal right in it that deserves the protection of law.

§4. TRADE NAME

244. Every business enterprise distinguishes itself through its unique name in the market known as the trade name. The CAMA 2020 compulsorily requires that every individual or business entity having a place of business in Nigeria registers it with the CAC within a period of twenty-eight days of commencing business. The essence of requiring the registration of every trading name is to afford CAC the opportunity to verify each trading name and ensure that more than one person or business entity is not assigned the same trading name because such would be confusing to the general public and might encourage free riding whereby consumers that are familiar with a particular trade name believe albeit erroneously that another business entity with a similar trading name is the one they are used to, and has the same quality of goods or services. Towards preventing this situation from occurring, the registration requirement of a business name is mandatory.

245. Similarly, under section 852 CAMA 2020, there are restrictions in respect of trade name use. Thus, unless authorized by law or any appropriate agency, no business entity is allowed to use words like 'state', 'government', 'municipal', 'national', 'regional'. This is because such words are capable of conveying the impression that the business entity is related to the government and therefore authentic or financially strong to be relied on. Also, words like ‘bank’, ‘insurance’ or ‘finance’ are reserved for only entities that are regulated and given special licence to operate by a regulatory body such as the Central Bank or the National Insurance Commission. Under CAMA 2020, the registrar-general reserves the right not to register a name if it is deemed offensive and contrary to public interest or policy.[152]

246. It should further be noted that every trade name is required to end with an abbreviation that reveals the nature of their legal personality, so that the public can know at a glance what the extent of liability is, in the event of default of payment or insolvency. Thus, ‘Plc.’ is used to show that a business entity is a public limited company. If it ends with ‘Ltd’, then it is a private limited company. If the company is limited by guarantee, the suffix is ‘Ltd/Gte’, and for unlimited companies, ‘Unlimited’ or ‘Ultd’ is used as their suffix. Importantly also, business names registered under Part E of CAMA 2020 are not in themselves legal entities and are not legally separated from their owners. Their individual owners only trade under the name and style registered in Part E; thus, the proper entity to be sued for issues emanating from the business registered under Part E is the business owner. However, for companies registered under Part A of CAMA, they enjoy a legal personality that is separate from their owners.

247. If a company registered under Part A commits a wrong for which a legal action against it is necessary, only the company can be sued and not the shareholders. If, however, there is liability imposed on the company, the shareholders, in the cases of public or private liability companies, are liable only to the extent of their unpaid up shares. If it is a company limited by guarantee, the members are liable to the statutory minimum sum of NGN 100,000.[153] If it is an unlimited liability company, the members’ liabilities are not restricted to any sum; they will be jointly and personally liable until the entire debt owed by the company is repaid. Once a trade name is registered, the company must publish it on its business premises, design corporate seal, stationary, etc., that reflect its trade name.

§5. Goodwill

248. Goodwill is the good reputation or brand name enjoyed by a commercial entity. Being an intellectual property, goodwill is an intangible asset and is often governed by the ordinary principles of contract law. It is the difference between the fair market value of a company’s assets (less its liabilities) and the market price or asking price for the overall company. In other words, goodwill is the amount in excess of the company’s book value that a purchaser would be willing to pay to acquire it. Goodwill is built as a result of consistent business patronage and customer loyalty over a period of time.

152. Section 852(1)(c), CAMA 2020.
153. *Ibid.*, at s. 26(12).

249. Goodwill can be quite vague even though it constitutes an important factor where a business is sold or transferred, acquired or where a merger occurs. A key advantage of goodwill is that where a business is being sold, it places the purchaser in a competitive position in the market.

250. While goodwill is described as the difference between the fair market value of a company's assets (less its liabilities) and the market price or asking price for the overall company, its value is not straightforward and is often subject to negotiations during business transactions.[154]

§6. COMMERCIAL PROPERTY RIGHTS

251. Commercial property, or commercial real estate, refers to real estate that is owned or used by a business entity.

252. The principal land legislation in Nigeria is the Land Use Act (LUA).[155] The LUA of 1978 stipulates that all land comprised in the territory of each state and such land be held in trust and administered for the use and common benefit of all Nigerians. This implies that the highest interest a person or company can own on land in Nigeria is a mere right of occupancy as it was confirmed by the Supreme Court of Nigeria in the case of *Nkwocha v. The Governor of Anambra State.*[156]The right to own a property in Nigeria is a constitutional right enshrined in the 1999 Constitution, and any derogation from such right must be justifiable within the exceptions permitted by the Constitution.

253. Transactions affecting land in Nigeria are required to be evidenced in writing owing to section 4 of the Statute of Frauds 1677, and failure to comply with this requirement renders such contracts unenforceable. Notwithstanding this rule, where the sale is carried out under customary law, other circumstances such as part-performance constitute sufficient evidence of a binding contract. As stated previously, any transaction or instrument that confers, vests, transfers, limits, charges or extinguishes any interest or right in any property be registered.

254. Transactions relating to the transfer of title or creation of a security interest in land are registered at the relevant lands registry of the state where such transactions took place. According to section 191 CAMA 2020, a company has power to borrow money for the purpose of its business objects and may charge or mortgage its undertakings or properties and issue debentures. Debentures,[157] therefore, are

154. *I. Oyewobi,* What Valuation of Business and Goodwill Means, *Vol. 8(2) Int'l J. Bus. & Mgmt. Invention, 60–66 (2019).*
155. See the Land Use Act, 1978.
156. *See Nkwocha v. Governor of Anambra State & 2 Ors* (1984) JELR 43602 (SC).
157. *See* ss 196–200 CAMA 2020.

instruments issued by the company to its lender to acknowledge the indebtedness by the company, the instruments which are more often than not by deed.[158]

255. Furthermore, where a corporate body creates a charge or mortgage over its real property, the documents creating the security interest are required to be registered at the CAC within ninety days of its execution.[159]

158. *See Union Bank of Nig. Ltd. v. Tropic Foods Ltd* [1992] 3 NWLR (Pt. 228) 321.
159. *See* s. 222 CAMA 2020.

Chapter 6. Bankruptcy and Related Institutions

256. The inability to repay debt to one's creditors when the debts have become due and payable could lead to the filing of a bankruptcy petition against the debtor. Bankruptcy refers to a formal process by which a court-appointed liquidator gathers up a debtor's assets and distributes them to his creditors according to their rights. Unlike in the United States where the term 'bankruptcy' refers to both natural and legal persons under the US Bankruptcy Code 1978, in Nigeria, the term 'bankruptcy' is used to refer to a bankruptcy trustee's process of gathering and distributing the assets of an individual debtor, for which the Bankruptcy Act 1990 is the applicable law.[160] There is some stigma attached to being declared an undischarged bankrupt which often boils down to being disqualified from holding certain elective and other public offices or from practising any regulated profession (except as an employee).[161]

257. In the Nigerian sense, there is a distinction between bankruptcy and insolvency. Whereas the former exclusively refers to individuals, the latter is used to describe companies that are unable to repay their debts of NGN 200,000 and above,[162] after the creditor has made a demand and twenty-one days have lapsed since the demand, and the debt remains unpaid: the foregoing distinction and their explanations were similarly treated by Njemanze.[163] For insolvent companies, the laws that are applicable are certain provisions of the Companies and Allied Matter Act (CAMA) 2020.[164] Nigeria does not yet have a specific legislation for corporate insolvency – there is a bill on that which is currently pending at the National Assembly.

258. Bankruptcy may be voluntary or involuntary. It is voluntary where a debtor makes an assignment of all his properties for the benefit of his creditors or files a petition for bankruptcy proceedings; it is involuntary where the creditors take the initiative by filing a bankruptcy petition against the debtor.

259. In a bankruptcy process, a creditor can obtain a final judgment order against the debtor, and execute same on him after service of bankruptcy notice on the person.[165] Bankruptcy law protects both the debtor and creditor, and affords support or protection to the debtor from a multiplicity of debt recovery cases/suits from his creditors arising from his inability to repay or defray his debts to them individually. Adjudication in bankruptcy thus operates as collective process which consolidates

160. Bankruptcy Act, Cap B2, Laws of the Federation of Nigeria (LFN), 1990.
161. *See* ss 50 and 131 of the Bankruptcy Act 1990.
162. *See* s. 572 CAMA 2020.
163. *See* generally, L.O. Njemanze, *Understanding Bankruptcy, Trust and Executorships Law and Accounts* (Rhyce Kerex Publishers 2003).
164. *See* Chs 18–22 CAMA 2020 dealing with administration, liquidation, company voluntary arrangement.
165. *See* s. 1(a)(i) Bankruptcy Act, Cap B2, Laws of the Federation of Nigeria (LFN), 2004.

many suits or litigations into one proceeding usually against a single person.[166] For example, section 10 of the Bankruptcy Act reads:

> except as directed by the court, no creditor to whom the debtor is indebted to in respect of any debt provable in bankruptcy shall have any remedy against the property or person of the debtor in respect of the debt, or shall commence any action or other legal proceedings, unless with the leave of the court and on such terms as the court may impose.

260. Bankruptcy also releases or extricates a debtor adjudged bankrupt from all his debts at the material point in time allowing him to make a fresh start as soon as the court approves his discharge. Especially for corporate entities, one of the main functions of insolvency law as denoted also by the Cork Committee in the United Kingdom is to facilitate an enquiry, investigation or probe into the reasons or causes of the failure or insolvency of the debtor. In summary, a bankruptcy adjudication procures or secures a fair, equal and equitable distribution or sharing of the properties of a debtor among the debtor's proven creditors. Here, all creditors who prove their debts must partake in the distribution according to their rights in bankruptcy. For secured creditors, they would receive payment from the debtor's assets in which they have in rem security rights, while unsecured creditors would generally receive pro rata – that is, the equal treatment of creditors in the same class.[167]

261. According to the Bankruptcy Act,[168] certain conditions must be in place for a bankruptcy proceeding to be initiated. The Act provides that the acts complained of must be an act of bankruptcy as provided by the aforementioned law:

> A debtor commits an act of bankruptcy in each of the following cases-
>
> (a) if a creditor has obtained a final judgment or final order against him for any amount, and execution thereon not having been stayed, has a bankruptcy notice served on him, and does not, within fourteen days after service of the notice, comply with the requirements of the notice or satisfy the court[169] that he has a counter-claim, set off or cross demand which equals or exceeds the amount of the judgment debt or sum ordered to be paid, and which he could not set up in the action in which the judgment was obtained or the proceedings in which the order was obtained,
>
> (b) If execution against him has been levied by seizure of his goods under process in an action, or proceedings in the court, and the goods have either been sold or held by the bailiff for twenty-one days:

166. *See* s. 10(1) of the Bankruptcy Act, Cap B2. LFN, 2004.
167. Uwadineke C. Kalu, *A Critique of Voluntary or Debtor Initiated Bankruptcy Adjudicatory Process and the Need for Legislative Reformation in Nigeria*, Vol. 1 J. Int'l L. Juris. 41–55 (2010).
168. Bankruptcy Act, Cap B2, Laws of the Federation of Nigeria (LFN), 1990.
169. 'Court' means the Federal High Court sitting in its bankruptcy jurisdiction. *See* s. 142 Bankruptcy Act, 1990.

(c) If he files in the court a declaration of his inability to pay his debts or presents a bankruptcy petition against himself.[170]

262. Section 4 of the Bankruptcy Act further provides that a creditor shall not be entitled to bring a bankruptcy petition against a debtor unless:

(a) the debt owing by the debtor to the petitioning creditor, or if two or more creditors join in the petition, the aggregate amount of debts owing to the several petitioning creditors, is not less than N2,000;
(b) the debt is a liquidated sum, payable either immediately or at some certain future time;
(c) the act of bankruptcy on which the petition is grounded has occurred within three months before the presentation of the petition; and
(d) the debtor is ordinarily resident in Nigeria, or within a year before the date of the presentation of the petition, has ordinarily resided or had a dwelling-house or place of business in Nigeria, or has carried on business in Nigeria, personally or by means of an agent or manager, or is or within the said period has been a member of a firm or partnership of persons which has carried on business in Nigeria by means of a partner or partners or an agent or manager.[171]

§1. Insolvency

263. In Nigeria, the CAMA governs issues relating to insolvency and winding up of companies. An insolvent company is one that in respect of any debt above NGN 2,000, it owes a creditor, is unable to satisfy payment of the debt after the debt has been demanded and three weeks have elapsed since the demand. Section 409 CAMA states that a company shall be deemed unable to pay its debts if:

(a) a creditor, by assignment or otherwise, to whom the company is indebted in a sum exceeding 2,000 then due has served on the company, by leaving it at its registered office or head office, a demand under his hand requiring the company to pay the sum so due, and the company has for three weeks thereafter neglected to pay the sum or to secure or compound for it to the reasonable satisfaction of the creditor; or
(b) execution or other process issued on a judgment, decree or order of any court in favor of a creditor of the company is returned unsatisfied in whole or in part; or
(c) the court, after taking into account any contingent or prospective liability of the company is satisfied that the company is unable to pay its debts.

170. *See* s. 1 Bankruptcy Act 1990.
171. *See also* s. 7 of the Bankruptcy Act, 1990.

264. Where a company is deemed by the court to be unable to pay its debts, there are different steps that may be taken with winding up often seen as the last resort where all else fails. The CAMA provides for Corporate Restructuring, Corporate Rescue, Arrangement and Compromise, Mergers and Acquisitions, and Winding Up either voluntarily or by an order of the court.

§2. Corporate Rescue and Restructurings

265. Corporate rescue is a major intervention necessary to avert eventual failure of a company.[172] It is an alternative to immediate liquidation of the company, with the aim to prevent the death of the company. Company rescue often involves changes in the management of the company and is usually achieved through restructuring methods.

266. Corporate restructuring refers to the process of redesigning one or more aspects of a company. It entails any fundamental change in a company's business or financial structure. Corporate financial restructuring involves restructuring the assets and liabilities of corporations, including their debt-to-equity structures, in line with their cash-flow needs to promote efficiency, support growth and maximize the value to shareholders, creditors and other stakeholders. Thus rather than bring a company to its end as a result of a harsh operating environment, stiff competition or difficult regulatory compliance, ailing companies adopt various restructuring methods as survival strategies, many of which are available under the Nigerian corporate and investment law and practice.

267. Corporate restructuring methods may be either internal or external. Internal options involve the company alone with its members or creditors, while external options involve the company and other third parties.[173] Internal restructuring options include: Arrangement and Management Buy-Out, while external options include: Mergers and Acquisitions, Takeover, Purchase & Assumption and Cherry-Picking.

I. Arrangement

268. This means any change in the rights or liabilities of members, debenture holders or creditors of a company or any class of them or in the regulation of a company, other than a change effected under any other provision of CAMA or by the unanimous agreement of all parties affected thereby.[174] Arrangement may be on Sale or via Compromise.

---

172. A. Belcher, *Corporate Rescue* 12 (Sweet and Maxwell 1997).
173. For more details, *see* Nelson C.S. Ogbuanya, *Essentials of Corporate Law Practice in Nigeria* 579 (Novena Publishers 2010).
174. *See* s. 710 CAMA 2020.

269. Under an Arrangement on Sale under section 714 of CAMA 2020, a company may by special resolution resolve that the company be put into members' voluntary winding up and that the liquidator be authorized to sell the whole or part of its undertakings or assets to another body corporate in consideration or part consideration of fully paid shares and distribute the same in specie among the members of the company in accordance with their rights in the liquidation. The consideration may be in the form of cash, shares, debentures or policies. This method of winding up of a company usually results in the rebirth of the company in another form either as a new company or providing funds for a restructuring scheme.

270. A dissenting member of the company may by writing addressed to the liquidator and left at the registered office or head office of the company, within thirty days after the passing of the resolution, in respect of any of the shares held by him, require the liquidator to either abstain from carrying the resolution into effect or purchase such shares at a price to be determined either by agreement in the case of a private company in which aliens do not participate or by Securities and Exchange Commission in the case of a public company or private company in which aliens participate.[175]

271. Section 715 CAMA provides that where a compromise or arrangement is proposed between a company and its creditors or any class of them, the court may, on the application of the company or any of its creditors or members or, in the case of a company being wound up, of the liquidator, order a meeting of the creditors or class of creditors, or of the members of the company, or class of members, as the case may be, to be summoned in such a manner as the court directs. Thus, arrangement by way of compromise enables a company to alter the rights of its members or creditors with the sanction of court. A compromise may be between a company and creditors to exchange debentures for shares or the company and its members to consolidate and subdivide shares.

II. Management Buy-Out

272. Management Buy-Out is the acquisition of a company or its subsidiaries by the management team of said company with or without third-party financing.[176] This option enables the management team to salvage the company rather than allow it to be subject to a takeover or merger and acquisition. It is especially favourable where the management wishes to retain the vision and mission of the company. The funding to actualize this could be from internal source or third-party financing.

---

175. Section 714(4). Subsection (3) provides that any member who fails to signify his dissent with the stipulated period shall be deemed to have accepted the resolution.
176. Rule 238 Securities and Exchange Commission Rules 2007 as amended in 2010. This rule further sets out the guide to embarking on a Management Buy-Out.

III. Mergers and Acquisitions

273. The above-stated terms are often used interchangeably; however, they are quite distinctive. A merger is a business combination which involves the fusion of two or more corporate entities largely on equal terms, while an acquisition is essentially the purchase by one company of all or substantial interest of another company.

274. In Nigeria, the industry that has mostly benefitted from this pattern of restructuring is the banking industry. In 2019, there was an amalgamation of Diamond Bank plc and Access Bank plc into one entity subsequently called Access Bank plc. Although both parties initially insisted that it was a merger, the Chief Executive Officer of Access Bank, Herbert Wigwe, in a later interview with Bloomberg Daybreak revealed that it actually acquired Diamond Bank plc. in a deal worth about USD 200 million.

275. The relevant institutional and regulatory agencies involved in mergers and acquisitions are as follows:

(a) Securities and Exchange Commission.
(b) Central Bank of Nigeria.
(c) Federal High Court of Nigeria.
(d) Nigeria Stock Exchange.
(e) Corporate Affairs Commission.

IV. Takeover

276. Section 131 of the Investments and Securities Act (ISA) 2007 describes takeover as a process which results in the acquisition/purchase of a substantial interest by an individual or company (the acquirer) in another company (target company), sufficient enough to give the acquirer substantial control over either management or overall affairs of the target company. In Nigeria, acquisition of between 30% and 50% (or as may be provided by the Securities and Exchange Commission from time to time) of the voting rights of the target company's called-up shares by an individual of the company qualifies for takeover.[177]

V. Purchase and Assumption

277. This is an external restructuring option which seeks to reduce loss of investment by allowing another company or investors to purchase the liabilities of the failing company and assume ownership of its assets, usually at auction price. The assumed company takes up the status of the purchasing company through a

177. Section 131(1) ISA 2007. *See* further Rules 235–238 SEC Rules and ss 146–147 ISA for conditions and steps to proceed with a takeover bid.

judicial assent. The transaction is perfected by a duly executed Deed of Purchase and Assumption executed by the involved parties filed along with the required court process at the Federal High Court.[178]

VI. Cherry-Picking

278. This option of restructuring allows the healthy company to examine the books of the ailing company to enable it to pick out those aspects it can save by integrating it with its own operations.[179]

§3. Winding Up and Dissolution of a Company

279. A corporation dies upon winding up or dissolution. In *Tate Industries Plc v. Devcom M.B Ltd,*[180] the court stated that 'a winding-up proceeding is signing the death warrant of a company or the pronouncement of the death of the company. It is a very serious matter.' In some cases, despite different avenues taken to rescue a company, it may fail. Where this occurs, the life of the company may be ended under the Company and Allied Matters Act in two ways:

(1) By the process of winding up as provided under the Act.
(2) The Commission strikes off the name of the company from the register of companies for being defunct.[181]

I. Modes of Winding Up

280. The winding up of a company may be effected:[182]

(a) by the court; or
(b) voluntarily; or
(c) subject to the supervision of the court.

A. Winding Up by the Court

281. According to section 571 CAMA 2020, a company may be wound up by the court if:

---

178. Nelson C.S. Ogbuanya, *Essentials of Corporate Law Practice in Nigeria* 631 (Novena Publishers 2010).
179. *Ibid.*
180. [2004] 17 N.W.L.R [Pt. 901]CA 182 at 225, paras E–G.
181. Section 692 CAMA 2020.
182. *See* s. 564 CAMA 2020.

(a) the company has by special resolution resolved that the company be wound up by the court;
(b) default is made in delivering the statutory report to the Commission or in holding the statutory meeting;
(c) the number of members is reduced below two;
(d) the company is unable to pay its debts;
(e) the court is of the opinion that it is just and equitable that the company should be wound up.

282. The court having jurisdiction to wind up a company is the Federal High Court within whose area of jurisdiction the registered office or head office of the company is situated.[183]

283. A review of section 564(1) of CAMA 2020 reveals that a petition for winding up on the grounds of default in delivering the statutory report or holding statutory meetings can only be brought by a shareholder and only after the expiration of fourteen days after the last day on which the meeting should have held.

284. By section 572 CAMA, a Company shall be deemed to be unable to pay its debts if:

(a) a creditor, by assignment or otherwise, to whom the company is indebted in a sum exceeding NGN 200,000 then due has served on the company, by leaving it at its registered office or head office, a demand under his hand requiring the company to pay the sum so due, and the company has for three weeks thereafter neglected to pay the sum or to secure or compound for it to the reasonable satisfaction of the creditor; or
(b) execution or other process issued on a judgment, decree or order of any court in favour of a creditor of the company is returned unsatisfied in whole or in part; or
(c) the court, after taking into account any contingent or prospective liability of the company, is satisfied that the company is unable to pay its debts.

285. Reiterating this, the court in *Oriental Airlines Ltd v. Air Via Ltd*[184] stated that the essential requirements for winding up a company due to inability to pay debts are:

(a) there must be an existing debt;
(b) the debt is due;
(c) a formal demand is made;
(d) the company is unable to pay.

183. *See* s. 570(1) CAMA 2020.
184. [1998] 12 N.W.L.R (Pt. 577) 271 at 279–280.

286. It is pertinent to note that a company will not be deemed to be unable to pay its debt even though it appears to be so where the debt is disputed in good faith and if there is no evidence of due demand for payment. In *Tate Industries Plc v. Devcom M.B Ltd*, the Court of Appeal Lagos Division held that where a debt is disputed bona fide, an order of winding up will not be made. In such case, the creditor must seek his remedy in an action to establish the debt.[185]

287. Furthermore, where there is no evidence of due demand for payment of such debt, the petition for winding up will be declared incompetent and the court would decline jurisdiction to hear the petition. According to section 572 CAMA, the demand is a condition precedent to compulsory winding up of a company as a result of inability to pay its debt.

288. Section 573 of CAMA provides for who may petition for the winding up of a company. It states:

> An application to the court for the winding up of a company shall be by petition presented subject to the provisions of this section, either by -
>
> a. the company;
> b. a creditor, including a contingent or prospective creditor of the company;
> c. the official receiver;
> d. a contributory;
> e. a trustee in bankruptcy to, or a personal representative of a creditor or contributory;
> f. the Commission under section 366 of this Act;
> g. a receiver if authorised by the instrument under which he was appointed; or
> h. by all or any of those parties, together or separately.

289. A company can be wound up on just and equitable grounds[186] where the company is unable to carry out its objectives; is formed for fraudulent purposes; has no business or assets or is discriminatory against its minority or members.

B. The Procedures for Winding Up by the Court

290. The following are the mandatory steps to be taken where the winding up procedure is by the court:[187]

(a) Filing of the Petition with the Affidavit verifying the petition.
(b) Service of the Petition.
(c) Advertisement of the Petition.

---

185. *See* Ch. 10 below for a more detailed treatment.
186. Section 571(f) CAMA 2020.
187. Winding Up Rules Cap C20 L.F.N 2004.

(d) Hearing to show compliance with the rules.
(e) Filing of Notice of Intention to Appear, Affidavit in Opposition and Affidavit in Reply by the Respondent.
(f) Appointment of provisional liquidator.
(g) Filing and hearing of summons for costs.
(h) Filing of list of names and addresses of persons who wish to appear.
(i) Hearing of the Petition.
(j) Making a winding up order.

291. The court may at any time after an order for winding up, on the application of either a liquidator or the official receiver or any creditor or contributory, and on proof to the satisfaction of the court that all proceedings in relation to the winding up ought to be stayed, make an order staying the proceedings either altogether or for a limited time, on such terms and conditions as the court thinks fit.[188]

C. Voluntary Winding Up

292. According to section 620 CAMA, a company may be wound up voluntarily:

(a) when the period, if any, fixed for the duration of the company by the articles expires, or the event, if any, occurs, on occurrence of which the articles provided that the company is to be dissolved and the company in general meeting has passed a resolution requiring the company to be wound up voluntarily;
(b) if the company resolves by special resolution that the company be wound up voluntarily.

293. Where a company passes a resolution for voluntary winding up, it shall, within fourteen days after the passing of the resolution, give notice of the resolution by advertisement in the Gazette or two daily newspapers and to the Commission.[189] A voluntary winding up shall be deemed to commence at the time of the passing of the resolution for voluntary winding up.[190]

294. Where it is proposed to wind up a company voluntarily, the directors of the company or, in the case of a company having more than two directors, the majority of the directors, may at a meeting of the directors make a statutory declaration, to the effect that they have made a full enquiry into the affairs of the company and that, having so done, they have formed the opinion that the company will be able to pay its debts in full within such period, not exceeding twelve months from the commencement of the winding up.

188. Section 601(1) CAMA 2020.
189. Corporate Affairs Commission (CAC).
190. *See* ss 621 and 622 CAMA 2020.

295. A winding up where such declaration has been made and delivered in accordance with the provisions above is referred to as a members' voluntary winding up. However, where no such declaration is made, it is referred to as a creditors' voluntary winding up.[191]

II. Winding Up Subject to the Supervision of Court

296. If a company passes a resolution for voluntary winding up, the court may on petition order that the voluntary winding up shall continue but subject to such supervision of the court, and with such liberty for creditors, contributories, or others to apply to the court, and generally on such terms and conditions, as the court thinks just.[192]

297. The court in making the supervision order may appoint an additional liquidator to act with the existing liquidator.[193] Upon a supervision order, the liquidator subject to any restrictions imposed by the court will exercise all his powers without the sanction or intervention of the court in the same manner as if the company was being wound up voluntarily.

191. *See* ss 626–633 CAMA which provide for the procedures applicable to a members' voluntary winding up, while ss 634–641 contain the provisions applicable to a creditor's voluntary winding up.
192. Section 649 CAMA 2020.
193. Section 652(1) CAMA.

Chapter 7. Negotiable Instruments

298. A negotiable instrument is a document guaranteeing the payment of a specific amount of money, either on demand or at a set time, with the payer usually named on the document. It is a document of title or evidence of indebtedness that is transferable in trading as a substitute for money. Negotiable instruments are unconditional orders or promise to pay, and include cheques, drafts, promissory notes, warehouse receipts, and bills of exchange. In Nigeria, the Bill of Exchange Act governs the law with respect to negotiable instruments. A negotiable instrument to be clear therefore is a document contemplated by a contract, which: (1) warrants the payment of money, the promise of or conveyance of which is unconditional; (2) specifies or describes the payee, who is designated on and memorialized by the instrument; and (3) is capable of change through transfer by valid negotiation of the instrument. Negotiability and transferability are closely related.

299. Generally, there are seven features a negotiable instrument ought to possess:

1. It must be in writing.
2. It must be signed by the maker or drawer.
3. It must be an unconditional promise or order to pay.
4. It must be payable in money.
5. It must be for a fixed amount of money.
6. It must be payable on demand or at a definite time.
7. It must be payable to order or bearer, unless it is a cheque.

300. Other scholars have included features such as popularity and evidence.[194]

§1. Bill of Exchange

301. Section 3 of the Bill of Exchange Act defines it as an unconditional order in writing, addressed by one person to another, signed by the person giving it, requiring the person to whom it is addressed to pay on demand or at a fixed or determinable future time a sum certain in money to or to the order of a specified person, or to bearer.[195] An instrument which does not comply with these conditions, or which orders any act to be done in addition to the payment of money, is not a bill of exchange.

194. *See* A.C. Onuorah, *Negotiable Instruments and the Nigeria Financial System*, Vol. 2(5) Int'l J. Bus. Mgmt & Tech. 72–80 (2018).
195. Bill of Exchange Act, Cap 35, Laws of the Federation of Nigeria, 1990.

§2. Types of Bills of Exchange

302.

(a) Inland Bill: This is a bill which is or on the face of it purports to be both drawn and payable within Nigeria; or drawn within Nigeria upon some person resident therein.[196]
(b) Foreign Bill: This is any other bill different from an inland bill.[197]
(c) Inchoate Bill: This is a bill lacking in some materials particular, for example, where the space for amount payable is left blank or where the space for payee is left blank. There is a prima facie authority to the holder of such a bill to fill in the omission within a reasonable time.[198]

303. There are three main parties to a bill of exchange: the drawer, drawee and the payee:

Drawer: This is the person who writes and signs the bill.
Drawee: This is the person on whom the bill is drawn.
Payee: This is the person to whom the money stated in the bill is payable. He may be the drawer or any other person to whom the bill has been endorsed. Other parties include the following:
Acceptor: This is the person who accepts the bill. In practice, the drawee is the acceptor but a third person may accept a bill on behalf of the drawee.
Holder: The payee or endorsee of a bill or note who is in possession of it, or the bearer.[199]
Endorser: The person, either the drawer or holder, who endorses the bill to any one by signing on the back of it is called an endorser.
Endorsee: The person in whose favour the bill is endorsed.
Drawee in case of need: This is a person who is introduced at the option of the drawer. Any endorser may insert the name of such person, and the effect of it is that a resort may be had to him in case the bill is dishonoured for non-acceptance or non-payment or in any other need.
Acceptor for honour: The person who may voluntarily become a party to a bill as acceptor in the event of the refusal by original drawee to accept the bill if demanded by the notary. The acceptor for honour offers to accept the bill *supra protest* with a view to safeguard the honour or prestige of the original drawer or any other endorser, as the case may be. This happens when the bill gets dishonoured and a formal certificate of dishonour, known as protest, is issued by the Notary Public to the holder of a bill in question.[200]

196. Section 4(1) Bill of Exchange Act.
197. *Ibid.*
198. *See* s. 20 Bill of Exchange Act.
199. Section 2(1) Bill of Exchange Act.
200. *See* s. 65 Bill of Exchange Act, 1990.

304. Section 22 of the Bill of Exchange Act declares capacity to incur liability as a party to a bill of exchange to be coextensive with capacity to contract. Therefore, where a bill is drawn or endorsed by an infant, minor or corporation having no capacity or power to incur liability on a bill, the drawing or endorsement entitles the holder to receive payment of the bill, and to enforce it against any other party. The liabilities of the various parties are further documented in sections 53–58 of the Act.

§3. Discharge of a Bill of Exchange

305. A bill is discharged if the orders contained thereon have been carried out and this may happen under the following circumstances:

i. By payment in due course by the drawer or acceptor in the good faith and without notice of any defect in the title of the holder.[201]
ii. When an acceptor of a bill becomes the holder of the bill at or after maturity in his own right, for example, if the bill was endorsed to him for value.[202]
iii. By waiver or renunciation of the holder or other party entitled to the proceeds of the bill. Renunciation must however be made by the drawee. A holder in due course who takes bill before its maturity and is not aware of the renunciation will however not be affected by the renunciation.[203]
iv. By cancellation of the bill or the party's signature. Here it is important to note the distinction between intentional and unintentional cancellation. Unlike intentional cancellation, unintentional cancellation or a mistaken cancellation does not discharge a bill. The onus, however, is on the person who asserts the existence of mistakes or the lack of intention to prove same: cancellation by a holder of a bill or his agent discharges any party liable on the bill if the cancellation is of that person's signature – so also will any endorser who would have had a right of recourse against the party whose signature is cancelled be discharged.[204]
v. By material alteration of a bill. Where the order on the bill or its acceptance is materially altered without the assent of the parties liable on the bill, the bill is discharged except as against a party who has himself made, authorized or assented to the alteration and subsequent himself made, authorized or assented to the alteration and subsequent endorser.[205]
vi. By acceptance of honour. This is the acceptance of a bill which has been dishonoured by a person with original liability on the bill, usually to save face or to protect the honour of any party liable on the bill. A payment of honour may however discharge the bill.

201. Section 59(1) Bill of Exchange Act.
202. Section 61, Bill of Exchange Act.
203. Section 62, Bill of Exchange Act.
204. Section 63(1)(2)(3), Bill of Exchange Act.
205. *See* s. 64, Bill of Exchange Act.

vii. When a bill is lost and replaced by another, the finder of the lost bill obtains no right to sue drawee or acceptor or drawer on the bill.[206]

§4. Cheques

306. A cheque is a bill of exchange drawn on a banker payable on demand.[207] It is a negotiable instrument that contains an unconditional order to the bank to pay a certain sum mentioned in the instrument, from the drawer's account, to the person to whom it is issued, or to the order of the specified person or the bearer. A cheque is that document which orders a bank to pay a specific amount of money from a person's account to the person in whose name the cheque has been issued. The person writing the cheque, known as the drawer, has a transaction banking account where their money is held.

§5. Types of Cheques

307.

Crossed Cheque: This type of cheque typically has two transverse parallel lines at the top left corner of some cheques, which may or may not have the words – & Co., A/c payee or Non-Negotiable. The amount on such cheques is credited to the account of the payee.
Open Cheque: This is also known as uncrossed cheque; it is one on which cash is payable at the counter of the bank, or it is transferred to the bank account of the person whose name is written on the cheque. It is negotiable; i.e., it is transferable in nature.
Bearer Cheque: This refers to the cheque which can be cashed by the person whose name is written on the cheque or anyone who presents the cheque before the bank for payment. It is negotiable in nature, which can be transferred by simply delivering it and so endorsement is not needed. No identification of the presenter or holder is required in case of a bearer cheque.
Order Cheque: It is the cheque which becomes payable to the person or organization whose name is specified on the cheque or to his order.
Self-Cheque: This type of cheque is used by a person who wants to withdraw money from his own account, by writing 'self' as the name of the payee.
Blank Cheque: This is a cheque which is only signed, but the name of the payee and date are not specified.
Stale Cheque: Typically, a cheque bears a date and is valid up to three months of the stated date. If a cheque is presented before the bank, after the expiry of the reasonable period, i.e., three months after the date, it is called stale.
Post-Dated Cheque: This occurs where a cheque is drawn containing a future date.
Antedated Cheque: This occurs where a cheque is drawn containing a prior date.

---

206. Section 69 Bill of Exchange Act, 1990.
207. Section 73 Bill of Exchange Act, 1990.

Traveller's Cheque: This is a cheque issued by a bank for a fee, containing a fixed amount. It is used to make payment in a foreign country, after endorsement by the signature of the holder.
Cheque Crossing: Crossing a cheque simply instructs the banker to pay the specified sum through the banker only, i.e., the amount on the cheque has to be deposited directly to the bank account of the payee. It ensures that the funds are transferred to the bank account only and not cashed upon the receipt of the cheque.

308. According to section 78 of the Bill of Exchange Act,[208] a cheque may be crossed either generally or specially:

General crossing: Where a cheque bears across its face an addition of the words 'and company' or any abbreviation thereof between two parallel transverse lines either with or without the words 'not negotiable'; or two parallel transverse lines simply, either with or without the words 'not negotiable', that addition constitutes a crossing, and the cheque is crossed generally.
Special crossing: Where a cheque bears across its face an addition of the name of a banker, either with or without the words 'not negotiable', that addition constitutes a crossing, and the cheque is crossed specially, and to that banker.

309. A crossing is a material part of a cheque. It is therefore unlawful for any person to obliterate or add to or alter a crossing.

§6. Promissory Notes

310. A promissory note is an unconditional promise in writing, made by one person to another, signed by the maker, engaging to pay, on demand or at a fixed or determinable future time, a sum certain in money to, or to the order of, a specified person or to bearer.[209]

§7. Essential Features of a Promissory Note

311.

(a) It is a written document.
(b) There must be a clear and unconditional promise to pay a certain sum to a specified person or on demand.
(c) It must be drawn and duly signed by the maker.
(d) It must be properly stamped.
(e) It specifies the name of the maker and payee.
(f) The amount to be paid must be certain, given in both figures and words.
(g) Payment is to be made in the country's legal currency.

208. Cap 35, LFN 1990.
209. Section 85(1) Bill of Exchange Act.

312. A promissory note is inchoate and incomplete until delivery thereof to the payee or bearer.[210]

210. Section 86 Bill of Exchange Act.

Chapter 8. Stocks, Commodities, Securities and Its Institutions

313. A stock (also known as 'share' or 'equity') is a type of security that signifies proportionate ownership in an issuing corporation. This entitles the shareholder or stockholder to that proportion of the corporation's assets and earnings. Stocks and other forms of securities are typically traded on the stock exchange. In Nigeria, this capital market is referred to as the Nigerian Stock Exchange (NSE).

314. A stock exchange or securities exchange is a facility where stockbrokers and traders can buy and sell securities, such as shares of stock and bonds and other financial instruments. A stock exchange is an organized and regulated financial market where securities (stocks, bonds, notes, shares) are bought and sold at prices governed by the forces of demand and supply.

315. The NSE is a company limited by guarantee and was founded in 1960. The NSE is regulated by the Securities and Exchange Commission, which has the mandate of surveillance over the Exchange to forestall breaches of market rules and to deter and detect unfair manipulations and trading practices. The Investment and Securities Act, 2007 is the relevant law establishing the Securities and Exchange Commission and also regulating the securities market to ensure the protection of investors, maintain a fair efficient and transparent market.

316. The first section of the Act[211] provides that a body to be known as the Securities and Exchange Commission shall be established and the Commission shall be a body corporate with perpetual succession and a common seal which may sue and be sued in its corporate name. It further provides that the Commission shall have power to acquire, hold or dispose of any property, movable or immovable for the purpose of carrying out any of its functions.

317. A commodity is a basic good used in commerce that is interchangeable with other commodities of the same type. Commodities are most often used as inputs in the production of other goods or services. Commodities are raw materials or agricultural products that can be bought and sold or objects that come out of the earth such as wheat, cattle, soybeans, corn, oranges, gold, uranium, copper, aluminium, coal, cotton, and oil. Commodities are traded in bulk on an exchange market. In Nigeria, this market is the Nigerian Commodity Exchange (NCX).

318. A commodity exchange is an exchange where various commodities, derivative products, agricultural products and other raw materials are traded. It is an organized, regulated market that facilitates the purchase and sale of contracts whose values are tied to the price of commodities.

319. The NCX was originally incorporated as a stock exchange on 17 June 1998. It commenced electronic trading in securities in May 2001 and was converted to a

211. Investments and Securities Act, 2007 (hereinafter referred to as the ISA).

commodity exchange on 8 August 2001 and brought under the supervision of the Federal Ministry of Commerce. The main regulatory organization that has oversight of commodity exchanges in Nigeria is the Security and Exchange Commission (SEC). The ISA is also the relevant law governing the commodities market as its definition of securities includes commodities, futures, contracts, options and other derivatives.[212]

320. Securities under the ISA refer to debentures, stocks or bonds issued or proposed to be issued by a government, a body corporate; or any right or option in respect of such debentures, stocks, shares, bonds or notes; or commodities, futures, contracts, options and other derivatives, all of which may be transferred by means of any electronic mode approved by the Commission (SEC) and which may be deposited, kept or stored with any licensed depository or custodian company.[213]

§1. The Securities and Exchange Commission

321. As previously stated in this chapter, the Securities and Exchange Commission[214] has oversight function with respect to the regulation of securities in Nigeria. The ISA provides that there shall be established a body to be known as the Securities and Exchange Commission which shall be a body corporate with perpetual succession and power to sue or be sued. It further provides that the Commission shall have power to acquire, hold or dispose of any property, moveable or immovable for the purpose of carrying out its functions.[215]

322. Section 13 of the ISA provides for the functions and powers of the Commission which includes but are not limited to registration of securities; registration and regulation of the securities exchanges, commodity exchanges, futures, options and derivatives Exchange, capital trade points; regulation of securities business; protection of public interest and investors; regulate cross-border securities transactions; intervene in the control and management of failing capital market operators; prevent unfair and fraudulent trade practices; and perform other functions and exercise other powers necessary to give full effect to the provisions of the ISA.[216]

---

212. *See* s. 315 of the Investment and Securities Act.
213. *Ibid.* Note that subsequent use of the term 'securities' in this chapter encompasses all terms such as stocks, commodities, and futures as defined under the Act.
214. Hereinafter referred to as SEC.
215. Section 1(1)(2)(3) ISA.
216. Read Section 13 further to see all functions and powers as provided under the ISA.

§2. Registration of Securities Exchanges

323. Securities exchanges are defined under the Act as an exchange or approved trading facility such as a commodity exchange, metal exchange, petroleum exchange, options or futures exchange, over the counter market, and other derivative exchanges.[217]

324. Securities exchanges such as the NSE and the NCX are required by law to be registered. The ISA provides that no security exchange may commence operation until it has been duly registered with the Commission. It further provides that an application for registration shall be made to the Commission in the specified form after the conditions for registration as provided by section 29 of the ISA have been met. According to section 32 of the ISA, securities exchanges are required to inspect and conduct enquiries and audits into its members, then in turn file a detailed report with the Commission on its surveillance and enforcement activities.[218]

325. Capital market operators are persons (individuals or corporate) duly registered by the Commission to perform specific functions in the capital market. Section 38 of the ISA provides for the registration of capital operators and the conditions to be met in order to be registered.

§3. Registration of Securities

326. All securities of a public company and all securities or investments of a collective investment scheme[219] are required to be registered with the Commission and the Commission will in turn issue a certificate of registration[220] in respect of the securities and investments registered by it. No securities or investments are to be transferred, issued, sold, or offered to the public without being registered. Anyone in contravention of this requirement is liable on conviction to a fine of NGN 1,000,000 or a term of imprisonment of three years.[221]

327. Similarly, section 56 of the ISA provides that a capital market operator shall keep a register of the securities in which he has an interest and must register particulars of securities in which he has an interest within seven days of acquisition of the interest.

217. Section 28 of the ISA.
218. Section 32, ISA.
219. *See* s. 315 of the ISA.
220. Certificate of registration is any certificate or licence issued by the Commission as a part of its registration functions under the ISA.
221. *See* s. 54, ISA.

§4. Invitations to the Public

328. The ISA provides for invitation of the public to make an offer for the purchase of securities. An invitation to the public is an offer or invitation to make an offer which is published, advertised, or disseminated by newspaper, broadcasting, cinematograph or any means whatsoever. It is an invitation which is calculated to result in shares, debentures, etc., becoming available for subscription or purchase by members of the public.[222]

329. Section 67 of the ISA provides that only a statutory bank or a public company whether quoted or unquoted may extend invitations to the public to acquire or dispose of any securities. Any invitation made to the public which is in breach of this section, all persons or body corporate making the invitation shall be liable to a penalty of NGN 5,000,000 in the case of a body corporate and NGN 100,000 in the case of an individual.[223]

§5. Conduct of Securities Business

330. The ISA prohibits certain cash transactions in excess of an amount periodically determined by the Commission. Furthermore, a securities dealer is expected to issue a contract note in respect of every securities transaction.[224]

331. According to section 99 of the ISA, contract notes are expected to include:

(a) the name and style under which the securities dealer carries on his business as a securities dealer and the address of the principal place at which he so carries on his business;
(b) the name and address of the person to whom the securities dealer gives the contract note;
(c) the date on which the transaction took place and, if outside a securities exchange or capital trade point, a statement to that effect;
(d) the number, amount and description of the securities which are the subject of the contract;
(e) the price per unit of the securities;
(f) the amount of the consideration;
(g) the rate and amount of commission (if any) charged;
(h) the amounts of all stamp duties or other duties and taxes payable in connection with the contract; and
(i) if the settlement amount with or without benefit is to be added to or deducted from the settlement amount in respect of right to a benefit purchased or sold together with the securities, the first-mentioned amount and the nature of the benefit.

222. Section 69, ISA.
223. *See* further Part IX of the ISA.
224. *See* ss 97 and 98, ISA.

332. Section 105 of the ISA states that a person shall not create, or cause to be created, or do anything which may create a false or misleading appearance of active trading in any securities on a securities exchange or capital trade point or with respect to the market for the price of any such securities. Furthermore, a person shall not in any form take actions that may result in rigging the market. The Act further provides that no person shall fraudulently induce another to deal in securities.[225] Insider trading is also prohibited as a person who is an insider of a company shall not buy or sell or otherwise deal in the securities of the company which are offered to the public for sale or subscription if he has information which he knows is unpublished price sensitive information in relation to those securities.[226]

I. Which Court Has Jurisdiction to Hear Matters Arising from Security Trading?

333. There shall be established a body to be known as the investment and securities tribunal (hereinafter called the Tribunal) to exercise the jurisdiction, powers, and authority conferred on it by the Act. Therefore, the investment and securities tribunal is the Court of First Instance with respect to disputes and other matters arising from securities trading.[227]

334. Section 284 of the ISA provides for the jurisdiction of the Tribunal as follows:

(1) The Tribunal shall, to the exclusion of any other court of law or body in Nigeria, exercise jurisdiction to hear and determine any question of law or dispute involving:
  - (a) a decision or determination of the Commission in the operation and application of this Act, and in particular, relating to any dispute:
    - (i) between capital market operators;
    - (ii) between capital market operators and their clients;
    - (iii) between an investor and a securities exchange or capital trade point or clearing and settlement agency;
    - (iv) between capital market operators and self-regulatory organization.
  - (b) the Commission and self-regulatory organization;
  - (c) a capital market operator and the Commission;
  - (d) an investor and the Commission;
  - (e) an issuer of securities and the Commission; and
  - (f) disputes arising from the administration, management and operation of collective investment schemes.

225. Section 108, ISA.
226. Read Further Part XI of the Investment and Securities Act which deals with prohibited conducts in respect to securities trading. Sections 115 and 116 provide for criminal liability of anyone who contravenes this part of the Act and the compensation to be paid to aggrieved persons.
227. Section 274 of the ISA. *See* further ss 275 and 276 ISA which provide for the composition and constitution of the Tribunal.

(2) The Tribunal shall also exercise jurisdiction in any other matter as may be prescribed by an Act of the National Assembly.
(3) In the exercise of its jurisdiction, the Tribunal shall have the power to interpret any law, rules or regulation as may be applicable.

335. The ISA provides that the Tribunal shall give its judgment in writing and a certified true copy of the decision of the Tribunal shall be supplied to the parties upon request. Furthermore, an award or judgment of the Tribunal shall have the same effect as though from the Federal High Court upon registration of the award or judgment with the Chief Registrar of the Federal High Court by the Tribunal.[228]

336. The power of appeal lies with the Court of Appeal; therefore, anyone dissatisfied with the verdict of the Tribunal has recourse to Court of Appeal while further appeals at the instance of the affected parties or the Commission lie with the Supreme Court.[229]

---

228. *See* 293 of the Investments and Securities Act, 2007.
229. Sections 295 and 297 of the ISA.

Chapter 9. Commercial Contracts

337. A commercial contract refers to a legally binding agreement between parties in which they are obligated to do or restrain from doing particular things. A contract is an agreement which gives rise to enforceable obligations. In *Orient Bank (Nig.) Plc v. Bilante International Ltd*, the court defined a contract to mean an agreement between two or more parties which creates reciprocal legal obligations to do or not to do particular things. For a contact to be valid, there must be mutuality of purpose and intention.[230]

338. The importance of contracts cannot be overemphasized because without it, commercial and trading activities would break down. The law of contract pervades almost all spheres of human activities of commercial flavour. Contract law applies to sales of goods, agencies, insurance, labour relations, company law, banking law and franchises and services.

§1. Classification of Contracts

I. Formal and Simple Contracts

339. A formal contract is a contract made by deed, while other contracts whether in writing or by word of mouth are simple contracts.

340. A contract by deed must be in writing and must be sealed and delivered. Therefore, it must be completed and given full legal effect by signing, sealing and delivery of it by the party executing to the other party. A contract by deed (under seal) is enforceable by the party in whose favour it is executed even in the absence of a consideration.

341. A simple contract as previously stated may be in writing or may be oral.[231] Under a simple contract, only a party that has furnished consideration can bring an action for enforcement unless they can prove a detrimental reliance under the promissory estoppel doctrine. According to Skinner C.B. in *Rann v. Hughes*,[232] all contracts are by the laws of England distinguished into agreements by speciality (contracts under seal) and agreements by parol (simple contracts) nor is there any such third class as contracts in writing. If they be merely written and not specialities, they are parol, and a consideration must be proved.

230. [1997] 8 NWLR (Pt. 515) 37 at 76.
231. An oral contract is referred to as parol contract.
232. (1778) 7 Term Rep. 350.

II. Express and Implied Contracts

342. A contract is express when the terms of the contract are clearly stated, while in the case of an implied contract, its terms are not. All material terms of the contract are clearly spelt out in an express contract and the contract comes into existence after the terms have been agreed upon. An implied contract is usually construed from the conduct of the parties and not from their words or correspondence.

III. Bilateral and Unilateral Contracts

343. A bilateral contract consists of an exchange of promises, the offeror promising to do something in exchange for the offeree's promise to do something else in return. There is typically no performance in this case and the consideration is referred to as executory consideration.

344. In the case of a unilateral contract, consideration consists of actual performance in return for a promise and the performance is referred to as executed consideration.

IV. Principles or Elements of Contract

345. The elements of a valid contract are generally accepted to be offer, acceptance and consideration. However, intention to enter into legal relations has been added as a fourth element. Furthermore, Niki Tobi, J.C.A. in *Orient Bank v. Bilante Int.*[233] added a fifth element which is capacity to contract.

A. Offer

346. An offer is a clear and definite undertaking or promise made by one party (called the offeror) with the intention that it shall become binding on him as soon as it is accepted by the party (called the offeree) to whom it is addressed.[234] An offer must be specific and unambiguous.

347. It is pertinent to note that there is no limit to the number of persons an offer can be made to. Therefore, a contract can be said to exist between the offeror and the person or persons accepting said offer. In the case of *Carlill v. Carbolic Smoke Ball Co.*,[235] it was stated that an offer can be made not only to an individual or a group of persons but also to the whole world.

---

233. *Ibid.*
234. I.E. Sagay, *Nigerian Law of Contract* 10 (Spectrum Books 2000).
235. [1893] 1 Q.B 256.

348. An offer may also be made expressly or implied. The test of existence of a contract in a case where an offer is implied is objective; will a reasonable man infer from the surrounding circumstances (the conduct of the parties) if there is indeed an offer? In *Major Oni v. Communications Associates,*[236] the plaintiff made an offer to let his flats to the defendants. The latter modified the terms of the contracts by including the installation of air conditioners. The plaintiff immediately installed the air conditioners. It was held that this brought a valid contract into existence between the parties. By installing the air conditioners, the plaintiff had accepted the defendant's counter-offer by conduct.

1. Invitation to Treat

349. This is not an actual element of contract; however it is often confused with an offer. As previously stated, an offer must be clear and unequivocal in order to be binding. Where there is simply a preliminary move in negotiations which may lead to a contract, it is an invitation to treat. In the course of negotiating with a view to making a contract, several steps may be taken before an actual offer is made. There are various circumstances that constitute an invitation to treat and not an offer.

a) Auctions

350. An auctioneer's request for a bid is not an offer but an invitation to treat (i.e., an invitation to make an offer). It is the actual bid that constitutes an offer. Indeed it has been held that the offer is accepted by an auctioneer when he signifies his acceptance by the fall of his hammer.[237]

b) Display of goods for sale and advertisement

351. A display of goods in a shop is not an offer to sell goods but an invitation to a customer to make an offer to buy.[238] Therefore, a customer makes an offer to buy the goods when he takes them to the cashier to pay for the goods, and the cashier may then accept or decline his offer. In *Pharmaceutical Society of Great Britain v. Boots Cash Chemists,*[239] the Court of Appeal held that goods are merely displayed to enable customers to choose what they want and that the contract is not completed until the shopkeeper or someone on his behalf accepts the offer after the customer has indicated the items he needs.

352. However, an advertisement for the return of lost or stolen property is treated as an offer. This is because no further negotiations are expected to occur and such advertisement is made with the intention to be bound.

---

236. (Unreported) High Court of Lagos, Lambo, J., Suit No LD/625/71 delivered on 8 Jan. 1973 Casebook, p. 1.
237. *Payne v. Cave* [1789] 3 Term Rep.148.
238. *Timothy v. Simpson* [1834] 6 C & P 499.
239. [1953] 1 Q.B 401.

c) Tenders

353. An invitation to tender is merely an invitation for offers from interested parties and is not itself an offer. The person making the statement is not bound to sell to the person making the highest offer. Where, however, the person who invites the tender states in the invitation that he shall be bound to accept the highest offer, then such invitation for tender is an offer.

d) Contract of Vehicular Conveyance (Buses, Taxis, Trains Versus Passengers)

354. This issue has been the source of a raging controversy since the possibilities therein are endless. An important issue is to find out the exact point it become practically impossible for the parties to withdraw from the transaction. The point where the passenger gets into the vehicle and it commences moving can be taken to be acceptance, and the offer therefore must have been made by the bus company. When the passenger waited at the bus stop could be taken as an invitation to treat.

e) Sale of Shares

355. Where a company makes an offer to the public asking it to subscribe for shares in it, it does not offer to sell the shares but has made an invitation to the public to offer to purchase said shares. The company reserves the right to accept or reject those offers.

B. Acceptance

356. An acceptance is a final and unqualified expression of assent to the terms of an offer.[240] An acceptance must conform to the offer and must either be communicated to the offeror or the requisite act demanded by the offer must be done. Tobi J.C.A. in *Orient Bank (Nig) Plc. v. Bilante International Ltd*[241] defined an acceptance of an offer as 'the reciprocal act or action of the offeree to the offer in which he indicates his agreement to the terms of the offer as conveyed to him by the offeror'. It was further stated that acceptance may be manifested by conducts of the parties, by their words or by the documents passing between them.

1. Invalid Methods of Acceptance

a) Counter-Offer

357. Where there is a modification of an offer by the person to whom it is made, a counter-offer is said to have been made. The counter-offer thus becomes a fresh offer which the initial offeror, now the offeree, may accept or reject. According to Tobi J.C.A., 'where any fresh term is introduced by the person to whom the offer is

240. G.H. Treitel, *Law of Contract* 13 (Stevens & Sons 1990).
241. [1997] 8 NWLR (Pt. 515) p. 37.

made, his expression of assent amounts to a counter offer which in turn requires to be accepted by the person who made the original offer'.

b) Cross Offer

358. This occurs where two offers with identical terms are sent by two parties to each other using distant communication. In this case, there cannot be said to be acceptance since both parties only exchanged offers (promises) with neither party assenting. In *Tinn v. Hoffman,*[242] the court held that there was no contract as there was a mere exchange of promises.

c) Conditional Acceptance

359. In this case, acceptance is made subject to a particular condition. This cannot constitute valid or binding acceptance. In *Winn v. Bull,*[243] the defendant agreed to take lease of a house but communicated acceptance by saying that this is 'subject to the preparation and approval of a formal contract'. The court held that the contract was inchoate in the absence of formal documentation. The contract was therefore not binding as the acceptance was made conditional.

d) Acceptance in ignorance of offer

360. There was an initial controversy on this issue due to the court's decision in *Gibbon v. Proctors.*[244] In this case, the defendants published a handbill offering a reward to anyone who was able to provide useful information to the police which would lead to the arrest of an individual who had assaulted a young girl. The plaintiff supplied the information even before the handbill was printed. The court however held that the plaintiff was entitled to the reward.

361. This decision was roundly rejected by several scholars, and the case of *Fitch v. Snedaker*[245] has clarified this by holding that a reward cannot be claimed by one who did not know it had even been offered.

e) Acceptance of Tenders

362. Where a tender is made to supply goods in 'such quantities (not exceeding a stated amount) as you may order' the person to whom the tender is submitted does not incur any liability simply by 'accepting' it. He only becomes liable when he places an order for the goods.

---

242. [1873] 29 L.T. 271.
243. [1877] 7 Ch. D.29.
244. (1891) L.T. 594.
245. 38 N.Y. 248 (1868).

2. Communication of Acceptance

363. As a general rule, acceptance is only effective when it has been communicated to the offeror. It was held in *Union Bank of Nigeria Ltd v. Prof. A.O. Ozigi*[246] that an acceptance may be demonstrated in three ways: by the conduct of the parties, by the words of the parties and by the documents that have passed between them.

364. There are however exceptions to the aforementioned general rule. In the below cases, acceptance may be effective even though it is not communicated to the offeror or brought to his notice:

(a) Communication to offeror's agent.
(b) Where the terms of offer waive the requirement of communication of acceptance.
(c) Acceptance by post.

365. Typically, acceptance occurs the moment the offeror receives the offeree's reply. However, in the case of acceptance by post, acceptance takes effect when the letter of acceptance is posted. In this instance, acceptance is binding and the contract is said to be perfected when the acceptor places this acceptance in the mailbox for return mail even if, in fact, it never reaches the offeror. This was further espoused in the case of *Adams v. Lindsell*,[247] where it was held that a contract entered by post comes into being the moment the letter of acceptance is posted.

366. As with every general rule, there are exceptions to the rule that the contract comes into being once the letter is posted:

(a) Where the terms of contract state expressly or impliedly that the acceptance must be communicated factually.[248]
(b) The rule will not apply to acceptance made instantaneously.
(c) Where the rule would create utmost inconvenience and absurdity.

3. Revocation of Acceptance

367. Where acceptance is not by post, it can be revoked before it reaches the offeror. This cannot apply in the case of acceptance by post since posting constitutes acceptance. It has however been suggested that where the letter of revocation reaches the offeror before or at the same time as the letter of acceptance, it is valid since the position of the offeror is not prejudiced.[249]

246. [1991] 2 NWLR (Pt. 176), 77.
247. [1818] 1 B. & A. 681.
248. *Holwell Securities Ltd v. Hughes* [1974] 1 WLR 155.
249. *Countess of Dunmore v. Alexander* [1830] 9 S.C. 190 Ct. of Session.

4. Termination of an Offer

368. An offer can be terminated in the following ways:

a) Revocation

369. The general rule was established in *Payne v. Cave*[250] that an offer can be revoked at any time before acceptance takes place. In *Routledge v. Grant*,[251] the defendant offered to buy a house from the plaintiff and gave him six weeks to accept. Defendant withdrew the offer after three weeks. Plaintiff's purported acceptance at the end of six weeks was held insufficient to constitute the transaction into a contract as the offer had been properly revoked after three weeks of the offer.

370. However, the revocation must be communicated effectively directly or indirectly to the offeree before acceptance. In this case, mere posting of revocation without receipt of it does not suffice.

371. In the case of unilateral contracts,[252] due to its very nature, revocation depends on the nature of the offer. In some cases, the parties may understand that the offeror reserves the right to revoke at any time until performance is complete, while in other cases, it may be proper to hold that the offeror cannot revoke once performance has begun. In *Errington v. Errington*,[253] a father bought a house for his son and daughter-in-law to live in. He paid one-third of the purchase price in cash and borrowed the balance on a building society mortgage. He told the son and daughter-in-law that if they paid the weekly instalments, he would convey the house to them when the instalments were fully paid. They paid. It was held that so long as they were paying, the father's promise was irrevocable.

b) Lapse of Time

372. An offer may be terminated where there is no acceptance after an appropriate lapse of time. Where there is a stipulated time, an acceptance after said time is ineffective. However, where there is no stipulated time, such offer determines after the lapse of a reasonable time. In *Ramsgate Victoria Hotel Co. v. Montifiore*,[254] the court stated that an offer will lapse if it is open for a specific length of time and that time limit expires. Where there is no express time limit, an offer is normally open only for a reasonable time.

373. Reasonable time will depend on the circumstances of the case with respect to offers involving other types of subject matter and the means of communicating the offer.

250. [1789] 3 Term Rep 148.
251. [1828] 4 Bing 653, Com. Pl.
252. A unilateral contract is a contract agreement in which an offeror promises to pay after the occurrence of a specified act. Therefore, performance in this case constitutes acceptance.
253. [1952] 1 K.B. 290.
254. [1866] L.R.L.I. Exch. 109.

c) Rejection

374. An offer is terminated when the offeree communicates his rejection to the offeror. Hence, the offeree making a counter-offer and introduces a new offer amounts to a rejection of the original offer. In *Hyde v. Wrench*,[255] Lord Langdale held that the counter-offer offered by the offeree terminated the original offer. Hence, '... thereby rejected the offer previously made by the defendant (the offerer)'.

375. However, this should be distinguished from the situation when the offeree merely seeks further information from the offeror, and does not make a counter-offer. In *Stevenson, Jacques & Co. v. McLean*,[256] a mere enquiry would not be considered as rejection.

d) Death

376. The death of either the offeror or the offeree will result in a termination: the right to accept an ordinary offer is not transferable. The unaccepted offer of a deceased person cannot be converted into a contract binding upon his estate. In *Dickinson v. Dodds*,[257] Mellish L.J. stated that 'if a man who makes an offer dies, the offer cannot be accepted after he is dead'.

C. Consideration

377. In *Currie v. Misa*, Lush J. defined consideration as 'A valuable consideration, in the sense of the law, may consist either in some right, interest, profit, or benefit accruing to the one party, or some forbearance, detriment, loss or responsibility, given, suffered, or undertaken by the other.' Consideration posits some detriment to the promisee in that he may give value and some benefit to the promisor who in turn receives the value.

378. In order to sustain an action, the plaintiff must prove either a benefit conferred on him by the defendant or on someone else at the instance of the defendant or a detriment suffered by him in the implementation of the terms of the bargain.

379. A moral obligation does not constitute consideration. In the case of *Eastwood v. Kenyon*,[258] moral obligation was dismissed as the basis for an action. Also, in *Faloughi v. Faloughi*, Kalgo J.C.A. held that natural love and affection was not a true or real consideration. It was stated incapable of estimation in terms of value.

380. Only a person who has furnished consideration in a contract can bring an action to enforce a promise given to the defendant in that contract. Therefore, a

255. (1840) 3 Beav. 334.
256. (1880) 5 Q.B.D. 346.
257. [1876]2 Ch. D. 463.
258. (1840) 11 A. & E. 438.

party that has furnished no consideration cannot enforce that contract. Consideration can be said to be absent in the following cases:

(a) Gratuitous promise by the promisor. Where the promisor commits himself to perform a continuing act without a corresponding commitment or promise by the promise.
(b) Non-performance by the promise. Consideration fails where it is predicated on performance (which does not occur) by the person seeking to enforce the contract.
(c) Where consideration is furnished by a third party and not the promisee.
(d) Where the claim is in excess of the benefit provided for in an agreement.

1. Classification of Consideration

381. Consideration can be classified into Executory and Executed consideration. Consideration is executory when the offer and acceptance consist of promises, that is, the offeree making a promise in return for the offeror's promise. In this case, actual performance is to take place at a later date. An instance of executory consideration is in a contract for sale of goods since parties may agree that delivery of and payment for the goods are to be made in the future.

382. Consideration is however executed where the promise is made in return for actual performance. An instance of this could be offers of reward by the owner of a lost property to anyone who finds and returns it to him.

2. Past Consideration

383. The giving of a promise or the performance of the act stipulated for in the contract exhausts the promise given in return. Any further promise made subsequently by any of the two parties without fresh consideration from the other party is not actionable. Such a promise made is based on past consideration. It can more accurately be deemed to have been made with no consideration at all. In *Roscorla v. Thomas*,[259] the plaintiff bought a horse from the defendant. The defendant thereafter made a promise to the plaintiff that the horse was 'sound and free from vice'. The promise failed as the horse turned out not to be so. Plaintiff sued for the breach of promise.

384. The court held that the promise was made after the sale was over and was unsupported by fresh consideration. It was also held that the fact the sale did not itself imply a warranty, the horse was therefore sound and free from vice. In *Re*

259. [1842] 3 Q.B. 234.

McArdle,[260] a testator left a house jointly to his children. The wife of one of the children, who was living in the house with her husband, spent a lot of money making improvements and carrying out alterations to the house. Later on, the other children jointly signed a document agreeing to pay her 488 pounds for expenses in improving the house. It was held by the English Court of Appeal that the promise was not binding on the children. The plaintiff had completed the works on the building before the promise to repay her was made. Her consideration was deemed past.

3. Adequacy of Consideration

385. It is not the duty of the court to measure the comparative value of the parties' promises exchanged in the course of the transaction or to enquire into whether one party has got a better bargain than the other. In *Faloughi v. Faloughi*,[261] Kalgo, J.C.A., emphasized that it is within the exclusive domain of the parties to a contract to determine the consideration for the contract. And once the consideration is of some value in the eye of the law, even the courts have no jurisdiction to determine whether it is adequate or inadequate.

4. Sufficiency of Consideration

386. As stated previously, consideration need not be adequate. However, consideration must be valuable in the eye of the law. The value must be economic in nature even though it cannot be precisely quantified. Natural affection and sentimental motives are not sufficient consideration.

V. Intention to Enter Legal Relations

387. This is an essential element of contract. The law does not assert the existence of a contract merely because of the presence of mutual promises. In addition to an agreement and furnishing of consideration, parties must intend to create legal relations.

388. There are three instances in which a contract may be denied on the grounds that there is no intention to create legal liability.

VI. Domestic and Social Agreements

389. The rule is that domestic and social agreements are not binding due to the presumption of the absence of contractual intention. In *Spellman v. Spellman*,[262] a

260. [1951] Ch. 669.
261. [1995] 3 N.W.L.R (Pt. 384) 434 at p. 451.
262. [1961] 1 W.L.R 921.

husband promised to buy his wife a car in order to improve their strained relations. The court held that this was purely a domestic arrangement not intended to create any legal relations. If it is shown that in the case of spousal agreement, the spouses were not living in harmony when the agreement was concluded, then a good ground is established to make the agreement binding. In *McGregor v. McGregor*,[263] a husband and his wife had taken out cross summons against each other for assault. It was agreed in settlement that each should withdraw their actions and, among others, that the husband should pay the wife a weekly sum for maintenance of herself and the children. This agreement was held binding on the husband. The presumption of absence of contractual intention was rebutted by the hostile relations between the parties.

VII. Commercial Agreements

390. In this case, though the presence of contractual intention is presumed, it may be rebutted. There are two situations in which defendants have advanced the plea of absence of the contractual intention in order to escape liability:

(i) Where they assert that their promise was a mere puff not intended to be taken seriously or literally. The test for determining this is that of a reasonable man.
(ii) Where the agreement itself contains a clause expressly excluding the intention to enter into legal relations.

VIII. Intermediate Instances

391. These are agreements that can neither be classified as domestic and social agreements nor as commercial agreements. An example of this is the carpool arrangement between friends or co-workers. In *Coward v. Motor Insurers Bureau*,[264] the court held that in the absence of evidence that the parties intended to be bound contractually in a carpool transaction, the courts would be reluctant to hold such an arrangement created any legal contractual relation. Similarly, with respect to collective agreements, the court held in *Union Bank of Nigeria v. Edet*[265] that a collective agreement is unenforceable for lack of contractual intention.

IX. Sale of Goods

392. The law of sale of goods in Nigeria is principally governed by the Sale of Goods Act, 1893, an English law adopted in Nigeria before political independence as one of the statutes of general application in the country.

---

263. [1888] 21 Q.B.D. 424.
264. [1962] 1 All E.R. 531.
265. [1993] 4 N.W.L.R (Pt. 289) 512.

393. According to section 1(1) of the Sales of Goods Act, a contract of sale is one whereby a seller transfers or agrees to transfer the property in goods to the buyer for a money consideration called the price. A contract of sale could be absolute or conditional.[266] Where under a contract of sale the property in the goods is transferred from the seller to the buyer, the contract is called a sale, but where the transfer of the property in the goods is to take place at a future time or subject to some condition thereafter to be fulfilled, the contract is called an agreement to sell.[267] An agreement to sell becomes a sale when the time elapses or the conditions are fulfilled subject to which the property in the goods is to be transferred.[268]

394. Okany[269] has stated that in addition to the ordinary elements of a contract, two other elements, namely, goods and monetary consideration, must also be present in a contract of sale of goods. In *Nidocco v. Gbajabiamila* and sundry other cases,[270] the Nigerian Supreme Court has held that failure to pay the purchase price under a sale of land is a fundamental breach which goes to the root of the contract of sale; and, second, that the effect of the contract without consideration is that it cannot be taken as complete, nor can the court decree specific performance of it.

395. Section 62 of the Sale of Goods Act defines goods to include all chattels personal other than things in action and money, and all corporeal movables except money. The term includes emblements, industrial growing crops, and things attached to or forming part of the land which are agreed to be severed before sale or under the contract of sale.

X. Formalities of a Contract of Sale

396. A contract of sale may be made in writing (either with or without seal), or by word of mouth, or partly in writing and partly by word of mouth, or may be implied from the conduct of the parties provided that nothing in this section shall affect the law relating to corporations.[271] Therefore, although a company has the powers of a natural person, if its memorandum stipulates that its contracts of sale should be in a particular format, they must be in that format.[272]

XI. Essential Elements of a Contract of Sale

397. For a contract to be valid, there must exist an offer, acceptance, consideration, and intention to create legal relations.[273] In addition, an enforceable contract

266. Section 1(2) Sale of Goods Act, 1893.
267. Section 1(3) Sale of Goods Act, 1893.
268. Section 1(4) Sale of Goods Act, 1893.
269. M.C. Okany, *Nigerian Commercial Law* (Africana FEP Publishers Ltd. 1992).
270. (2013) 56 (Pt. 1) NSCQR 230.
271. Section 3 Sale of Goods Act, 1893.
272. *See* s. 38 CAMA which provides for the capacity and powers of companies.
273. *See* Sagay, *Nigerian Law of Contract*, *supra* n. 91, Ch. 1.

must be valid with regard to capacity of parties; form of contract in relation to whether it is oral, written, or by deed; content, as it relates to express and implied terms; genuine consent, in that the contract must not have been induced by misrepresentation, mistake, duress or undue influence; and such contract must not be illegal or contrary to public policy. A contract which does not satisfy these relevant requirements may be void, voidable or unenforceable.[274]

398. From the foregoing, it follows that the following must be in place for a valid contract of sale to take place:

1. **Parties:** In a contract for sale of goods, there must be two parties present; the buyer and the seller. The parties could be two corporations with one as the buyer and the other as the seller.
2. **Offer and Acceptance:** Another important ingredient for a contract of sale is offer and acceptance. The offer most likely comes from the buyer and the acceptance comes from the seller. However, in some situations, this role may be reversed.
3. **Consent:** A contract of sale in which one of the parties is under duress would not be valid. The parties have to be aware of what they are doing and they should consent to it.
4. **Capacity:** Capacity to contract in sales of goods is governed by the general law relating to capacity to contract and to transfer and acquire property. However, where necessaries are sold to an infant, a drunkard or a person with mental incapacity, such persons must pay a reasonable price. Necessaries mean goods suitable to the condition in life of such infant or minor or other person, and to his actual requirements at the time of the sale and delivery.[275]
5. **Price:** The price in a contract of sale of goods serves as the consideration. Exchange of goods simpliciter cannot, therefore, come within the confines of sale of goods. Section 8(1) of the Sale of Goods Act provides that the price in a contract of sale may be fixed by the contract, or may be left to be fixed in a manner thereby agreed, or may be determined by the course of dealing between the parties. Where the price is not determined in accordance with the foregoing, the buyer must pay a reasonable price.[276] Furthermore, where there is an agreement to sell goods on the terms that the price is to be fixed by the valuation of a third party, and such third party cannot or does not make such valuation where the goods or any part thereof has been delivered to and appropriated by the buyer, such buyer must pay a reasonable price for them; and second, where such third party is prevented from making the valuation, by the fault of the seller or buyer, the party not at fault may maintain an action for damages against the party at fault.[277]

---

274. *Ibid.*
275. Section 2 Sale of Goods Act, 1893.
276. Section 8(2) Sale of Goods Act, 1893. What is 'reasonable price' is a question of fact dependent on the circumstances of each particular case.
277. Section 9(1) & (2) Sale of Goods Act.

6. **Goods:** Section 62 of the Act defines goods to include all chattels personal other than things in action and money, and all corporeal movables except money. There must be some goods or interest in goods to be transferred. By section 16 of the Act, where there is a contract for the sale of unascertained goods, no property in the goods is transferred to the buyer unless and until the goods are ascertained. There are different categories of goods and they are provided for by the virtue of section 5 of the Act. Goods may be categorized as: (a) existing goods, (b) specific (or ascertained) goods, (c) goods sold by description, (d) future goods:
   (a) Existing goods: These are goods owned or possessed by the seller at the time of the contract of sale.
   (b) Specific (or ascertained) goods: These are goods that would be manufactured or acquired by the seller after the conclusion of the contract of sale. They are not in the possession of the seller at the time of the contract. They are delivered to the buyer at a future date.
   (c) Goods sold by description: These are goods that are not yet specified. They are goods sold by description, but which were not identified or agreed upon at the time of the contract but are included in a particular class of goods.
   (d) Future goods: These are goods not yet in existence, and goods in existence but not yet acquired by the seller. That is to say, goods yet to be acquired or manufactured by the seller after the contract has been made.
7. **Time:** Section 10 Sale of Goods Act states that time for payment is not considered of the essence except it is stipulated by the terms of the contract. It is further provided that whether or not any other stipulations as to time would be of the essence is determined by the agreement between the parties. If there is no stipulation as to the time for delivery, by the provisions of section 29(2) of the Act, it is stated that the goods should be delivered within a reasonable time. This goes to show that although time of payment is not prima facie of the essence, the time of delivery is important. Thus in the case of *Amadi Thomas v. Thomas Aplin & Co Ltd*, the goods were to be delivered at a particular time but the seller did not comply with the time stipulated. The court ruled that the time of delivery is of the essence. Thus the failure to stick to the time provided by the contract was a breach of the contract of sale.

§2. Actions for Breach of Contract of Sale

399. Under the Sale of Goods Act, both the buyer and seller have rights and remedies available to them in the instance of a breach.

I. Rights Available to a Seller under a Contract of Sale

400. According to section 38(1) of the Sale of Goods Act, a seller of goods is deemed to be an unpaid seller when the whole of the price has not been paid or tendered to him; or when a bill of exchange or other negotiable instruments has been received as conditional payment, and the condition on which it was received has not been fulfilled by reason of the dishonour of the instrument. This clarifies who has rights as a seller and what remedies are available to him should the buyer default in making payment for the goods delivered to him. As is to be noted, the completion of a contract of sale is signified by the payment of the purchase price. Accordingly, when the seller collects the full payment for the goods which he has duly delivered to the buyer, all his rights over the goods are completely extinguished. In order to protect a seller who has delivered in the case where the buyer reneges on his own part, section 39 of the Act outlines his rights:

(1) Subject to the provisions of this Act, and of any statute in that behalf, notwithstanding that the property in the goods may have passed to the buyer, the unpaid seller of goods, as such, has by implication of law:
  (a) a lien on the goods or right to retain them for the price while he is in possession of them;
  (b) in case of the insolvency of the buyer, a right of stopping the goods *in transitu* after he has parted with the possession of them;
  (c) a right of resale as limited by this Act.

(2) Where the property in goods has not passed to the buyer, the unpaid seller has, in addition to his other remedies, a right of withholding delivery similar to and coextensive with his rights of lien and stoppage *in transitu* where the property has passed to the buyer.

401. Section 41(1) of the Act further provides for the seller's right of lien and empowers the seller to retain possession of the goods until payment is made or price tendered, but only in circumstances where the goods have been sold without any stipulation as to credit; where the goods have been sold on credit, but the term of credit has expired; or where the buyer has become insolvent. The unpaid seller would lose his right of lien or retention of the goods when he delivers the goods to a carrier or other bailee or custodier for the purpose of transmission to the buyer without reserving the right of disposal of the goods; when the buyer or his agent lawfully obtains possession of the goods; or where he has waived his right of lien.[278] Section 42(3) of the Act states that the unpaid seller of goods, having a lien or right of retention thereon, does not lose his lien or right of retention by reason only that he has obtained judgment for the price of goods.

II. Remedies Available to a Seller under a Contract of Sale

402. The Act provides for two remedies available to a seller in the event of a breach:

---

278. Section 43 Sale of Goods Act, 1893. *See* further ss 44–48 of the Act which provide for the seller's rights of stoppage *in transitu* and Resale.

Action for the price: Where, under a contract of sale, the title in the goods passes to the buyer, and the buyer wrongfully neglects or refuses to pay for the goods according to the terms of the contract, the seller may maintain an action against him for the price of the goods. Where also the price is payable on a day certain irrespective of delivery, and the buyer wrongfully neglects or refuses to pay such price, the seller may maintain an action for the price, although the property in the goods has not passed, and the goods have not been appropriated to the contract.
Damages for non-acceptance: Where the buyer wrongfully neglects or refuses to accept and pay for the goods, the seller may maintain an action against him for damages for non-acceptance. The measure of damages is the estimated loss directly and naturally resulting, in the ordinary course of events, from the buyer's breach of contract. The Nigerian Supreme Court held in *Aminu Ishola v. Afribank*[279] that in general, the damages to which a plaintiff who has been deprived of his chattel is entitled to is, prima facie, the value of the chattel together with any special loss which is the natural and direct result of the wrongful act. The court went further to state that the object of awarding damages for each of contract is to put the injured party so far as money can do it in the same position as if the contract had been performed.

403. It is worthy of note that an injured party is expected to take steps to mitigate his loss; otherwise, his claim for damages may be affected. In *Okongwu v. Nigeria National Petroleum Corporation*,[280] the Supreme Court stated that a plaintiff must take all reasonable steps to mitigate the loss to him consequent upon the defendant's wrong and cannot recover damages from any such loss which he could have avoided but had failed, through unreasonable action or inaction to avoid.

III. Remedies Available to a Buyer under a Contract of Sale

404. Available to the buyer is an action for damages for non-delivery of goods specified under the contract of sale. Therefore, where the seller wrongfully neglects or refuses to deliver the goods to the buyer, such buyer may maintain an action against the seller for damages for non-delivery.[281] The measure of the damages is the estimated loss directly and naturally resulting, in the ordinary course of events, from the seller's breach of contract. The Supreme Court held in *Artra Industries (Nigeria) Ltd. v. Nigerian Bank for Commerce and Industry*[282] that damages for breach of contract are not awarded for anticipated gross income but for net income or profit, such that in considering a claim for loss of anticipated profit, the projection of an anticipated profit in a feasibility report without more has no weight and is not acceptable as proof of such anticipated profit.

279. (2013) 54.2 NSCQR 717.
280. (2015) 4 NSCQR 412.
281. Section 51(1) Sale of Goods Act, 1893.
282. (1998) 4 NWLR (Pt. 546) 357.

405. An aggrieved buyer also has a remedy in specific performance which the court may grant upon his application. This is a remedy ordered by the court requiring the fulfilment of a legal or contractual obligation when monetary damages are inappropriate or inadequate. In any action for breach of contract to deliver specific or ascertained goods, the court may, if it thinks fit, on the application of the plaintiff, by its judgment or decree, direct that the contract shall be performed specifically, without giving the defendant the option of retaining the goods on payment of damages. The judgment or decree may be unconditional, or upon such terms and conditions as to damages, payment of the price, and otherwise, as to the court may seem just, and the application by the plaintiff may be made at any time before judgment or decree.[283] This remedy is however purely discretionary and the court may decide either to grant or not to grant it.

406. The Sale of Goods Act also grants the buyer a remedy for breach of warranty by the seller. Section 53(1), however, provides the buyer is not allowed the right to reject the goods or repudiate the contract but rather a remedy of set-up against the seller; the breach of warranty in diminution or extinction of the price; or of maintaining an action against the seller for damages for the breach of warranty. This remedy derives from the fact that there is always the implied warranty by the seller that the goods shall be free from any charge or encumbrance from any third party not declared or known to the buyer. The measure of damages for breach of warranty is the estimated loss directly and naturally resulting, in the ordinary course of events, from the breach of warranty.[284]

§3. Commercial Services

I. Distribution

407. Distribution is the process of making a product or service available for the consumer or business user who needs it. This can be done directly by the producer or service provider, or using indirect channels with distributors thereby ensuring that products reach target customers in the most direct and cost-efficient manner. A manufacturer or company may make its products and brand available to consumers via different means such as Distributors, Franchising and Authorized Dealers.

II. Distributors

408. A manufacturer or a supplier of goods may appoint an independent third party – the distributor – to market its goods. The independent third party purchases the goods on his own account and trades under his own name as an authorized distributor. A distributor is therefore a company that buys and sells products from

283. Section 52, Sale of Goods Act, 1893.
284. Section 53(2) Sale of Goods Act. *See* further s. 53(3)(4) of the Sale of Goods Act.

another company. The distributor usually warehouses these products at a facility it owns or leases. It then sells the products to retailers and/or directly to consumers.

409. A distribution agreement is a legally binding contract between the owner of the products and the distributor. This agreement specifies the rights, costs and responsibilities of the parties in relation to the distribution of the products. The distributor purchases the products from a company that makes the products, but does not have any ownership in the company or manufacturer itself. There is no specific legislation that governs distributorship agreements in Nigeria: it is simply a creature of contract, provided that such agreement does not offend any provisions of the Federal Consumer and Competition Act 2019, in respect of monopoly.

III. Franchise

410. The International Franchise Association defines a franchise as the agreement between two legally independent parties which gives a person or a group of people the right to market a product or a service using the trade name or trademark of another business. In Nigeria, this has been one of the vehicles through which foreign direct investments are experienced. A franchise is a contractual relationship where the franchisor allows a franchisee to use its trade name, marks and brands while exercising continuing control over the franchisee. The franchisor is obliged to provide training and assistance to a franchisee and requires a franchisee to make an initial and continuing payments to the franchisor. The franchisee purchases the right to market and sell the items under the trademarked name of the franchisor.

411. A franchise agreement is a legally binding contract between the franchisor and franchisee that details the rights, responsibilities, obligations and compensation of both parties in relation to the purchase and operation of the franchise. Nigerian courts typically enforce forum selection agreements.[285] A franchise being a creature of contract, the applicable law will be the law chosen by the parties and stipulated in their franchise. In the same manner, the court or forum will be determined generally by the parties' choice unless they failed to include one, in which case, the place of performance (Nigerian franchisee) will be applicable.

IV. Authorized Dealers

412. This is an individual or a business concern, which is involved in the activities of buying goods for their account and then selling it off from their stock. A dealer does commercial trading as part of its regular business. The dealer is the middleman between the distributor of goods and the consumer. They are the authorized sellers of a particular commodity in a particular area.

---

285. *See* Sonar *(Nig) Ltd. v.* Nordwind [1987] 4 NWLR (Pt. 66) 520.

413. The aforementioned commercial services have no specific legislation governing them in Nigeria. However, they are regulated under the various commercial/ contract laws in the country. Laws affecting these services include Company Laws, Tax Laws, Intellectual Property Laws, Labour Laws and Employment Laws. Where any of the parties are foreigners, Immigration Laws, Foreign Investment Laws, Foreign Exchange Laws, etc., also apply.

414. Agreements with respect to the above services in Nigeria are typically governed by:

(a) The Company and Allied Matter Act 2020.
(b) The PDA 1970.
(c) Investment and Securities Act 2007.
(d) Trademarks Act 1990.
(e) Copyright Act 1988 Cap 68, Laws of the Federation of Nigeria 1990, etc.

415. The regulatory agencies include the CAC; Securities and Exchange Commission (SEC); NIPC; Nigerian Copyright Commission; Registrar of Trademarks, Patents and Industrial Design; and National Office for Technology Acquisition and Promotion.

§4. Contracts with Middlemen

416. A person who is employed by both the seller and purchaser of goods, or by the purchaser alone, to receive them into his possession, for the purpose of doing something in or about them; as, if goods be delivered from a ship by the seller, to a wharfinger, to be by him forwarded to the purchaser, who has been appointed by the latter to receive them; or if goods be sent to a packer, for and by orders of the vendee, the packer is to be considered as a middleman. He is also understood as one who has been employed as an agent by a principal, and who has employed a subagent under him by authority of the principal, either express or implied. He is not in general liable for the wrongful acts of the subagent, the principal being alone responsible.

§5. Commercial Agency

417. An agent is a person who acts on behalf of another called the Principal in his dealings with third parties. The *Black's Law Dictionary* defines agency as 'a fiduciary relationship created by express or implied contract or by law, in which one party, agent, may act on half of another party, the principal, and bind that other party by words or actions'. Agency is a fiduciary relationship created by express or implied contract or by law in which one party (the agent) may act on behalf of another party (the principal) and bind that other party by words or action. The Nigerian Court of Appeal in *Mikano International Ltd v. Ehumadu*[286] clarified that: 'Agency is the relationship that exists between two persons, one of whom expressly or impliedly consents that the other should represent him or act on his behalf, and the other who consents to represent the former or so to act.'

418. The one who is to be represented or on whose behalf the act is to be done is called the principal and the one who is to represent or act is called the agent. Any person other than the principal and the agent may be called a third party. The basic idea behind the law of agency is that the law recognizes that a person need not always do things that change his legal relations in person, and he may use the services of another person to change them or to do something during the course of which they may be changed.

419. The law of agency, therefore, is an area of commercial law dealing with a set of contractual, quasi-contractual and non-contractual fiduciary relationships that involve a person, called the agent, that is authorized to act on behalf of another (called the principal) to create legal relations with a third party.

420. According to the Nigerian Supreme Court,[287] the relationship of principal and agent may arise in five ways, namely:

(1) by express appointment, whether orally or by letter of appointment or indeed, by a power of attorney;
(2) by ratification of the agent's acts by the principal;
(3) through the doctrine of estoppel;
(4) by implication of law in the case of agency by necessity; and
(5) by presumption of law in the case of cohabitation.

§6. Classification of Agents

421. **Classification on the basis of extent of authority:** This is dependent on the scope of the authority given and the extent to which their exercise affects the position of the principal as well as the nature of the acts performed by the agent (e.g., general acts in all affairs in relation to a particular business) and special (acts on some special occasions or for some particular purpose) agents.

422. **Classification according to the nature of liability imposed by the agent:** For instance, a *Del credere* agent who is an agent who, in consideration of extra remuneration called *del credere* commission, guarantees to his principal that third parties with whom he enters into contracts for and on behalf of the principal shall

286. (2013)1 CLRN 83.
287. *See Vulcan Gases Ltd v. G.F. Industries Gasvenwertung A.G* (2001) 5 SC (Pt. 1), 1.

pay any sums becoming due under these contract. Upon default of payment, he himself must pay for the goods, and for this additional service, the *del credere* agent receives a higher commission than an ordinary sales agent.

423. Classification in terms of the particular function performed by the agent:

Mercantile agent: A commercial **agent** who in the ordinary course of his business has authority to sell goods, to consign goods for sale, to buy goods or to raise money on the security of goods on behalf of his principal. Examples of mercantile agents are as follows:
Factors: A salesman who sells in his/her own name on behalf of others, taking a commission (called a factorage) for services. A factor is a mercantile fiduciary transacting business in his own name and not disclosing his principal.
Brokers: A person who in the ordinary course of his business is employed to make contracts with third parties for the purchase of goods or property or for the sale of his principal's goods or property of which he is not entrusted with possession or document of title. A broker's function is to arrange contracts for property in which he or she has no personal interest, possession, or concern. The broker is an intermediary or negotiator in the contracting of any type of bargain, acting as an agent for parties who wish to buy or sell stocks, bonds, real or personal property, commodities, or services. Rules applicable to agency are generally relevant to most transactions involving brokers.
Estate agent: Estate agent is a person or business that arranges the selling, renting, or management of properties and other buildings. Estate agency is a fiduciary relationship whereby a person (referred to as 'an estate agent') acts as an intermediary between a principal (property owner/landlord) and another party (property buyer/tenant).
Partners: Agency partner is a person/firm who necessarily not has a decision-making in the company but holds a share profit whenever a lead is generated or some work has been assigned via affiliation.
Auctioneer: An agent authorized to sells goods at public sale. It is the job of an auctioneer to organize the goods for sale at an auction, as well as to oversee the bidding, often encouraging bidders to compete with each other to drive the price up.

I. Parties to an Agency Relationship

424. From the foregoing, you may have realized that there are three parties in an agency relationship. They are the principal, the agent, and third parties that deal directly with the agent who is acting on behalf of the principal. An agency relationship is a fiduciary relationship.

II. Formation of an Agency Relationship

425. In *Niger Progress Ltd v. North East Line Corporation,*[288] the Supreme Court stated that an agency can arise impliedly from the nature and condition of the parties or from the circumstances of the relationship. According to the apex court, the relationship of principal and agent may arise in three ways: by agreement (express or implied); by ratification and by operation of law.

426. Generally, an agency relationship may arise in the three following ways:

Agency by Express or Implied Agreement: An agency is created by express appointment when the principal appoints the agent by express agreement with the agent. This express agreement may be an oral or written agreement between the principal and the agent. An agency by implied agreement in situations where an agent appointed to conduct a particular trade or business does all such things as are necessarily incidental to the conduct of such trade or business. It may also arise where it is implied from the conduct of the parties. The law will imply such an agreement if the parties have, by their conduct, consented to a state of affairs which is explicable only in terms of agency.
Agency by Estoppel: Estoppel is the principle of law which prevents a person from asserting a reverse of what he has previously represented, if an innocent *representee* has materially changed his position in reasonable reliance on the previous representation. It arises when A makes a representation to a third party, whether by words or conduct, that B is his agent, and subsequently that third party deals with B as A's agent in reliance on such representation. A will not be permitted (is estopped) to deny the existence of the agency if to do so would cause damage (usually financial loss) to that third party. In agency by estoppel, the authority of the agent is described as only apparent or ostensible but not actual, as the principal has, in fact, not granted the agent such authority to act on the principal's behalf.
Agency by estoppel may be created where a retiring partner retires without making a public announcement to that effect and the remaining partners enter into contract with persons who had previously dealt with the firm and who are aware of his membership but unaware of his retirement, in order to bind the affected partner by such contracts as he has by his conduct, held himself out as a continuing partner. In *Scarf v. Jardine,*[289] a member of the partnership retired without notifying the public. It was held that the retired partner was bound by contracts made by the remaining partners with persons who had previously had dealings with the firm or who were aware of his membership.
Agency by Ratification of the Principal: Agency by ratification arises when a person (the principal) ratifies (i.e., approves and adopts) an act which has already been done in his name and on his behalf by another person (the agent) who in fact had no actual authority (whether express or implied) to act on his (the principal's) behalf when the act was done. Ratification only creates an agency relationship between the

288. (1989) NWLR (Pt. 107) 68 (1989) 4 SC.
289. [1882] 7 AC 345. *See* further *Drew v. Nunn* (1879) 4 QBD 661.

principal and the agent in respect of the act ratified by the principal, but not in respect of any other act, whether past or future.

§7. Ratification is Retroactive

427. In other words, its effect is that it relates back to the time when the agent made the contract and the principal becomes liable and entitled under the contract as if the agent had acted with authority. In *Buron v. Denman*,[290] where the defendant, a British Naval Officer/Commander, forcibly freed some slaves belonging to the plaintiff. Subsequent ratification by the Secretary of State and the Admiralty Lords was held to render the defendant's act an 'Act of State' for which he could not be made personally answerable.

428. The person who ratifies an act of another person must have been in existence and have the legal capacity to carry out that act himself both at the time when the act was done and at the time of ratification. A person may lack legal capacity on grounds of bankruptcy, infancy or mental incapacity.

429. **Agency by Operation of Law:** This is also referred to as Agency of Necessity. This arises when a person ('A') is faced with an emergency in which the property of another person ('B') is in imminent jeopardy and it becomes necessary, in order to preserve the property for A to act for and on behalf of B. In this case, A acts as an agent of necessity of B. Agency of necessity arises only when it is practically impossible for the agent to communicate with the principal before the agent acts on behalf of the principal. Authority to act in case of emergencies cannot usually prevail over express instructions to the contrary given by the principal.

§8. Duties of an Agent to His Principal

430.

(1) Duty to act on behalf of and be subject to the control of the principal.
(2) Duty to act within the scope of authority or power delegated by the principal.
(3) Duty to discharge his or her duties with appropriate care and diligence.
(4) Duty to avoid conflict between his or her personal interests and those of the principal.
(5) Duty to promptly hand over to the principal all monies collected on the principal's behalf.
(6) Duty not to disclose any confidential information.
(7) Duty not to delegate his duty.

290. (1848) 2 Ex., 167.

§9. Duties of a Principal to His Agent

431.

(1) Duty to compensate the agent as agreed.
(2) Duty to indemnify the agent against claims, liabilities and expenses incurred in discharging duties assigned by the principal.

I. Remedies Available to the Principal for Agent's Breach of Duty

432. The principal may avail himself of one or more of the following remedies where the agent breaches his duty:

(1) Termination of the Agency relationship.
(2) Rescission and Damages.
(3) Action for Accounts.
(4) Private possession.
(5) Action for Conversion.

II. Remedies Available to the Agent for Principal's Breach of Duty

433. Where the agency relationship is contractual and the principal commits a breach of the agreement, the agent has most of the remedies available to a contracting party:

(1) Action for Damages.
(2) Right of Set-off.
(3) Right of lien.
(4) Accounts.
(5) Withholding of further performance.
(6) Right of stoppage *in transitu.*

§10. Insurance

434. Insurance is a means of protection from financial loss. It is a form of risk management, primarily used to hedge against the risk of a contingent or uncertain loss. An entity which provides insurance is known as an insurer, insurance company, insurance carrier or underwriter. A person or entity who buys insurance is known as an insured or as a policyholder. The insured receives a contract, called the insurance policy, which details the conditions and circumstances under which the insurer will compensate the insured. The amount of money charged by the insurer to the policyholder for the coverage set forth in the insurance policy is called the premium.

435. In Nigeria, the Insurance Act 2003[291] governs issues with respect to insurance but does not offer a specific definition of the term. Section 102 of the Insurance Act, however, provides that insurance includes 'Assurance'. Insurance has been described as a transaction in which the insurer (the insurance company) for a certain consideration (premium) promises to reimburse (indemnify) the insured or render services in the case of certain accidental losses suffered during the subsistence of the agreement. Under section 50 of the Act, there is a policy of no insurance premium, no cover, to help protect insurance companies from liabilities where the insured did not pay any premium as consideration for entering into the insurance contract. Section 50(1) states that 'the receipt of an insurance premium shall be a condition precedent to a valid contract of insurance and there shall be no cover in respect of an insurance risk unless the premium is paid in advance'.

I. Types of Insurance

436. Section 2 of the Insurance Act 2003 divides insurance into two main classes: life insurance business and general insurance business. These classes have different types of insurance business under them. Under life insurance, there shall be three categories: (1) individual life insurance business; (2) group life insurance and pension business; and (3) health insurance business. In the case of general insurance, there shall be eight categories: (1) fire insurance business; (2) general accident insurance business; (3) motor vehicle insurance business; (4) marine and aviation insurance business; (5) oil and gas insurance business; (6) engineering insurance business; (7) bonds credit guarantee and suretyship insurance business; and (8) miscellaneous insurance business.

A. Persons Who May Carry on Insurance Business

437. No persons shall commence or carry on any class of insurance business in Nigeria, except a company duly incorporated as a limited liability company under the CAMA, 1990 or a body duly established by or pursuant to any other enactment to transact the business of insurance or reinsurance. Only an insurer registered by the Commission under this Act shall commence insurance business in Nigeria.[292]

B. Duties of an Insurer

438. An insurer who employs the services of an insurance agent and every person who acts for an insurer in that behalf shall maintain a register showing the name and address of every insurance agent and the date on which his services were

291. Insurance Act 2003, Cap A52 Laws of the Federation of Nigeria.
292. Sections 3 and 4 Insurance Act 2003. Section 102 defines Commission as the National Insurance Commission constituted under Act 1 of 1997.

employed and, where applicable, terminated. Where an insurance business is transacted through an insurance agent, the agent shall immediately pay to the insurer any premium collected by him.

Chapter 10. Commercial Securities

§1. Introduction

439. In March 2020, Nigeria was ranked the biggest economy in Africa. What this means for the country is that it will become an attractive hub for foreign direct investors. From the business perspective, a prudent investor intending to do business in Nigeria would most probably want to know what the various modes of taking commercial securities are, the applicable law, and how they are generally perfected and enforced. Given the heightened relevance of this preliminary enquiry for prospective investors or those advising them, this section is dedicated to highlighting the various securities available in securing payment obligations and how they are created, perfected, ranked, and enforced in the event of a debtor's repayment default or insolvency.

§2. The Various Types of Commercial Security

440. Commercial security could be created against two categories of assets, namely, tangible and intangible assets. Intangible assets are those that cannot be physically felt. They are regarded as 'choses in action' because if there is an infringement of right in them, the holder of right in them can only assert ownership or remedy the infringement through a court action. Examples of such intangible assets are shares, debt, bank accounts, IP, etc. Being properties and also conferring property rights, rights in intangible assets can be used to secure a repayment obligation as stipulated under section 2 of the STMA Act 2017.

441. Tangible assets are those that are capable of being felt physically and could either be a personal (movable) asset or a real (immovable) asset. Examples of movable assets are cars, laptops, televisions, etc., while the examples of immovable assets are land and buildings. All the categories of asset mentioned above can be used to secure repayment obligations in Nigeria.

§3. Personal Properties

I. Shares

442. Shares are usually defined as units of ownerships in a company. In other words, paid-up shares are assets and could be used by the shareholder to secure a lending transaction. There are two principal ways of creating a security over shares – the equitable mortgage and legal mortgage. The equitable mortgage of shares constitutes a deposit of the instrument that records the shares to the mortgagee, after the mortgagor has provided the former with a share transfer form that evidences the transaction. There is an additional requirement of providing the mortgagee with a signed resolution of the mortgagor's company management wherein approval is given for the transfer of the shares.

443. Where it is a legal mortgage, perfection requires the mortgagee to be registered as a shareholder of the company and in its register of shares, and there is an undertaking to transfer back the shares to the mortgagor, following a discharge of the underlying debt. There is also the requirement to stamp the transfer document as required by the Stamp Duties Act or any current regulation made in respect of it by the minister.

444. About a decade ago, Nigeria introduced the possibility to own shares in dematerialized form, and for this, Nigeria's Central Securities and Clearing System (CSCS) was created wherein owners of shares that were represented by paper instruments lodged in their share certificates for dematerialization. Under the CSCS arrangement, parties to a lending transaction (lender and borrower), wherein shares in the CSCS are used as security, must sign a joint memorandum which authorizes the CSCS authority to place a lien on the agreed number of shares, on the arrangement to lift the lien upon the discharge of the debt or occurrence of an agreed condition.

445. It is important to note that the STMA Act 2017 has modified the above understanding a little bit under section 31, which states that 'a holder of a negotiable instrument or title document shall have priority over a perfected security interest in the negotiable instrument or the title document where the holder – gave value; acquired the negotiable instrument or the title document without knowledge that the transaction is in breach of the security agreement to which the security interest relates, and took possession of the negotiable instrument or the title document.'

446. Section 31 respects the overarching rule of perfection under the STMA Act which is that the first security interest to be registered in the collateral registry has priority over another registered subsequently in respect of the same collateral. Given that possession of a negotiable instrument or title document is a method of perfection under the STMA Act, the Act is of the position that a secured party in possession of such instrument already perfects it, as a result, and in that case, there is no need for registration at the National Collateral Registry.

II. Deposit Account

447. Under the STMA Act, a deposit account is recognized as a collateral that can be used to secure a repayment obligation. Typical examples are escrow accounts where a lender and borrower agree with their common banker to create an account which shall be funded by the party with the repayment obligation to serve as collateral, with the understanding that the bank shall release the fund to the secured party upon the satisfaction of specified conditions.

448. Generally, a borrower's deposit account that is funded is an asset which his creditor can use to secure repayment, and in the event of default, proceed to satisfy his indebtedness from the proceeds of the account. An example is a judgment creditor, who is authorized under the law to commence a garnishee proceeding, an ex parte type of proceeding wherein the creditor obtains judgment on the strength of his own application without the judgment debtor being heard on the matter. The judgment is then enforced by mandating the debtor's banker or anyone holding his assets to release them for satisfaction of the judgment debt.

449. It is important to note that a banker's right of set-off is held pre-eminent under section 29 of the STMA Act over that of a secured creditor with a perfected security interest over the same bank account. Thus, where a customer of a bank owes the bank as well as a secured creditor, the latter's perfected right in the deposit account will not be able to rank in priority over that of a banker in control of the deposit account because of his pre-eminent right of set-off. In the words of section 29 of the STMA Act: 'a financial institution's rights of set off shall have priority over a perfected security interest that extends to a deposit account. A transferee of funds from a deposit account or cash other than from a deposit account takes the funds or cash free of a security interest unless the transferee acts in collusion with the Grantor or Borrower in violating the right of the creditor … '.

III. Assignment of Rights in Contract

450. Before 2017, the rule that governed assignment of rights in contract, especially accounts-receivable/book debts, was the rule in *Dearle v. Hall.*[293] The rule is a creature of equity and is to the effect that where an owner of debt assigns portions of them to assignees, their priority will be determined by the order in which they notified the account debtor. The rule operates as an exception to the general rule which says that between two equities, the first in time to be created prevails in a priority contest. Thus, unlike the general rule, the rule in *Dearle v. Hall* is a notification system that creates agility of race towards the account debtor.

451. However, the STMA Act has rendered the rule in *Dearle v. Hall* inoperative in Nigeria, and generally replaced its notification system with the registration system in the National Collateral Registry, which gives priority to assignees of accounts, on the basis of who registered first at the registry, and not who first notified the account debtor. Sequel to this is that section 25 of the STMA Act nullifies any contractual obligation not to assign without consent of the counterparty not first had and obtained.

452. It provides that 'a secured creditor may transfer a secured obligation notwithstanding any agreement with the Grantor or the Borrower limiting the right to transfer the secured obligation and without having to obtain consent of the Grantor or the Borrower. A security interest that is transferred shall have the same priority as it had at the time of the transfer. A transfer of security interest perfected by registration is valid without registering an amendment financing statement in the Registry'. Investors must know about section 25 of the STMA Act, given that most lending contracts contain non-assignment clauses.

---

293. [1828] 3 Russ 1.

§4. Aircraft and Vessels

453. Section 2(c) of the STMA Act explicitly stated that the Act does not apply to any interest created by a transfer, assignment or mortgage in movable property governed by a law for which a registry has been established with regards to ships and aircraft. The Maritime Shipping Act is the principal legislation in Nigeria that governs transactions involving vessels, especially in the context of using them as collateral to secure a repayment obligation. In order to properly obtain a security interest in a vessel registered in Nigeria, the consent of the Federal Ministry of Transport must be first sought and obtained in writing. Thus, such application for consent must be submitted to the Director General of Nigerian Maritime Administration and Safety Agency (NIMASA) for approval, alongside a resolution from the board of directors of the ship-mortgagor, authorizing the mortgage transaction. Usually, there is a nominal fee to be paid (NGN 20, or about 30 cents of USD), over the deed of mortgage that has been duly stamped.

454. In addition to the above formalities regarding taking security in a vessel, the duly stamped deed of mortgage must be registered with the registries of the CAC and the NIMASA as well as the relevant ports of registry. In the case of a mortgage over an aircraft, the duly stamped deed of mortgage must be registered with the Nigerian Civil Aviation Authority. Where a vessel registered in Nigeria is used as collateral under a mortgage transaction, sale of the vessel requires the consent of the Minister of Transport first sought and obtained.

§5. Stamp Duty Charges on Personal and Real Collateral Assets

455. The Stamp Duty Act in Nigeria stipulates transactions that require the purchase of stamps which must be affixed on the document as a precondition for perfection. Thus, if a document transfers or creates a security interest over assets, such document is subject to a stamp duty calculated on the basis of ad valorem, if the document is executed in Nigeria within forty days of being executed or if outside of Nigeria, thirty days of such document's receipt in Nigeria.

456. If a debenture or a legal mortgage secures an amount, the stipulated charge by the Stamp Duty Act is 0.375% of the amount being secured. However, in practice, this price scale is not followed, given that the Act empowers the minister to adjust rates to match inflation. Thus, what happens in practice is that the borrower presents the finance document to the Stamp Duties Commissioner to assess and determine the rate to be paid ad valorem based on their current charges. At the moment, 0.125% is the prevailing stamp duties charge that is used to calculate ad valorem charges on documents creating a security interest over an asset of the borrower.[294]

457. The charge of 0.125% can boil down to high amount of stamp duty charges if the debenture seeking to be perfected secures a large sum. What parties to a lending transaction do in practice, especially where there is a line of credit opened in favour of the borrower, is to agree and allow the borrower to pay stamp duties only to the extent of the amount received, with the borrower's promise that each time a sum is credited by the lender, the former will endeavour to pay stamp duty to cover up the new sum, so that the lender could remain secured up to the amount advanced. In Nigeria, this is known generally as 'upstamping', and failure to upstamp leaves the lender's additional monetary advance unsecured, and in the event of default or insolvency, cannot therefore be satisfied on the basis of the underlying asset, but personally against the debtor; or if in the context of insolvency, *pari passu* payment with the general body of unsecured creditors, because the new advance would be treated as unsecured credit.

458. Under the law, where a transaction involves governments of specified countries or per treaty, multilateral financing institutions, such as Africa Reinsurance Corporation, payment of stamp duties would be exempt. Other than these exemptions, payment of stamp duties where required is highly important for security documents executed in Nigeria because while failure to stamp will not in principle render the transaction or the document void, such unstamped document will not be admissible in evidence in the event of any dispute. In practice, security documents are stamped before they are presented for registration if they are registrable documents. The registrars of documents at the CAC will not accept a registrable but unstamped document, for registration. If they are not registrable documents, then they must be stamped as a precondition for being used as evidence for what they purport to claim. The CAC registry usually charges 1% of the amount secured for private companies and where it is a public company, 2% ad valorem is payable.

459. Where the asset in question is land, an additional requirement of obtaining the Governor's consent under the LUA is a precondition for validity and admissibility as evidence, as stated under section 22 of the Act. The applicable fees vary, depending on the state in question in Nigeria. Also, the document which alienates an interest in land must be registered in the land registry of the particular state where the land is situated, and fees chargeable by the state's land registry also vary.

294. N. Okafor, O. Okafor & C. Okolie, *Lending and Taking Security in Nigeria: Overview Taxes and Fees on Loans, Guarantees and Security Interests* (Practical Law 1 Jun. 2016), https://uk.practicallaw.thomsonreuters.com/4-524-5665?transitionType=Default&contextData=(sc.Default)&firstPage=true.

§6. Security Over Future Assets

460. A frequently asked question by prospective investor in Nigeria is whether they could create a security interest in their debtor's future assets. The answer is in the affirmative. Presently, there are two floating securities that can be created in Nigeria, namely, floating charge as stipulated in the CAMA, 2020, especially under section 222 thereof. A floating charge in Nigeria has the same understanding and function as in England, the country of its birth. Thus, a floating charge is only created by private or public companies over their assets, and the encumbrance serves as collateral for credit.

461. Under this arrangement, the floating chargor-company can continue to use their charged assets in the ordinary course of business without having to seek and obtain a prior consent from the floating chargee, before disposing them. This arrangement continues until *crystallization,* which is the occurrence of an agreed event such as default in repayment or the debtor-company ceasing to be a going concern. Crystallization converts a floating charge to a fixed charge and becomes immediately perfected, given that perfection was completed by registering the charge document under section 222. This is unlike a fixed charge where the security interest attaches to the debtor's company-specific assets from the moment the security agreement was validly concluded.

462. With respect to the second floating security, section 15 of the STMA Act provides that a security interest can be created on a debtor's present and after-acquired assets. The material distinction between the floating security under section 15 of the STMA Act and the CAMA floating charge is that while in the latter, attachment on the debtor's assets does not occur until crystallization, the former attaches on the debtor's assets in the beginning, and also the moment future assets are acquired into the debtor's business, and thus, does not require crystallization to attach.[295] In other words, it is a fixed cum floating security device.

463. Investors should therefore be aware of the coexistence of these two floating security devices. Section 2(3) of the STMA Act which is a newer law compared to CAMA explicitly stated that 'nothing in this Act shall prevent the creation of security interest in the form of charges by companies registered under the CAMA'. Of interest to further note is that a floating charge entitles the holder under section 205 CAMA to appoint a receiver-manager to manage the debtor-company. In practice, the appointed receiver is merely an extended helping hand of the secured creditor and could in the pursuit of narrow interests mismanage the assets or, in many cases, fraudulently transfer the assets to another company.

---

295. Section 203(2) CAMA 2020.

§7. Legal Restrictions on Certain Companies in Granting Security

464. In Nigeria, a person, in exercising the rights of ownership, is generally allowed to create a security interest over their assets. Where the person is a corporate person, one could look at the constitutional documents of the company (memorandum of association and articles) to determine what the powers of the company are, and what acts by its officers would amount to ultra vires. If an act that is unsupported by the constitutional documents of the company is performed, such act remains ultra vires and void unless ratified by the company's shareholders and board of directors prior to the time the act is challenged.

465. Two main companies exist in Nigeria, namely statutory and incorporated companies. The latter are creatures of statutes, and the powers of a statutory company are contained in the particular statute that created it or any secondary legislation that is made within the confines of the enabling statute. Thus if there is no express grant of the power to create security over its assets, such corporation would not be able to legally do so.

466. If the company in question is private or public, and registered by the Corporate Affairs Commission, the power to create a security over its assets must be contained in the memorandum of association and articles of the company.

467. In the case of commercial banks, they are considered a special kind of company and are regulated by the CBN. The law that primarily governs banks is the Bank and Other Financial Institutions Act, and the regulations made pursuant to its provisions by the CBN. Thus, as part of the regulation of banks by the CBN, commercial banks require the written approval of the CBN before it can grant a security over its assets. This helps the CBN to monitor the level of risks a particular bank is undertaking, and whether it is acceptable in line with prudential regulations, given that depositors' and existing creditors' funds are at a risk of loss when a bank mortgages its assets and acquires too many liabilities.

§8. Enforcement of Securities

468. Before the enactment of the STMA Act in 2017, four types of security devices, which were acquired from the English common law, were integral part of Nigeria's commercial law. These are mortgage, charge, pledge and lien. Mortgage is further divided into chattel and real mortgages, while charge is divided into floating and fixed charges. Coupled with this is the categorization of rights into legal and equitable. There were also those known as quasi security devices, like the hire purchase, conditional sale and equipment leasing. This group is also called retention of title devices, in that, respectively, the hirer, buyer or lessee is allowed to have possession (equitable ownership) of the underlying property, while the owner, seller or lessor retained the title (legal ownership) of the property until full payment has been made.

469. The STMA Act applies only to movable property, and adopts the functional approach under section 2 thereof, in determining whether a lending transaction is under its scope. Thus, if in a transaction, a borrower furnishes a personal (movable) asset in which he has right (whether legal or equitable) as security in exchange for a credit received from the lender, such a transaction is called a security interest transaction and the validity of the underlying security interest right of the secured lender in respect of creation, perfection, priority, and enforcement will be governed by the STMA Act.

470. This functional approach, which was borrowed from the United States model of secured transactions under Article 9 of the Uniform Commercial Code, subsumes all commercial security devices mentioned above that satisfy the functional approach of section 2, and it does not matter any more the name parties choose to christen their transaction, instead the function such transaction performs is what is important for determination whether it will be governed by the unitary system of the STMA Act.

§9. Letters of Guarantee

471. In Nigeria, a contract of guarantee is governed by the Statute of Frauds 1677. Section 4 thereof requires a contract of guarantee to be in writing as a precondition for enforceability. In the business circle, a guarantee from a reputable and deep pocket third party can be as good as securing payment with a security interest in a collateral of the borrower. Even though a letter of guarantee is frequently being used in Nigeria to secure repayment obligations, such obligations of guarantors are of a secondary nature, and entail the secured party to first seek repayment from the primary debtor, and only after a demand to the borrower for payment has been made, and he failed to repay, will the secured lender's right to recover same from the guarantor be deemed ripen. Without first exhausting the possibility of getting repaid directly from the primary obligor, a cause of action premised on the guarantor's inability to repay would be deemed premature and unsustainable.

472. There are other variants – a letter of indemnity or a comfort letter. Both types are not covered statutorily under section 4 of the Statute of Frauds, but by common law contract, and thus, could be orally agreed upon, since a contract can be formed orally in Nigeria. In an indemnity contract, the party giving the indemnity promises to pay, and thus, there is no mandatory requirement to first exhaust the primary debtor: the secured party can bypass the primary debtor and demand directly from the party that gave the indemnity.

473. It is also possible that a parent company can give a letter of comfort, which merely vouches for the debtor's economic strength and the real likelihood of it (the child-company) honouring its promise to repay debt under the contract. What this means is that the parent company, by giving a letter of comfort, does not assume a repayment obligation in the event of default of the borrower-company, although if its assurance was baseless, it might expose itself to a suit for misrepresentation.

Although in the parent's defence, it could be argued whether it (parent company) owes the third party lender the duty to say the truth as to make it liable for negligence for breach of such duty.

§10. JUDICIAL AND SELF-HELP ENFORCEMENT OF SECURITIES

474. A breach of contract entitles the innocent party to seek remedies in court. Nigerian courts award either damages or specific performance as remedy for breach of contract. Generally, every security agreement stipulates what would constitute a breach and the avenues available for the innocent party to pursue remedy for the breach. While the right to seek a judicial intervention or remedy arises by an operation of law, the right to pursue remedy through a private channel must be agreed by the parties prior to the alleged breach, and such channel should not be in contravention of any law that is in force.

475. In Nigeria, a real mortgagee (the lender in mortgage transaction whereby a piece of land or building is the collateral) has the power to re-enter premises, or sell the mortgaged property after the contractual date of redemption, and an additional grace period of three months has lapsed. Such real legal mortgagee can also approach the court for a judicial foreclosure, which is an application that basically asks the court to allow him displace the mortgagor permanently, and thus, take over the mortgage property as both an equitable and legal owner.

476. A legal mortgagee exercising a power of sale arising from contract can either sell the asset privately or via a public auction. In any case, he is required to exercise good faith and be commercially reasonable in his dealings with the mortgaged property. However, where the mortgagee was commercially reasonable in the sale, yet the asset was not sufficient to satisfy the existing indebtedness, the deficiency sum becomes an unsecured debt, and generates only an in personam right against the debtor, which can only be recovered through a court action or by set-off.

477. In a secured lending transaction whereby a movable asset was used as collateral, the STMA Act applies. Where a borrower defaults, and the secured lender had furnished a notice of repossession, and ten days have lapsed since the notice, the Act under section 40 permits the lender to privately repossess the collateral. Where a secured lender repossesses, he can sell the collateral as is, and apply the proceeds to satisfy the underlying debt. Provided the secured lender was commercially reasonable and satisfied the good faith requirement, the borrower will be liable to repay any deficient sum; although the outstanding debt cannot be satisfied from any other asset of the debtor, but through a court action or a set-off given that the deficient sum is an unsecured debt.

§11. Debt Restructuring and Insolvency of a Counterparty

478. The corporate rescue philosophy is part of Nigerian law. Although there is no comprehensive and dedicated statute for insolvency and reorganization of debts, some alternatives exist. The Bankruptcy Act 1990 was adopted from England, and applies to the restructuring of debts of a human debtor as well as liquidation of their assets to satisfy creditors' indebtedness.

479. Where the debtor is a corporation registered with the CAC, some provisions of the CAMA 2020, particularly sections 715–717, and the Winding Up Rules under CAMA are applicable with respect to the restructuring of debt and winding up.

480. In Nigeria, corporate rescue could first begin with humble steps, whereby a company's management and their creditors try to work out a solution on how the company can be given a breathing space in the repayment obligations. However, being a workout, whatever that is agreed vis-à-vis debt relief will be a product of contract and the traditional remedies of breach and nothing more, are what the company will have in the event a creditor reneges. This is so because there is no court involvement from the beginning, except later, in the context of being requested to enforce the contract – so there is no form of arm-twisting or compulsory estoppel in a creditor-debtor company workout type of restructuring.

481. In the event, a statutorily backed kind of debt restructuring can be found in CAMA 2020. This is called the *schemes of arrangement* under section 710, whereby a debtor-company nominates a supervisor, and submits a debt restructuring proposal to court. This then follows an initiation of creditors' meeting, where each class of creditors is required to vote, and at least 75% of the debt holders in each class must approve the proposed plan. The plan must entail some kind of relief to the debtor-company in order to prevent it from total collapse.

482. If the 75% vote is obtained, the Federal High Court would confirm the voted plan. In the case of a public company, the court's confirmation only comes after the Securities and Exchange Commission has approved the voted plan. The 25% or less dissenting creditors would nonetheless be bound by the plan. However, in the event they choose to exercise their property rights by insisting on repayment, they will be paid off according to their rights in liquidation, which is based on the forced sale valuation of the corporate assets. The confirmed proposal must then be filed at the CAC registry in order to enter into effect.

483. The scheme of arrangement is a debtor-in-possession kind of process and is not regarded as an insolvency procedure because it is typically undertaken by a solvent company seeking to avoid liquidation. Its effectiveness lies in the theory that retention of the management who has a concrete knowledge of, as well as managerial experience about the company's business, assures more success compared to if they were ousted and replaced by people who will require time to get accustomed to the company's business, a luxury a company in distress would hardly afford. The CAMA 2020 introduced changes in respect of debt restructuring.

484. The changes are the introduction of the UK-type of administration, and the Company Voluntary Arrangement; the latter has a lot of resemblance with the schemes of arrangement in CAMA except that a scheme of arrangement process does not enjoy any form of moratorium, and the company's creditors have the right under their contract with the company, to commence a winding up process on the ground of inability to repay debt, or similarly, appoint a receiver-manager under section 203(2) CAMA if the scheme of arrangement process triggers and crystallizes an underlying floating charge.

485. There is also the likelihood that the debtor-company has signed certain executory contracts in which the termination clause in the contracts is to the effect that the commencement of any kind of debt restructuring process or insolvency will relieve the solvent counterparty from further performance or certain contractual obligations, and this could result in unquantifiable hardships that might have domino effects in relation to the debtor-company's debt obligations and doing business.

§12. Liquidation of Companies Due to Inability to Repay Debt

486. Liquidation is a terminal procedure. There are many grounds for which a company could be wound up, and one of it which concerns this discussion is a company's inability to repay debt under sections 571(d) and 572 of CAMA 2020. If a company owes debt amounting to NGN 200,000 (approximately USD 500) or more, and such debt has become due and payable, and the creditor has made a demand pursuant to the above sections of CAMA, and more than twenty-one days have lapsed since demand, and the debtor failed to repay, such creditor can bring a winding up petition to the Federal High Court to wind up the company so that its assets can be liquidated.

487. A section-572 debt in this regard must be undisputed to be able to sustain a winding up petition. If there is a dispute on the entire debt, that is, the debtor denies the existence of the debt obligation following the creditor's demand, then such denial will disable the winding up petition; the dispute must go on trial for resolution, wherein the court will establish the fact of debt after reviewing the evidence adduced by the litigants. It is only after the fact of the alleged debt of more than NGN 200,000 has been established that the creditor will proceed to submit an effective winding up petition that must satisfy the section 572 provision.

488. It is important to note that the foregoing about disputed debt will not apply if a portion of the debt is partly denied by the debtor-company, but the acknowledged portion is more than NGN 200,000. In which case, the acknowledged portion would be able to sustain a winding up petition regardless of the fact that the other part of the debt is disputed. All this entails that a party wanting to petition for winding up has the burden to gather the relevant pieces of evidence to establish the fact of the undisputed debt beyond NGN 200,000, along with evidence of demand satisfying section 572 of CAMA 2020.

§13. Liquidation and Distribution of Assets

489. Flowing from the above discussion, if a court decides in favour of the creditor in respect of the section 572 petition, a liquidator will be appointed to gather the assets of the debtor-company and distribute them to all those with valid claims against the company. In Nigeria, creditors are broadly divided into two types – secured and unsecured creditors. Secured creditors are those creditors with security interest (in rem) rights against the company's assets – in other words, there are specific assets of the company set aside to satisfy their debts. The payment is made, usually after deducting handling and other relevant administrative expenses involved in liquidating the encumbered assets. If the fund realized from sale of the in rem secured assets is not enough to repay a secured creditor, to the extent he is still owed, he becomes an unsecured creditor.

490. The unsecured creditors do not have security interest rights; they have a personal right against the debtor-company, and in liquidation, barring a few exceptions, they are treated equally by being repaid pro rata (*pari passu*). In the unsecured creditors class, there are preferential unsecured creditors and their debts are treated with preference. A few examples from section 657(1) of CAMA are taxes, wages of employees and workmen, provident fund deductions, etc.

491. A liquidator's main aim is to realize as much as possible a significant amount of the debtor-company's assets and accordingly distribute them to those with valid claims against the company. In a way, however, he is also considered the champion of unsecured creditors and this title comes with the power beyond mere asset-gathering. Thus, under section 663 of CAMA, a liquidator has powers to disclaim certain contracts he deems onerous, and in addition to that, can also investigate and void transactions that qualify as fraudulent.

492. The avoidance powers achieve two main aims. First, the voided contracts on the ground of being onerous as well as the voided transfers deemed to be fraudulent preferences all help to swell the pool of assets that are available for distribution to the unsecured creditors. Second, if the liquidator's investigations lead him to ascertain the directors' fraudulent activities while in office, he will be mandated as an officer of court, to report such activities so that adequate punishment will be meted against the directors; this will serve as deterrence to those who manage companies in that capacity, not to misappropriate corporate assets and to generally comply with the fiduciary duties directors owe to the company they manage.

493. In conclusion, it should be noted that taking commercial securities to secure a repayment obligation comes with certain material risks, ranging from failure to comply with statutory requirements to failure to perfect the security itself against the debtor's collateral. Either of this could, in egregious cases, lead to voidance of security due to a breach of statute, or in a milder case, a loss of priority to other creditors due to failure to perfect the security.

Part II. Economic Law

Chapter 1. General Principles of Economic Law

494. Over the centuries, several definitions of economics have been propounded. However, what most of these definitions have in common is that it is the study of the scarce resources, commodities, goods and services and how they are allocated to individuals in the society with unlimited wants/needs.

495. Economic law therefore discusses the laws which regulate this allocation of scarce resources to individuals. It regulates the relations arising from economic activities. Economic law broadly covers the law of trade, commercial law and investment/finance law.

496. Some economic law principles include but are not restricted to free movement, equality of access to credit, free competition, state planning, state intervention in economic activities, state shareholdings, etc. As it is often the case when it comes to laws in Nigeria, some of the applicable laws were borrowed from England and are not often no longer compatible with the existing realities in the country.

§1. Free Movement

497. This is a pertinent area of economic law in that it provides for laws regulating the free movement of goods and services both locally and internationally. Without a common market and rules regulating or staying obstructions to free movement of goods and services, it will be almost impossible for an economy to generally thrive. Economic laws concerning freedom of movement seek to prevent any measure hindering free trade. Mostly, these laws seek to remove barriers to trade, thereby fostering economic growth and competitiveness which in turn boosts employment and prosperity in such economy.

498. In Nigeria, there are several impediments to free movement of goods such as taxation, custom duties, poor security, poor infrastructure (road networks). International movement of goods (trade) faces a big challenge of high duties and levies, for instance, importation of rice is subject a levy of 20% and import duty of 10%, which is in fact a reduction from the 100% it was pegged at in 2013. Nigeria, according to the World Bank Ease of Doing Business Report 2020, ranks 131st out of 190 countries.[296]

499. The recent policy of 'buy locally to grow the Naira' did not consider the market realities in the country and is indeed offensive to the equal market access principle of the WTO, which does not allow discriminatory policies between foreign and domestic goods in a member country's market. Locally, several challenges to free trade or movement of goods and services abound such as the current Boko Haram Crisis which poses a huge challenge to movement of goods from the northern part of the country; poor security (police response time and general availability to investigate crimes); lack of transport and road infrastructure and a generally lower product quality.

500. The impact of the Boko Haram Crisis on the economy of Northern Nigeria which inadvertently affects the entire nation cannot easily be quantified. Several businesses have had to shut down with several persons migrating to other safer regions and the displacement of thousands from their homes, farms and cattle. According to Shiklam (2012) quoted by Oladayo Nathaniel:[297]

> The Maiduguri Monday Market said to be the biggest market in the city is reported to have been seriously affected as hundreds of shop owners, especially Southerners are said to have closed their businesses and left the troubled city. About half of the 10,000 shops and stalls in the market were said to have been abandoned by traders who have fled the city.

501. The inability of the government to tackle these issues which restrict free movement continues to have adverse effects on the economy and increase poverty, which in turn creates even more security issues from frustrated and disgruntled youths who resort to violence and crime to get what they perceive as 'their rights' from the economy. This is indeed a vicious cycle.

§2. EQUALITY

502. Economic equality in a simple term is 'equal life chances'. This means equal access to opportunities, equal pay for equal work regardless of gender and tribe and other factors, equal channels of distribution of goods and services to all nooks and crannies of the country regardless of tribal identity. The ability of an economy to provide equal opportunities for its citizens has a vast positive impact on the general growth and development.

---

296. The World Bank Ease of Doing Business Report, 2020, https://www.doingbusiness.org/content/dam/doingBusiness/country/n/nigeria/NGA.pdf.

297. *See* generally, Oladayo N. Awojobi, *The Socio-Economic Implications of Boko Haram Insurgency in the North-East of Nigeria*, Vol. 11(1) Int'l J. Innovation & Sci. Res. 144–150 (2014).

503. Equality in Nigeria however is rather elusive with the ever-widening gap between the rich and the poor. Despite the recent economic growth with the country emerging from the 2015 recession, the growth is hardly reflected in the lives of the masses with many living on less than USD 1 daily. Theresa May, the British Prime Minister in an August 2018 visit to South Africa, stated that Nigeria with over eighty-seven million people living on less than USD 1.90 a day is home to more very poor people than any nation in the world. It is somewhat shocking therefore that in an economy faced with such poverty levels, the combined wealth of the richest people in the country could end poverty at the national level.

504. This gross inequality in Nigeria's economy also applies to its industries with the existing tax policies favouring the rich and choking the microbusinesses out of existence. According to former Governance Adviser/Regional Coordinator, Department for International Development, Dr Sina Fagbenro-Byron, 'We have to put in place, anti-trust laws. We have to empower small holder farmers in order to increase food production. We have to go back to micro financing. Micro-financing deals with small holdings and small areas. Our economy can only be diversified when those who have the creative elements to run the economy has access to finance.'[298]

§3. Free Competition

505. Competition law seeks to promote free market competition without allowing for anticompetitive conduct by companies. It seeks to prohibit market dominance, conducts that restrict free trading and competition between firms or companies. It also supervises mergers and acquisitions of large conglomerates so as not to stifle other companies who may be in the same business.

506. In 2019, the Nigerian Senate passed the Federal Competition and Consumer Protection (FCCP) Act.[299] The purpose of the Act is to establish a FCCP Commission and Tribunal for the development and promotion of fair, efficient and competitive markets in Nigeria, facilitate access to safe products by all citizens and protect the rights for all consumers in Nigeria.

507. Prior to the Act, the laws regulating competition in Nigeria had been embedded in various pieces of legislation relating to the regulation of different sectors of the economy. A few prominent examples are the ISA 2007, the Nigerian Communications Act 2003, among other laws. These laws all contain provisions that deal with competition as it relates to the specific sector they regulate. It is surprising that an economy as large as Nigeria's waited until 2019 to have an adequate law to protect its businesses and consumers from unhealthy competition in the market.

---

298. *See* ThisDay Business Newspaper (6 Sep. 2018).
299. Federal Competition and Consumer Protection Act 2019.

508. Fortunately, in general, the Act will end misleading, unfair and unconscionable marketing and trading practices as well as seek to eliminate monopolies at all levels of the Nigerian market, prohibit abuse of dominant market position and penalize restrictive trade and business practices.[300] Notably, section 73 of the Act prohibits market dominance and clarifies factors taken into account when accessing market dominance.

§4. State Planning

509. This is generally the government's effort at allocating resources to suit the various demographics in the country, rather than leaving it to market forces. Since the Independence of Nigeria in 1960, several attempts have been made by the different regimes of government to implement plans to allocate resources fairly and equitably, and, consequently bring about economic growth. These attempts have however hardly been successful due to inefficiency, mediocrity and mostly corruption in governance. Economic plans such as the Structural Adjustment Programme; the National Economic Empowerment and Development Strategy; the Strategy for Attaining the Millennium Development Goals; and the 7-Point Agenda were promised to be implemented by different governments upon taking power, but none have been quite successful in bringing about the much-desired change the Nigerian economy so desperately needs.

510. The most recent of these plans in Nigeria is the Vision 20:2020 which states that 'by 2020 Nigeria will be one of the 20 largest economies in the world, able to consolidate its leadership role in Africa and establish itself as a significant player in the global economic and political arena'. This vision focuses on two main objectives which are to make efficient use of human and natural resources to achieve rapid economic growth and translate the economic growth into equitable social development for all citizens.[301]

511. Based on the most recent nominal Gross Domestic Product (GDP) data from the World Bank, Nigeria is not among the world's top twenty economies with respect to GDP size. In 2010 when the vision 20:2020 was created, Nigeria was the thirtieth and as of 2016, it was the twenty-sixth largest economy in the world. However, in 2019, according to the World Bank, Nigeria was once again in the thirtieth position.[302] Without resolving the issues that plagued previous economic programmes, it will certainly be difficult for this particular vision to be effective, especially with the recent health crisis of COVID-19 pandemic, which is envisaged to cost so many lives and affect the global economy more than the 2008 financial crisis.

---

300. Section 3 of the Federal Competition and Consumer Protection Act.
301. National Bureau of Statistics, December 2010. 'Nigeria Vision 20:2020, Abridged Version', Federal Government of Nigeria. Pp. 2.
302. *See* http://databank.worldbank.org/data/download/GDP.pdf.

§5. State Intervention

512. State intervention in the economy of any given nation has been a source of argument among economists. Free market economists are of the opinion that government intervention should be strictly limited to providing the enabling environment because going beyond that tends to cause an inefficient allocation of resources. However, there are some who argue that there is a strong case for government intervention in different fields of the economy. Free market economists believe that the market is the best judge of when and how to produce; that governments are likely to make wrong decisions due to influence from political pressure groups; and that government intervention takes away the individual's decision on how to spend and allocate scarce resources. Arguments in favour of government intervention believe that it leads to a fairer distribution of income and wealth; that it can overcome prolonged recession and reduce unemployment; and that markets may underproduce merit goods.

513. The most recent intervention of the Nigerian government in the economy besides privatization of a lot of previously state-controlled sectors is the diversification from oil dependence. Recently, governments have been taking aggressive looks at the agricultural and SME sectors.

§6. State Shareholding

514. This can also be referred to as state ownership. This occurs when enterprises or property interests are vested in the state and not on individuals or companies. State shareholding entails the government's involvement in the state's economic development and growth.

515. The benefits of state-owned enterprises include providing goods and services at a cheaper rate, protecting the citizens from being exploited by privately owned companies, providing job opportunities, generally creating an enabling business environment and playing a supervisory role to the key sectors in the economy. Despite these benefits, state-owned enterprises are susceptible to negative work attitudes from employees and high levels of bribery and corruption. These disadvantages are the bane of the existence of government establishments in Nigeria.

516. For instance, it is commonplace to visit the court registry at 2:00 p.m. on a weekday to file a case and be told by a clerk that he is about to close for the day. In some cases, people have to wait for a public official to finish with their prayers during work hours before they are attended to. Also, it is common to see that someone who arrived later than you did might be attended to before you, simply because they offered some bribes to the public official. Or you may need to bribe a court bailiff before they can ordinarily do their job. And so on. These are typical scenarios in government establishments. In Nigeria, several sectors are being privatized with certain benefits in view – e.g., revenue generation, relief on the already overburdened federation account, improved performance and efficiency, expanded share ownership, and efficient allocation of resources, etc.

517. One of the sectors that has received the benefit of privatization in the country is the power sector. On 30 September 2013, under Goodluck Jonathan's regime, the Power Holding Company of Nigeria ceased to exist and the Nigerian Electricity Regulatory Commission was formed. The agency, as provided in the Electricity Reform Act,[303] was tasked with monitoring and regulating the Nigerian Electricity Industry, with issuing licences to participants and with ensuring compliance with market rules and operating guidelines.

303. *See* s. 88, Electric Power Sector Reform Act, 2005.

Chapter 2. Law of Establishment and Supervision of Economic Activities

518. Economic activities are primarily undertaken to earn income. These activities could involve business transactions, trade, agriculture, etc., and there are laws that govern their establishments and supervisions.

§1. Restrictions on Freedom to Exercise a Particular Trade or Profession

519. Freedom to exercise a trade or profession of one's choosing is fundamental; however, the government is typically allowed to put a reasonable restriction on this right in the interest of the general public. The government, under the general mandate or powers contained in the Exclusive list of the Constitution, to protect the lives and property of the citizens and residents, has the power to restrict any trade considered immoral, illegal or injurious to public health and public welfare.

520. Section 40 of the 1999 Constitution guarantees citizens and residents the freedom to be a part of any trade union, or association for the protection of their interests.[304] In other words, the government has powers to control the economy in such a manner as to secure the maximum welfare, freedom and happiness of every citizen on the basis of social justice and equality of status and opportunity.[305] The government is further empowered to control the economy in such a way that wealth or the means of production and exchange is not concentrated in the hands of a few.[306]

§2. Professional Qualification Requirements

521. The various professions in Nigeria are regulated at various levels – by the regulatory body of that profession and also by the courts. For instance, the legal and medical professions are respectively regulated by the Nigeria Bar Association (NBA) and Nigeria Medical Association (NMA). The NBA regulates lawyers while the NMA regulates medical doctors and dentists. Similarly, the Nigerian Society of Engineers regulates the engineering profession.

522. There are other professions in Nigeria and each is governed by a specific body. These professional bodies oversee the quality of practice of their professions and ensure members' strict compliance with the relevant codes of conduct. Where a member breaches their professional code of conduct, the disciplinary arm of the association could act as quasi-judicial body to try such a misconduct. And where a

304. *See* Ch. IV of the Constitution of the Federal Republic of Nigeria for other rights enshrined therein.
305. Section 16 of the Constitution.
306. Section 16(2)(c) of the Constitution.

member is found to have breached the code of conduct, they could have their practicing licence withdrawn. For lawyers, the primary legislation that governs their profession is the Legal Practitioners Act, while the law that governs medical and dental professionals is the Medical and Dental Practitioners Act.

523. The quality of educational programmes for the various professions in Nigeria is highly monitored to ensure that the professional aspirants are equipped with competent skills that will serve society. Apart from the requirement to be educationally sound, there is also emphasis for aspirants to possess good character and respect for human dignity, over and above pecuniary interests. The Nigerian legal education is divided into two parts – first, the aspirant studies a five-year bachelor of laws (LLB) programme at a university accredited by the National University Commission to teach the LLB programme, and a one-year barrister and solicitor qualification programme at the Nigerian Law School, before they are called to the Nigerian Bar to practise law.

524. Medical and dental students study a six-year bachelor of medicine and surgery and bachelor of dental surgery, respectively, at a university accredited by the National University Commission to teach these medical programmes. Upon graduation, they are required to do a one-year compulsory housemanship at a qualified hospital.

525. The court is also a regulator of these professional bodies. Thus, where an alleged misconduct of a member is also an offence under Nigerian law, the High Court would have jurisdiction to try the member, and where it finds them guilty, would have them punished accordingly. From time to time, there are rogues who impersonate these professions, and they are always caught and tried in court for justice.

§3. Financial Requirements for the Prudential Control of Banks

526. The primary legislation for the regulation of banks in Nigeria is the Banks and Other Financial Institutions Act which gives the CBN powers to supervise and regulate banks and other financial institutions in Nigeria. The CBN is the regulator of all banking businesses.

527. Prudential guidelines are made to address various aspects of banks operations such as risk management, corporate governance, KYC (know-your-customer) and anti-money laundering/counter financing of terrorism and loan loss provisioning. It has been made a mandatory regulatory requirement in all banks by the CBN.

528. The guidelines require the classification of credit into performing and non-performing credit. Non-performing credit is categorized into three:

(1) Substandard credit: Credit facilities on which unpaid principal and interest remain outstanding for more than 90 days but not more than 180 days.

(2) Doubtful credit: Credit facilities on which unpaid principal and interest remain outstanding for at least 180 days but less than 360 days and are not secured by legal title to lease assets or perfected collateral in the process of collection or realization.
(3) Bad credit: Credit facilities on which unpaid principal and interest remain outstanding for 360 days or more and are not secured by legal title to leased assets or perfected collateral in the process of collection or realization.

529. Prudential guidelines also require a general provision of at least 2% of all risk assets.

530. Other guidelines include the following:

Liquidity rule: This is the restriction of a proportion of a bank's deposits that can be lent out. It mandates banks to hold onto a percentage of their deposits as liquid assets. In Nigeria, banks are obliged to hold at least 30% of their deposits as liquid assets and of which one-third must be held in treasury bills.
Legal lending limit (single obligor limit): This is the maximum amount a bank is allowed to lend to a single borrower or an individual in relation to its total shareholder funds. In Nigeria, it is 20% of shareholders' funds.
Capital Adequacy ratio: This measures the extent to which a bank's equity cushion can absorb its risk assets in the event of obligor default. The CBN stipulates a minimum capital adequacy ratio of 10%.

Chapter 3. State Incentives for Economic Activities

531. Nigeria is a member of the WTO, and as such has the international obligation to respect the WTO legislation, primarily the GATT, GATS, and TRIPS. The notable principles of the WTO in this sense are the Most Favoured Nation and National Treatment. Nigeria, being a developing country from the perspective of the WTO, is also eligible to some of the benefits which allow it to generate policies that promote new business activities and reduce poverty.

532. Economic development incentives include tax incentives (tax exemptions, tax deductions and tax credits), subsidies, state grants and investments.

§1. Tax Incentives

533. Tax incentives are fiscal measures that are used to attract local or foreign investment capital to certain economic activities or particular areas in a country.[307] They are special arrangements in tax laws to attract, retain or increase investment in a particular sector, stimulate growth in specific areas and assist companies or individuals carrying on identified activities. The underlying basis is to ensure overall growth of the economy and even development of all sectors.[308]

534. The government, exploring the provisions of the tax law and NIPC Act, provides fiscal incentives that drive economic growth by encouraging businesses with tax exemptions, deductions and credits. Tax incentives if properly implemented can boost investments, increase employment, take improvement to less developed areas, aid research and technology development and just generally raise economic welfare.

535. The various thirty-six states in Nigeria also use tax incentives to compete among themselves for investments, jobs, and income.[309] In Nigeria, incentives are granted based on sectors and they are reviewed regularly to ensure that they are indeed fit for purpose. Foreign investors are expected to voluntarily plough back into the economy in return for tax concessions granted to them, and based on the WTO obligation, there must be no discrimination between domestic and foreign products in the Nigerian market. The Tax incentives used in Nigeria are as follows:

307. United Nations, *Tax Incentives and Foreign Direct Investment: A Global Survey* (2000) United Nations Conference on Trade and Development (ASIT Advisory Studies No. 16), https://unctad.org/system/files/official-document/iteipcmisc3_en.pdf.
308. O.O. Ifueko, *Tax Incentives for Foreign Investors in Nigeria* (The Nigerian Investors Business Forum 2012).
309. N. Francis, *State Tax Incentives for Economic Development* (Tax Policy Center 28 Feb. 2016), https://www.taxpolicycenter.org/publications/state-financing-incentives-economic-development/full.

- Reduced Corporate Income Tax Rate: This form of incentive sets a lower tax rate to attract investment in specific sectors and is targeted at the income of investors who meet the specific criteria.
- Loss Carry Forwards: In Nigeria, pioneer companies are allowed to carry losses forward for one year, while for continuing businesses, losses can be carried forward for a maximum of four years.
- Zero/Reduced Tariffs: Government can either reduce or eliminate tariffs on imported capital equipment in order to reduce the cost of investment or increase tariffs in order to protect the local market from influx of import competition.
- Zero/Reduced Tax on Dividend: In Nigeria, certain dividends are exempt from taxation or have reduced taxation in order to attract investment. They include: dividend received by a pioneer company, dividend from small businesses in the manufacturing sector for the first five years, dividend received from investment in wholly export-oriented business.
- Export Promotion Zones: This is an incentive provision for exporters within the nation's customs territory which provides an attractive environment for doing business, especially in an otherwise unattractive environment.[310]

536. As many advantages that may result from tax incentives, there are costs that arise with it. For instance, the loss of the revenue that may have been collected; lack of transparency often associated with granting these concessions; and the cost of ensuring compliance and enforcement.

§2. Subsidy

537. This is a form of financial aid or support extended to an economic sector with the aim of promoting economic and social policy. Subsidies come in different forms such as cash grants, interest-free loans, low-interest loans, tax breaks, etc. The most common form of subsidies is those to the producer and consumer. Consumer subsidies typically reduce the price of goods and services to the consumer. Although Nigeria's economy is largely import-based, under the WTO, subsidies contingent on export performance are prohibited.

538. It is interesting to note that many people in Nigeria understand the term 'subsidy' almost exclusively as 'fuel subsidy', since the term has dominated politics and national discourse, given that crude oil has been the mainstay of the economy. Subsidy on petroleum products has been a regular feature of the fiscal policy since the discovery of crude oil in commercial quantity in the 1980s. The perception has been that since the country is a major producer of oil, it should be made available to its citizens at a low price. The implementation of oil subsidy was in an effort to increase quality of life, aid the poor, and also ensure that prices of goods and services remain affordable due to the impact the price of oil has on other sectors of the economy.

---

310. B.C. Opara & N.C. Opara, *Analysis of Government Policies and Nigerian Firms Export Marketing Strategies*, 8 Int'l Bull. Bus. Administration 2010.

539. Sadly, due to several factors such as corruption and embezzlement of the funds, inability of the budget to keep up with the payments, the subsidy on fuel has been removed with the attendant results being increase in fuel prices from NGN 65–145 per litre and the consequent increase in prices of products and services. Subsidies have however been maintained on kerosene and diesel is presently deregulated.

540. Another important subsidy in the country is agricultural subsidy. With the shift from total reliance on petroleum products to other sectors of the economy like agriculture, it is important to encourage more persons to go into the sector as a way of attaining self-sufficiency in food, and generally boosting economic growth. Agricultural subsidies and grants are provided by the Ministry of Agriculture.[311] Agricultural insurance is also subsidized by 50% in order to encourage more farmers to insure their farms and stay in business in case of natural disasters. This kind of subsidy is not in contravention to the WTO obligation.

§3. State Grants and Investments

541. For most businesses, whether small or large, access to finance is key to achieving their goals. Small businesses often find this a challenge as most banks are unwilling to lend and would rather lend to large businesses in a bid to reduce their risk.

542. In the face of this challenge, government often steps in with grants and favourable investment policies. The aim of state financing is to provide capital for start-ups and for existing businesses to expand and create more jobs. There are several types of programme the government uses to achieve this primary objective, for instance, capital access, loan participation, loan guarantee, collateral support and direct loans.

543. Nigeria has several grant programmes to encourage entrepreneurs to set up businesses. Examples of such grants are as follows:

(a) Federal Government grants for Agriculture.
(b) National Institutes of Health grant.
(c) Cybertipline Grant (grants to small businesses that provide services and programmes that help eradicate sex trafficking and exploitation of children).
(d) Bank of Industry grants (a youth empowerment programme where young people are empowered and grants are released to them to begin small-scale businesses).
(e) YouWin Connect Nigeria (a yearly programme by the Federal Government to support ideas and already existing businesses, job creation and wealth creation).
(f) Social Intervention Fund (for artisans and owners of SMS businesses across the nation).

---

311. Federal Ministry of Agriculture and Rural Development.

544. Banks and other large corporations in the country are also encouraged by the government to engage in these forms of grants to SMEs and start-ups as part of their Corporate Social Responsibility.

Chapter 4. Competition Law

545. Competition law promotes and maintains healthy market competition, and regulates anticompetitive conducts by companies. It is referred to as 'Anti-trust Law' in some jurisdictions and 'Anti-monopoly Law' in others. In simple terms, competition law acts as an umpire in the market 'jungle' where profits can be made by unscrupulous manufacturers to the disadvantage of consumers. According to Justice Dimgba, it is a set of rules, disciplines and judicial decisions maintained by governments relating either to agreements between firms that restrict competition or to the concentration or abuse of market power on the part of private firms.[312]

546. There is that persistent danger that market players, especially those more financially buoyant, may manipulate enforcement gaps in competition law to maximize profits and abuse their market power. Thus, the primary objective of the competition law is to regulate the activities of manufacturers and protect the consumers from abuses. It also regulates anticompetitive behaviours such as price fixing and rigging and concentration of economic power. When the law protects the market to the extent that both the buyer and seller are price takers, there are economic benefits, boosting growth, efficiency and innovation.[313]

547. It follows therefore that the main aim of competition law is consumer protection.

548. In Nigeria, the FCCP Act, 2019 is the primary law that regulates competition. In addition to this, the various aspects of the economy are regulated by specific industry regulators. For instance, the Nigerian Communications Act 2003 created the National Communications Commission to regulate matters bordering on communications, and similar pieces of legislation, like the Electric Power Sector Reform Act 2005 and the Investment and Securities Act 2007, all created regulatory bodies that oversee matters in these areas of the economy.

549. Thus, the Investment Securities Act empowers the Securities and Exchange Commission to regulate the Securities market. Part XII of the Act, in particular, provides the rules guiding mergers, acquisitions and takeovers, and strictly curtails adjustments which might affect competition in the relevant market.

550. The FCCP Act, 2019 repealed the previous Consumer Protection Act, 2004; it establishes the FCCP Tribunal for the development and promotion of fair, efficient and competitive markets in the Nigerian economy, and to facilitate access by all citizens to safe products, secure the protection of rights for all consumers in Nigeria and for other related matters.[314]

---

312. *See* generally, N. Dimgba, *The Need and the Challenges to the Establishment of a Competition Regime in Nigeria* (2008). Retrieved 13 Jul. 2020 from https://independent.academia.edu.
313. T. Buthe, *The Politics of Market Competition: Trade and Antitrust in a Global Economy* (2008), https://leitner.yale.edu/sites/default/files/files/resources/papers/Buthe_chapter_all_2014-03-20.pdf.
314. The Federal Competition and Consumer Protection Act 2019 (Preamble).

551. The main objectives of the FCCP Act are to promote and maintain competitive markets in the Nigerian economy,[315] promote economic efficiency,[316] protect and promote the interest and welfare of consumers by providing consumers with competitive prices and product choices, and also seeks to prohibit restrictive business practices which prevents, restricts or distorts competition or constitutes an abuse of dominant position of market power in Nigeria, and also contribute to the sustainable development of the Nigerian economy. The Act is applicable to all undertakings and all commercial activities within or having effect in Nigeria.[317]

§1. Establishment of the Commission

552. The FCCP Act establishes the FCCP Commission ('the Commission') for the purpose of carrying out the functions, duties and responsibilities conferred on it by virtue of the provisions of the FCCP Act.[318] As also hinted earlier, it provides for the establishment of a Competition and Consumer Protection Tribunal,[319] to arbitrate over every conduct prohibited under the FCCP Act. The Tribunal shall hear appeals from or review any decision from the exercise of powers of any sector-specific regulatory authority in a regulated industry in respect of competition and consumer protection matters; issue such orders as may be required of it under the FCCP Act; and make any ruling or such other orders as may be necessary or incidental to the performance of its functions under the FCCP Act.[320]

§2. Restrictive Practices

553. Similarly to the provisions of Articles 101–102 of the Treaty of the Functioning of European Union, restrictive practices under the FCCP Act are ways in which people involved in an industry, trade or profession, protect their own interests rather than having a system which is fair to the public, employers and other workers.[321]They are activities carried out by enterprises to inhibit competition. Instances of restrictive practices are as follows:

- Abuse of dominant market position.
- Restricting entry of new competitors into a specific market.
- Restraining fair and open competition.
- Collusion to fix prices (cartels).
- Contracts in restraint of trade – non-compete agreements for former employees.

315. Section 1(a).
316. Section 1(b).
317. Section 1(c) & (d).
318. Section 3(1).
319. Section 39.
320. Section 48.
321. *The Collins English Dictionary* (HarperCollins Publishers 2007).

554. Part VIII of the FCCP Act provides for restrictive agreements. It provides that 'any agreements among undertakings or the decision of an association of undertakings that has the purpose of actual or likely effect of preventing, restricting or distorting competition in any market shall be unlawful and subject to Section 61 of this Act void and of no legal effect whatsoever'.[322]

555. The FCCP Act (or 'the Act') lists out the prohibited acts[323] and they include the following:

(a) Directly or indirectly fixing a purchase or selling price of goods or services subject to section 108 of the Act.
(b) Dividing markets by allocating customers, suppliers, territories or specific types of goods and services.
(c) Limiting or controlling the production or distribution of any goods or services, markets, technical development or investments, subject to section 109 of the Act.
(d) Engaging in collusive tendering, subject to 110 of the Act.
(e) Making the conclusion of an agreement subject to acceptance by other parties of supplementary obligations which, by their nature or according to commercial usage, have no connection with the subject of such agreement.

556. Section 64 prohibits any term or agreement for the sale of any goods or services if the purport of such term or agreement is to establish or provide for the establishment of minimum prices to be charged on the resale of the goods or services in Nigeria.

§3. Monopoly

557. A monopoly exists where a specific person or enterprise is the only supplier of a particular commodity. A monopolistic market is typically dominated by one supplier and exhibits features such as high prices and excessive barriers to trade.

558. According to the Act, where it appears to the Commission that there are grounds for believing that a monopoly situation may exist in relation to the production or distribution of goods or services of any description, or in relation to exports of goods or services of any description from Nigeria, it shall cause an investigation to be held into a particular sector of the economy or into a particular type of agreements across various sectors to determine the extent of the situation in relation to the market.[324]

559. The Act identifies a situation of monopoly to exist in relation to the following:

322. Section 60. Section 61 provides for agreements authorized by the Commission.
323. Section 60(2).
324. Part X, s. 77 of the Federal Competition and Consumer Protection Act 2019.

(a) The supply of goods of any description.
(b) The supply of services of any description.
(c) The exports of goods of any description from Nigeria, to the extent it has an effect on competition in a market in Nigeria.[325]

§4. Abuse of Dominant Position

560. This occurs where a company restricts competition due to its position of strength in a given market.[326] A dominant position is not indicative of abuse; this only occurs where that power is abused. Abuse of market dominance can be divided into: exclusionary and exploitative conducts.

561. An exclusionary conduct occurs where other companies that may be as efficient as the dominant company are barred from the market, while an exploitative conduct occurs where the dominant party uses its position to charge prices or apply conditions that would be impossible in a competitive market.

562. According to the Act, 'abuse of dominant position in a relevant market occurs where an undertaking enjoys a position of economic strength enabling it to prevent effective competition being maintained on the relevant market and having the power to behave to an appreciable extent independently of its competitors, customers and ultimately of the consumers'.[327] An undertaking will be generally considered to be in a dominant position if it is able to act without taking account of the reaction of its customers, consumers or competitors.[328]

563. Section 74 of the Act provides for the consequences of abuse of dominant position in a market while 74(2) states that an undertaking that abuses its dominant position in a market commits an offence under this Act and shall on conviction be liable to a fine of not less than 10% of its turnover in the preceding business year or such higher percentage as the court may determine under the circumstances of the particular case.

§5. Mergers and Acquisitions

564. Mergers and acquisitions are transactions in which the ownership of companies, other business organizations, or their operating units are transferred or consolidated with other entities.[329] Legally, a merger occurs where there is a

325. Section 78 of the Act.
326. Section 73(1) of the Act expressly prohibits the abuse of dominant position in a market.
327. Section 71(2).
328. Section 71(1).
329. Part XII.

consolidation of two entities into one entity, while an acquisition occurs where one entity takes ownership of another entity's assets, which could also include the liabilities.

565. According to the Act, a merger occurs when one or more undertakings directly or indirectly acquire or establish direct or indirect control over the whole or part of the business of another undertaking.[330] A careful review of section 93(1)(b) of the Act, which clarifies the various means by which a merger can be achieved, covers the legal definitions of both mergers and acquisitions.

566. Section 94 of the Act covers the Commission's powers to approve mergers. The Act further provides that when considering a merger or a proposed merger, the Commission shall determine whether or not the merger is likely to substantially prevent or lessen competition. This is done by assessing the strength of competition in the relevant market and the probability that the undertakings in the market, after the merger, will behave competitively or cooperatively, taking into account any factor that is relevant to competition in that market, including the actual and potential level of import competition in the market; the ease of entry into the market, including tariff and regulatory barriers; whether the merger or proposed merger will result in the removal of an effective competitor, etc.[331]

§6. Offences Against Competition

567. Sections 108–114 of the Act provide for specific offences against competition and outline the consequences of being liable for such offences.[332] They are: price fixing, conspiracy, bid-rigging, obstruction of investigation or enquiry, offences against records, giving of false or misleading information and failure to attend or give evidence.

§7. Law of Unfair Competition and Trade Practices

568. Unfair competition laws are designed to protect consumers and businesses against deceptive business practices. Some instances of unfair competitive practices include: trademark infringements, trade defamation and misappropriation of business trade secrets. Most of these instances border on commercial law and were discussed previously.

330. Section 93(1)(a).
331. Section 95(1) & (2).
332. Part XIV.

§8. CONCLUSION

569. The FCCP Act on the face of it looks promising as it covers both competition regulations and consumer protection and enforcement. It is expected that the Commission will ensure compliance by appointing experts in antitrust laws, economics, intellectual property, etc., to carry out its activities.

570. The importance of competition law cannot be emphasized, hence the heightened importance it has enjoyed across various jurisdictions in the world. Nigeria can no longer afford to delay the enforcement of the provisions Act because if left unbridled, the untoward and unregulated trade practices will continually relegate the markets to the background and have extremely adverse effects on the economic and trade growth of the country.

571. As is often the case with laws in Nigeria, problems with implementation and enforcement should be anticipated and steps taken to ensure this Act do not face the same challenge. It is pertinent that all relevant stakeholders be better educated on the competition law and policies with those in charge of administering it being taught on the subject then passing this information down to consumers by means of seminars and webinars.

Chapter 5. State Regulation of the Conditions of Commercial Transactions

572. As mentioned in the previous chapter, the underlying motive for the regulation of commercial transactions by the state (laws) is the protection of consumers. According to Aniagolu J.S.C. in *Constance Ngonadi v. Nigerian Bottling Co. Ltd*:[333]

> nothing appears to be elementary in this country where it is often the unhappy lot of consumers to be inflicted with shoddy and unmerchantable goods by some pretentious manufacturers, entrepreneurs, shady middlemen and unprincipled retailers whose avowed interests seems only and always, to be to maximize their profits leaving honesty a discounted and shattered commodity.

573. Consumer protection laws ensure the rights of consumers as well as fair trade, competition and accurate information in the marketplace. For instance, government typically requires businesses to disclose detailed information about products especially where public health and safety is involved.

§1. Price and Supply Regulation

574. Price regulation refers to the policy of setting prices by a government agency, legal statute or regulatory authority. Supply regulation refers to policies regulating the amount of goods and services available to consumers.

575. Section 89(1) of the FCCP Act, 2019 provides that 'for the purpose of regulating and facilitating competition only, the President may, from time to time, by order published in the Federal Gazette, declare that the prices for goods or services specified in the order shall be controlled in accordance with the provisions of this Act'.[334]

576. The Act further provides for situations in which the President may make such regulations: where competition is lessened or likely to be absent; where it is necessary for the price and supply to be regulated in the interests of the consumers; and where such regulation is necessary to remedy the effects of the absence of competition.[335] Before such order as previously discussed can be made by the President, the Commission must submit a report to the President assessing the state of competition in the relevant market and providing recommendations on the desirability and likely effects of implementing price regulation.[336]

333. [1985] 1 NWLR (Pt. 4) 739, where the plaintiff/appellant sustained severe injuries from a brand of Kerosene refrigerator which was sold to her by the defendant/respondent.
334. Part XI of the Federal Competition and Consumer Protection Act.
335. Section 89(2)(a)(b)(c) of the Federal Competition and Consumer Protection Act, 2019.
336. Section 89(3). *See also* s. 90.

577. According to section 91 of the Act, an undertaking (establishment) shall not supply regulated goods and services for prices other than the authorized price. It further provides for the penalties for contravention of the provision.

§2. CONSUMER LAW

578. Simply, Consumer Law provides protection to the consumer when they purchase a product or service. Consumer protection has been earlier discussed in the previous chapters and will be reviewed lightly here.

I. Institutional Aspects of Consumer Law

579. Consumer protection is of utmost importance to all market economies and as a result, many countries established institutions and relevant legislation to protect consumers. A consumer could be described as an individual who purchases, uses, maintains or disposes a product or service for private consumption. He may also be regarded as any person who hires any services for a consideration or any beneficiary of such services, provided the service is availed with the approval of the person who has hired the services for a consideration.

580. Consumer protection institutions refer to agencies established by the state for the purpose of ensuring that consumers are protected against harmful business practices and providing for redress when consumers suffer injury. In Nigeria, prior to 2019, the principal regulation for consumer protection used to be the Consumer Protection Council Act. It provided for the establishment of the Consumer Protection Council whose functions were outlined in section 1(1) of the Act.[337] However, the current law is the FCCP Act, which also establishes the FCCP Commission to be in charge of enforcement of matters bordering on consumer and competition. In addition to the FCCP Commission, there are other consumer protection agencies such as the Standard Organization of Nigeria, Nigeria Industrial Standard, National Agency for Food and Drugs Administration and Control and Electricity Regulatory Agency/Commission. This may lead to duplication of functions and rivalry among its agencies. However, the FCCP Act provided for a Tribunal to adjudicate over consumer protection issues.

II. General Principles of Consumer Protection

581. The Consumer Bill of Rights as presented to the USA congress in 1962 by John F. Kennedy includes the following:

(a) The right to know or the right to information.
(b) The right to be heard.

337. The Consumer Protection Council Act, s. (1) Cap C25, L.F.N., 2004.

(c) The right to safety.
(d) The right to choose.
(e) The right to satisfaction of basic needs.
(f) The right to redress.
(g) The right to consumer education.
(h) The right to representation and right to healthy environment.

582. In 1985, the United Nations issued guidelines on consumer protection. These guidelines were revised in 2015 and are now referred to as the United Nations Guidelines on Consumer Protection 2016. The guidelines ensure the following:[338]

(a) The protection of consumers from hazards to their health and safety.
(b) Promotion and protection of the economic interests of consumers.
(c) Consumer's access to adequate information to enable them to make informed choices.
(d) Consumer's education, including education on the environment, social and economic impacts of consumer choice.
(e) The availability of effective consumer dispute resolution and redress.
(f) The freedom to form consumer and other relevant groups or organizations and the opportunity of such organizations to present their views in decision-making processes affecting them.

583. On 20 July 2004, the European Commission Directorate-General for Health and Consumer Protection published ten basic principles of consumer protection:

(1) Buy what you want where you want.
(2) If it does not work, send it back.
(3) High safety standards for food and consumer goods.
(4) Know what you are eating.
(5) Contracts should be fair to consumers.
(6) Sometimes, consumers can change their minds.
(7) Making it easier to compare prices.
(8) Consumers should not be misled.
(9) Protection while you are on holiday.
(10) Effective redress for cross-border disputes.

584. Consumer rights principles as covered by the repealed Consumer Protection Council of Nigeria[339] and the new FCCP Act mostly replicate the consumer

338. Part III, Art. 5, (C)-(H) United Nations Department of Economic and Social Affairs, *United Nations Guidelines on Consumer Protection* (as revised in 2015, New York).
339. At http://www.cpc.gov.ng/index.php/consumers.

rights of John Kennedy: Right to Value for Money, Right to Safety, Right to Information, Right to Choose, Right to Redress, Right to Consumer Education, and Right to Representation.[340]

III. Representation of Consumer Interests

585. This right is intrinsic to upholding other basic principles of consumer protection. This right basically covers advocacy of consumer's interest and the ability to take part in the formulation of economic and other policies affecting consumers. Consumer representatives are an effective mechanism for ensuring that consumer's interests are heard and favourably acted upon.

586. A consumer representative is appointed to represent the interests of consumers. He must bring a consumer perspective to all discussions and decision-making of the board on which he sits.

IV. Qualities of an Effective Consumer Representative

587. An effective consumer representative must be able to:

(a) address issues from the perspective of the consumer;
(b) develop and maintain relationships with the people they represent;
(c) respect Diversity;
(d) be accessible to the consumer groups they represent;
(e) have a broad community network with which to consult regularly;
(f) work effectively in a team environment;
(g) understand, commit to and maintain confidentiality when it is required.

V. Consumer Information

588. These pieces of information ensure that consumers are well protected, informed and educated about the products and services they wish to consume.[341] Establishments have a duty to consumers to help them make informed decisions on products and services and also ensure that such information is accurate, relevant, current and timely. It is also important that such information is given in the prevailing language they understand.

589. According to section 115(2) of the FCCP Act, 'a notice, document or visual representation is in plain language if it is reasonable to conclude that an ordinary

340. Section 2 of the Consumer Protection Act lists the functions of the Council with respect to protecting consumer rights. Part XV of the Federal Competition and Consumer Protection Act, 2019 provides for the rights of consumers.
341. Section 115 of the Federal Competition and Consumer Protection Act, 2019.

consumer of the class of persons for whom the notice, document or visual representation is intended, with average literacy skills and minimal experience as a consumer of the relevant goods or services, could be expected to understand the content, significance, and import of the notice, document or visual representation without undue effort … '.

590. Consumers should also acquire the knowledge and skill to be an informed consumer. Ignorance often creates room for exploitation. Towards this goal, part of the responsibility of the Commission is to create awareness and organize educational programmes, campaigns and advertisements that educate consumers.

§3. Safety and Quality of Goods and Services

591. This refers the right to be protected against the marketing of goods and services which are hazardous to life and property. Consumers should insist on the quality of the products as well as on the guarantee of the products and services they are presented to buy and consume.

592. Section 132(1) of the FCCP Act provides that every consumer has a right to receive goods that are reasonably suitable for the purposes for which they are generally intended; are of good quality, in good working order and free of defects;[342] will be useable and durable for a reasonable period of time, having regard to the use to which they would normally be put and to all the surrounding circumstances of their supply; and comply with any applicable standards set by industry sector regulators.[343]

593. If a consumer has specifically informed an undertaking of the particular purpose for which the consumer wishes to acquire any goods, or the use to which the consumer intends to apply those goods, and the undertaking ordinarily offers to supply such goods or acts in a manner consistent with being knowledgeable about the use of those goods, the consumer has a right to expect that the goods be reasonably suitable for the specific purpose that the consumer has indicated.[344]

§4. Consumer Contracts

594. A consumer contract is a binding agreement between an establishment (undertaking) and a consumer concerning the sale or supply of goods and services,

342. Defects have been defined in *Holmdene Brickworks (Pty) Ltd v. Roberts Construction Co Ltd* [1977] (3) 670 (A), 684H as an abnormal quality or attribute which destroys or substantially impairs the utility or effectiveness of the *res vendita*, for the purpose for which it has been sold or for which it is commonly used.
343. Federal Competition and Consumer Protection Act, 2019.
344. Section 132(2). Also *see* s. 133(1) which provides for the implied warranty of quality. Further *see* s. 131 of Federal Competition and Consumer Protection Act, 2019.

for which the latter acted in a non-professional capacity and for personal consumption of the goods. Terms of such contract may be express or implied. It is express when clearly stated perhaps on the goods themselves while they are implied when they arise simply by virtue of the agreement to sell whether stated or not.

595. Generally, certain terms apply to a contract between an establishment and the consumer which both parties are expected to comply with. These will be listed below as some have been discussed previously:

(a) The establishment must adequately give information to the consumer before making the sale.
(b) The consumer has the right to change their minds and cancel/return an order within a reasonable time.
(c) The consumer should not have to pay more than the basic rate for goods and services.
(d) The establishment must deal fairly with the customer.[345]

596. Typically, there are three types of contract the aforementioned legislation covers:

Off-premises contracts: These cover four scenarios – where the consumer and seller are together and agree in a place that is not the seller's business premises; where the consumer and trader are together, the consumer makes an offer in a place that is not the seller's business premises; where the agreement occurs on the seller's business premises immediately after a meeting with consumer in a place that is not the seller's business premises; and where the contract is made with the consumer during an excursion organized by the trader with the aim of selling or promoting goods and services.
Distance contracts: Where the contract is made between a seller and a consumer where they are not together, which is negotiated and agreed by means of distance communication, e.g., phone, post or internet.
On-premises contracts: This refers to contract made on the seller's business premises.

597. Section 128 of the FCCP Act provides that 'An undertaking shall not: offer to supply, supply, or enter into an agreement to supply, any goods or services at a price that is manifestly unfair, unreasonable or unjust, or on terms that are unfair, unreasonable or unjust; market any goods or services, or negotiate, enter into or administer a transaction or an agreement for the supply of any goods or services, in a manner that is unfair, unreasonable or unjust; or require a consumer, or other person to whom any goods or services are supplied at the direction of the consumer, to

345. Sections 120–124 of Federal Competition and Consumer Protection Act, 2019.

waive any rights, assume any obligation, or waive any liability of the undertaking, on terms that are unfair, unreasonable or unjust, or impose any such terms as a condition of entering into a transaction.'[346]

§5. Sales Promotion and Commercial Practices

598. Consumer protection ensures that establishments do no engage in unfair commercial practices. Consumers are not to be misled or exposed to aggressive marketing, and any claim made by an establishment must be clear and accurate thereby enabling consumers to make an informed choice.

599. Section 125 covers the provision on aggressive marketing and states that an undertaking or any person acting on its behalf shall not use physical force, coercion, undue influence or pressure, harassment, unfair tactics or any other similar conduct against any person in connection with marketing of any goods or services or supply of goods or services to a consumer. When marketing a product or service, if the establishment or any person acting on its behalf gives the consumer a wrong impression or misrepresents a material fact to the consumer, or fails to correct a wrong impression on the part of the consumer, such establishment or person shall be liable in damages to the affected individual and shall have to make monetary restitution.[347]

§6. Consumer Redress

600. In light of the aforementioned rights and policies, an undertaking is expected to comply with when dealing with a consumer; what happens where such undertaking contravenes these rules and policies? Indeed, there are also regulations and methods by which the consumer may seek compensation. This is referred to as consumer redress.

601. Prior to 2019, the Commission charged to enforce the provisions of the Consumer Protection Council Act helps to provide speedy redress to consumers' complaints through negotiations, mediation and conciliations.[348] The Council operated through zonal offices and is assisted by committees set up in every state. The state committees had powers only to receive and mediate complaints between the complainants (consumers) and the defendants and control recurring abusive consumer practices. Where parties are unable to settle their differences, the committee was required to recommend to the Council what necessary compensation may be payable by the offending party to the injured consumer.

346. *See also* subs (2) for clarification on what qualifies as unfair, unreasonable or unjust contract terms.
347. Sections 125–126 of the Federal Competition and Consumer Protection Act, 2019. Also *see* s. 127 which provides for representation tests and publication testimonials.
348. The Consumer Protection Council Act, s. 1(1) Cap C25, L.F.N., 2004.

602. The current law, the FCCP Act, provides for redress under section 17 which lists the functions of the Commission created under it. The Act further states the options available to the consumer in seeking to enforce his consumer rights:[349] recourse to the establishment itself, recourse to the applicable industry regulator with sufficient jurisdiction,[350] recourse to the Commission under the Act,[351] and finally, recourse to the courts of law.[352]

§7. Environmental Rules Affecting Economic Output

603. As is the case with every attempt to regulate a market, there is always a trade-off between the benefits of such regulations and their impact on the production of goods and services. Different societies tend to weigh their economies in reaching the tough decision on whether to place greater emphasis on protecting their environment or on more economic output. Should more emphasis therefore be placed on growing the economy first or should more emphasis be placed on regulating the markets (competition)?

604. On this, economists are largely divided. However, most economies, e.g., Nigeria, with low GDP tend to place greater emphasis on economic growth, while those with higher levels of income are more concerned with market regulation (consumer protection). In Nigeria, this argument has also been waged, resulting in very little concern for market regulations and more focus on economic growth.

349. Section 147 of the Federal Competition and Consumer Protection Act.
350. Section 148 of the Federal Competition and Consumer Protection Act.
351. Section 149 of the Federal Competition and Consumer Protection Act.
352. Section 153, Part XVII of the Federal Competition and Consumer Protection Act.

Selected Bibliography

Journals and Books

Belcher, A. *Corporate Rescue.* London: Sweet and Maxwell, 1997.

Obilade, A. *The Nigerian Legal System.* London: Sweet & Maxwell, 1979, 83.

Oba, A.A. 'The African Charter on Human and Peoples' Rights and Ouster Clauses under the Military Regimes in Nigeria: Before and after September 11', *African Human Rights Law Journal* Vol. 2 (2004): 275.

Oba, A.A. 'Islamic Law as Customary Law: The Changing Perspective in Nigeria', *International & Comparative Law Quarterly* Vol. 51 (2002): 817.

Sanni, A. 'Fundamental Rights Enforcement Procedure Rules, 2009 as a Tool for the Enforcement of the African Charter on Human and Peoples' Rights in Nigeria: The Need For Far-Reaching Reform', *African Human Rights Law Journal* Vol. 11 (2011): 511–531.

Onuorah, A.C. 'Negotiable Instruments and the Nigeria Financial System', *International Journal of Bus, Management and Technology* Vol. 2(5) (2018): 72–80.

Oyebade, A. *The Foundations of Nigeria: Essays in Honour of Toyin Falola, Africa.* World Press Inc., 2003.

Afigbo, A.E. *The Warrant Chiefs Indirect Rule in Southern Nigeria 1891-1929.* Longman, 1972.

Burns, A. *History of Nigeria.* George Allen and Unwin Ltd, 1948.

Opara, B.C. & N.C. Opara. '*Analysis of Government Policies and Nigerian Firms Export Marketing Strategies*', 8 *International Bulletin of Business Administration* (2010).

BBC, 'David Cameron Calls Nigeria and Afghanistan "fantastically corrupt"', *BBC News.* (10 May 2016), https://www.bbc.com/news/uk-politics-36260193.

Nwabueze, B. *A Constitutional History of Nigeria.* C. Hurst & Co (Publishers) Ltd, 1982.

Black's Law Dictionary. 7th ed., West Group, 1999.

Adebayo, B. & S. Busari, 'Foreign Workers kidnapped from Nigeria Oil Rig', *CNN.* (29 April 2019), https://edition.cnn.com/2019/04/29/africa/foreign-oil-workers-nigeria-kidnap-intl/index.html.

Meek, C. 'The Religions of Nigeria', *Africa: Journal of the International African Institute.* Vol. 14(3) (1943): 106–117.

Orr, C.W.J. *The Making of Northern Nigeria.* London: Macmillan, 1911.

Eboh, C. 'Nigeria's NNPC Plans to Revamp Refineries to Cut Fuel Imports', *Reuters.* (22 March 2019), https://www.reuters.com/article/nigeria-refineries/nigerias-nnpc-plans-to-revamp-refineries-to-cut-fuel-imports-idUKL8N2193WQ.

Selected Bibliography

Robert, C. *Nigeria in Conflict.* Secker and Warburg, 1970.

Okonkwo, C. *Introduction to Nigerian Law.* Sweet & Maxwell, 1980.

Enweremadu, D.U. 'Nigeria's Quest to Recover Looted Assets: The Abacha Affair', *Africa Spectrum.* Vol. 48(2) (2013): 51–70. Doi:10.1177/000203971304800203.

Democracy. Longman Nigeria Ltd, 1985.

Awa, E. *Federal Government in Nigeria.* University of California Press, 1964.

Fapohunda, E. & M. Todaro. 'Family Structure, Implicit Contracts, and the Demand for Children in Southern Nigeria', *Population and Development Review* Vol. 14(4) (1988): 571–594.

Nwauche, E. 'The Nigerian Fundamental Rights (Enforcement) Procedure Rules 2009: A Fitting Response to Problems in the Enforcement of Human Rights in Nigeria?', *African Human Rights Law Journal* Vol. 10 (2010): 502.

Worugji, E. & R.O Ugbe. 'Judicial Protection of Women's Rights in Nigeria: The Regrettable *Decision in Mojekwu v. Iwuchukwu*', *University of Botswana Law Journal* Vol. 16 (2013): 59.

Kalu, E. *Constitutional Development in Nigeria: An Analytical Study of Nigeria's Constitution-Making Developments and the Historical and Political Factors That Affected Constitutional Change.* Cambridge University Press, 1960.

Toyin, F. *Colonialism and Violence in Nigeria.* Indiana University Press, 2009.

Ugobude, F. 'Culture: The Osu Caste System in Igboland', *The Guardian* (18 November 2018), https://guardian.ng/life/culture-the-osu-caste-system-in-igboland/.

Schwarz, F. *Nigeria the Tribes the Nation or the Race: the Politics of Independence.* MIT press, 1965.

Hetherington, G. *British Paternalism: 1920-1940.* London: Cass, 1970.

Treitel, G.H. 'The Deserted Wife's Right to Pledge Her Husband's Credit for Necessaries', *Modern Law Review* Vol. 16(2) (1953): 221–225.

Kirk, G. *Lugard and the Amalgamation of Nigeria.* London: Cass, 1968.

Hon. Justice Ayoola. 'Rationale, Objectives and the Scope of Law Reform', in *Law Development and Administration in Nigeria*, edited by Osibanjo & Kalu. Intec Printers Limited, 1990.

IBRD. 'Doing Business in Nigeria (2018)', *Comparing Business Regulation for Domestic Firms in 36 States and FCT Abuja with 189 Other Economies,* 33–56, https://www.doingbusiness.org/content/dam/doingBusiness/media/Subnational-Reports/DB_in_Nigeria_2018_w-bookmarks.pdf.

Anyaogu, I. 'How Poor Regulation Is Hurting Nigeria's Small Businesses', *Business Day* (29 July 2020), https://businessday.ng/features/article/how-poor-regulation-is-hurting-nigerias-small-businesses/.

Sagay, I. *Nigerian Law of Contract.* 2nd ed., Spectrum Law Publishing, 2001.

Omeje, J.C., E.I. Egwa, & V.O. Adikwu. 'Impact of Quota System and Catchment Area Policy on the University Admissions in North Central Nigeria', *SAGE Open* Vol. 6(2) (2016), Available at doi:10.1177/2158244016654951.

Smith, J.D. *A Culture of Corruption: Everyday Deception and Popular Discontent in Nigeria.* Princeton University Press, 2007.

Farrar, J.H. & A.M. Dugdale. *Introduction to Legal Method.* 2nd ed., Sweet &Maxwell, 1984.

Fabunmi, J.O. *Equity and Trusts in Nigeria.* Obafemi Awolowo University Press, 2006.

Carby-Hall, J.R. 'The Collective Agreement-Legal Enforceability?', *Managerial Law* Vol. 35(1/2) (1993): 1–24, pp. 3–4.

Fage, J.D. *A History of West Africa.* Cambridge University Press, 1969.

Cook, J. 'Tracing the Roots of Nigeria's Agricultural Decline', *Center for Strategic & International Studies* (5 May 2016), https://www.csis.org/analysis/tracing-roots-nigerias-agricultural-decline.

Hargreaves, J. *West Africa Partitioned.* Macmillan, 1974.

Post, K.W.J. *The Nigerian Federal Election Politics and Administration in a Developing Political System.* Oxford University Press, 1963.

Mohammed, K., Dutsin-Ma & A. Bello. 'The State of Nigerian Economy in the 21st Century; Privatization and Commercialization Programmes under Obasanjo/ Atiku Regime', *European Scientific Journal* Vol. 9(1) (2013): 88–98, https:// core.ac.uk/download/pdf/328023776.pdf.

Igweike, K. *Nigeria Commercial Law: Agency.* FAB Educational Books, 1993.

Awotokun, K. 'Local Government Administration under 1999 Constitution in Nigeria' Journal of Social Sciences Vol. 10(2) (2005): 129–134.

Gann, L.H. & P. Duignan (eds). *Colonialism in Africa 1870 1900*, V 2. Cambridge University Press, 1982.

Njemanze, L.O. *Understanding Bankruptcy, Trust and Executorships Law and Accounts.* Enugu: Rhyce Kerex Publishers, 2003.

Ogunmodimu, M. 'Language Policy in Nigeria: Problems, Prospects and Perspectives'. *International Journal of Humanities and Social Science* Vol. 5(9) (2015): 154–160.

Okany, M.C. *Nigerian Commercial Law.* Africana FEP Publishers Ltd, 1992.

Crowder, M. *The Story of Nigeria.* Faber and Faber, 1961.

Eboh, M. 'Oil Firms Spill 3,346 Barrels of Crude Oil in Eight Months – Investigation', Vanguard (29 September 2020), https://www.vanguardngr.com/2020/09/ oil-firms-spill-3346-barrels-of-crude-oil-in-eight-months-%E2%80%95-investigation/.

Rahmani, M. 'Constitutional Development in Nigeria 1945–1960' (Doctoral thesis, 2015 Liabbes University).

NAFDAC. 'Curbing Substandard, Falsified (SFS) and Counterfeit Medicines'. *NAFDAC* (11 November 2019), https://www.nafdac.gov.ng/curbing-substandard -falsified-sfs-and-counterfeit-medicines/.

Ogbuanya, Nelson C.S. Essentials of Corporate Law Practice in Nigeria. Novena Publishers, 2010.

Okafor, N., O. Okafor & C. Okolie. 'Lending and Taking Security in Nigeria: Overview Taxes and Fees on Loans, Guarantees and Security Interests'. *Practical Law* (1 June 2016), https://uk.practicallaw.thomsonreuters.com/4-524-5665? transitionType=Default&contextData=(sc.Default)&firstPage=true.

Princewill, N. 'Of Our Indigenous Greeting Culture'. *The Guardian* (16 June 2017), https://guardian.ng/opinion/of-our-indigenous-greeting-culture/.

Dimgba, N. 'The Need and the Challenges to the Establishment of a Competition Regime in Nigeria' (2008). Retrieved 13 July 2020 from https:// independent.academia.edu.

Selected Bibliography

Francis, N. 'State Tax Incentives for Economic Development'. *Tax Policy Center* (28 February 2016), https://www.taxpolicycenter.org/publications/state-financing-incentives-economic-development/full.

Dumka, N. *The Ethnic History of Nigeria*. Available at https://core.ac.uk/download/pdf/14051828.pdf.

Ifueko, O.O. 'Tax Incentives for Foreign Investors in Nigeria'. *The Nigerian Investors Business Forum*, Berne Switzerland, 2012.

Awojobi, O.N. 'The Socio-Economic Implications of Boko Haram Insurgency in the North-East of Nigeria'. *International Journal of Innovation and Scientific Research* Vol. 11(1) (2014): 144–150.

Olatunji, O.O. *The Yoruba History, Culture and Language*. Ibadan University Press, 1970.

Omoruyi, O. 'The Origin of Nigeria: God of Justice Not Associated with an Unjust Political Order: Appeal to President Obasanjo Not to Rewrite Nigerian History' (2002) http://www.nigerdeltacongress.com/tarticles/the%20origin_of_nigeria.htm.

Egbefo, O.D. 'Fifteen Years of Democracy, 1999-2014: Reflections on Nigeria's Quest for National Integration'. *African Research Review* Vol. 9(2) (2015): 59–77

Oyediran, O. (ed.) *The Nigerian 1979 Elections.* Macmillan Press Ltd, 1981.

Benson, O., L. Anyalebechi & I. Ariole. 'Promoting Indigenous Language in Nigeria: Issues and Challenges for the Library and Information Professionals', *Library Philosophy and Practice (e-journal)* Vol. 1472 (2017), http://digitalcommons.unl.edu/libphilprac/1472.

Fordham, P. *The Geography of African Affairs.* Penguin Books, 1965.

PBS NewsHour, 'Ethnicity in Nigeria' (5 April 2007), https://www.pbs.org/newshour/arts/africa-jan-june07-ethnic_04-05.

Tibenderana, Peter K. 'The Irony of Indirect Rule in Sokoto Emirate, Nigeria', *African Studies Review* Vol. 31(1) (1988): 67–92.

Premium Times, '83% of Nigeria Oil Blocs Owned By Northerners — Senate Committee Chair', *Premium Times* (6 March 2013), https://www.premiumtimesng.com/news/123398-83-of-nigeria-oil-blocs-owned-by-northerners-senate-committee-chair.html.

Uche, R.D. 'Quality of University Graduates and Human Resources Development in Nigeria', *Research in Education* Vol. 92(1) (2014): 49–58. Doi:10.7227/RIE.0004.

Sklar, R. *Nigerian Political Parties: Power in an Emergent African Nation.* Africa World Press, 2004.

Okafor, S.O. 'Ideal and Reality in British Administrative Policy in Eastern Nigeria', *African Affairs* Vol. 73(2) (1974): 293.

Adedini, S.A., S. Babalola, C. Ibeawuchi, O. Omotoso, A. Akiode, & M. Odeku. 'Role of Religious Leaders in Promoting Contraceptive Use in Nigeria: Evidence from the Nigerian Urban Reproductive Health Initiative', *Global Health, Science and Practice* Vol. 6(3) (2018): 500–514, https://doi.org/10.9745/GHSP-D-18-00135.

Hogben, S.J. & A.H.M. Kirk-Greene. *The Emirates of Northern Nigeria.* Oxford University Press, 1966.

Johnson, S. *The History of the Yoruba.* C.M.S Bookshop, 1937.

Ehindero, S.G. *The Constitutional Development of Nigeria: 1849-1989*. Ehindero (Nigeria) Ltd, 1991.

Olawale Elias, T. *The Nature of African Customary Law*. Manchester University Press, 1956.

Obiwuru, T.C., O.B. Oluwalaiye & A.T. Okwu. 'External and Internal Environments of Businesses in Nigeria: An appraisal', *International Bulletin of Business Administration* Vol. 12 (2011): 15–23.

Mamman, T. *The Law and Politics of Constitution Making in Nigeria, 1862-1989: Issues, Interests and Compromises*. Ed-Linform services, 1998.

The Collins English Dictionary. HarperCollins Publishers, 2007.

The Guardian. 'Worries Over Declining Training Scheme For Artisans', *The Guardian* (21 December 2020), https://guardian.ng/property/worries-over-declining-training-scheme-for-artisans/.

The World FactBook. https://www.cia.gov/library/publications/the-world-factbook/geos/ni.html.

The Worldwatch Monitor. 'Who Are the Fulani?'. Available at https://www.worldwatchmonitor.org/who-are-the-fulani/.

Obert, T. 'Transport Workers Strikes and the Imperial Response. Africa and Post World War II Conjuncture'. *African Studies Review* Vol. 31 (1988): 26.

Idemudia, U. 'The Resource Curse and the Decentralization of Oil Revenue: The Case of Nigeria'. *Journal of Cleaner Production* Vol. 35 (2012): 183–193.

United Nations. 'Tax Incentives and Foreign Direct Investment: A Global Survey' (2000) *United Nations conference on Trade and Development* (ASIT Advisory Studies No. 16), https://unctad.org/system/files/official-document/iteipcmisc3_en.pdf.

Kalu, U.C. 'A Critique of Voluntary or Debtor Initiated Bankruptcy Adjudicatory Process and the Need for Legislative Reformation in Nigeria'. *Journal of Intl Law and Jurisprudence* Vol. 1 (2010): 41–55.

Ige, V.O. & R.A. Oladapo, 'Variation in Compensation for Compulsory Property Acquisition: Ondo State, Nigeria Experience'. Pacific Rim Property Research Journal Vol. 24(2) (2018): 139–148.

Geary, W. *Nigeria under British Rule*. London: Methuen, 1927.

Akinbobola, Y. 'Bid to End Subsidy Stirs Protest in Nigeria'. *Africa Renewal* (April 2012), https://www.un.org/africarenewal/magazine/april-2012/bid-end-subsidy-stirs-protest-nigeria.

Sodiq, Y. *A History of the Application of Islamic Law in Nigeria* (Palgrave Macmillan, 2017), Chapter 6. Available at https://link.springer.com/content/pdf/bfm%3A978-3-319-50600-5%2F1.pdf.

Selected Bibliography

Table of Cases

Abacha v. Fawehinmi (2000) FWLR (Pt. 4) 553 at 586
AG Abia v. AG Federation (2003) 19 WRN 1
AG Lagos v. AG Federation (2003) 35 WRN 1
AG v. Blake [2001] 1 AC 268
Akenzua II, Oba of Benin v. Benin Divisional Council [1959] WRN LR 1
Akinfosile v. Mobil Oil (Nig) Ltd (1969) 3 ALR Comm 141
Alhaji Shugaba Abruraham Darman v. Minister of Internal Affairs (1981) 2 NCLR 459
B. Stobiliri & Co Ltd v. Obasi [1997] 9 NWLR (Pt. 520) 293 at 305
Bamgboye v. University of Ilorin & Ors (1991) 8 NWLR 129
Chanrai v. Khawam [1965] 1 All NLR 182
Countess of Dunmore v. Alexander [1830] 9 S.C. 190 Ct. of Session
Electronics Ltd v. Akhter Computer Ltd (2001) 1/BCLC/433
Esso West Africa Inc v. Alli (1968) 3 ALR Comm 317
Freeman and Lockyer v. Burkhurst Park Properties Ltd (1964) 1 ALL E.R. 630
Holmdene Brickworks (Pty) Ltd v. Roberts Construction Co Ltd [1977] (3) 670 (A), 684H
Holwell Securities Ltd v. Hughes [1974] 1 WLR 155
Imani & Sons Ltd v. BIL Construction Co Ltd (1999) NWLR 12 (Pt. 630) 253
James v. Midmotors (Nig) Ltd (1978) 11-12 S.C. 21
Major General George Innih (rtd) & ors v. Ferado Agro and Consortium Ltd [1990] 5 NWLR (Pt. 152) 604
Mojeku v. Mojeku (2004) 11 NWLR (Pt. 883) 96
Mojekwu v. Mojekwu [1997] 7 NWLR 283 CA; (2004) 11 NWLR (Pt. 883) 96 S.C.
Nkwocha v. Governor of Anambra State & 2 Ors (1984) JELR 43602 *(SC)*
Olusola Oyegbemi v. Attorney-General of the Federation (1982) 3 NCLR 895
Orient Bank v. Bilante Intl [1997] 8 NWLR (Pt. 515) 37 at 76
Oyenuga v. International Computers (Nigeria) Ltd (1991) 1 NWLR 415
Payne v. Cave [1789] 3 Term Rep.148
Shirlaw v. Southern Foundaries Ltd (1939) 2 K.B 206 at 227
Sonar (Nig) Ltd. v. Nordwind [1987] 4 NWLR (Pt. 66) 520
Timothy v. Simpson [1834] 6 C & P 499
Vulcan Gases Ltd v. G.F. Industries Gasvenwertung A.G (2001)5 SC (Pt. 1) 1
Webster v. Webster (1916) 1 K. B. 714
Wrotham Park Estate Co Ltd v. Parkside Homes Ltd [1974] 1 WLR 798

Table of Cases

Table of Legislation

Bankruptcy Act 1990
Bill of Exchange Act 1990
Companies and Allied Matters Act 2020
Constitution of the Federal Republic of Nigeria 1999
Evidence Act 2011
Federal Competition and Consumer Protection Act 2019
Fundamental Rights (Enforcement Procedure) Rules 2009
Hire Purchase Act 1967
Insurance Act 2003
Interpretation Act 2004
Investments and Securities Act 2007
Sale of Goods Act 1893
Sharia Court of Appeal Law (Northern Nigerian Laws 1963)
Supreme Court Ordinance 1914

Table of Legislation

www.ingramcontent.com/pod-product-compliance
Ingram Content Group UK Ltd.
Pitfield, Milton Keynes, MK11 3LW, UK
UKHW020143290926
15471UKWH00004B/672

9 789403 540559